The
Anguish
of
Snails

Volume 2 in the series

Folklife of the West

Series Editors:

Barre Toelken,
Department of English,
Utah State University

William A. Wilson,
Department of English,
Brigham Young University

Wristband by Tututni basketmaker Ellen DeGross. Photo by Ron Daines

The Anguish of Snails

Native American Folklore in the West

Barre Toelken

UTAH STATE UNIVERSITY PRESS
Logan, Utah

Utah State University Press
Logan, Utah 84322-7800

Printing of the color photos in this book was supported by donations (see page 203) raised through the efforts of Jean Irwin and Star Coulbrooke and with the assistance of the Utah Alliance for Arts & Humanities Education.

Cover photos by Ron Daines
Cover design by Jean Irwin
Text design and composition by Ian Hatch

Manufactured in Canada
Printed on acid-free paper

Library of Congress Cataloging-in-Publication Data

Toelken, Barre.
 The anguish of snails : Native American folklore in the West / Barre Toelken.
  p. cm. — (Folklife of the West ; v. 2)
Includes bibliographical references and index.
 ISBN 0-87421-556-0 (pbk. : alk. paper) — ISBN 0-87421-555-2 (hardback : alk. paper)
 1. Indians of North America—West (U.S.)—Folklore. 2. Folklore—Performance—West (U.S.) 3. Folklore—West (U.S.)—Classification. 4. Oral tradition—West (U.S.) I. Title. II. Series.
 E78.W5T64 2003
 398'.089'97078—dc21

                              2003006172

Contents

Illustrations

Dedication and Acknowledgments

THIS BOOK IS DEDICATED to the many Native American people whose traditions and expressions have illuminated my life and professional work. Some have died, and I need to acknowledge my debt to them in absentia: Tsinaabąąs Yazzie (Little Wagon), my adopted Navajo father, who said he could drive his wagon to the moon as long as I would help push it out of sand dunes and up the hills; Hugh Yellowman, storyteller, Yé'ii Bicheii dancer, deer chaser, moccasin maker, and lifesaving friend, whose stories spoke eloquently through the blessing (and curse) of tape recordings; Homer Damon, my half-Seneca maternal grandfather, whose Puritan New England family refused to tell him who he was; John Brown, my Navajo foster son, who killed himself in the line of duty; and too many Navajo friends whose faces I last saw while pushing the sand into their graves. Their frozen images will inhabit my mind forever.

The book is also dedicated to others still alive: Helen Yellowman, daughter of Little Wagon and my adopted sister, the mother of twelve, who nursed me back from the brink of death; Vanessa Brown, my Navajo daughter, mother of five, dancer of powwows, and known to her adopted Lakota Sun Dance family as Many Eagles Woman (Wanbli Ota Wi), who conquered the Catholic sisters long before it was fashionable; Peter DeCory, my Lakota son-in-law, who has rejoined the cultural and ritual circle of his people in the Sun Dance and the powwow; Native friends like Vic Charlo, Nora Dauenhauer, Ed Edmo, James Florendo, Verbena Green, N. Scott Momaday, Emory Sekaquaptewa, David Warren, George Wasson, James Welch, Willie Wright, all of whom heroically refused to vanish and who have performed their anguish and joy in art, story, song, food, dance, and—incredibly—humor.

I am also indebted to some non-Native trail guides, colleagues, advisors, and mentors who have proven beyond a doubt that it is possible to reach for understanding and share it with others: Joseph Epes Brown, Peter Corey, Richard Dauenhauer, Dennis DeGross, Larry Evers, Dell

Hymes, Virginia Hymes, Karl Kroeber, Phyllis Morrow, Jarold Ramsey, and Roger Welsch.

Other friends and colleagues who have helped me understand this book include Bonnie Glass-Coffin, Barry Lopez, Rose Milovich, Peter Nabokov, Elliott Oring, Leonard Rosenband, Jeannie Thomas, Rosanna Walker, Barbara Walker-Lloyd, Randy Williams, and William A. Wilson.

Five people need to be thanked in particular: Ron Daines, who gave his photographic help and his cultural know-how, in spades; Jean Tokuda Irwin, who organized the pictures in color and put together the most appealing cover; Star Coulbrooke, who made the gifts of friends look like so many colored shots; Judy McCulloh, who volunteered her time and expertise as indexer, when it became apparent that I could not; and John Alley, of USU Press, who accepted an early form of this ten years ago and still pursued it until it came to ground.

And to Miiko, who nursed me back from the edge of death—what can I give more than this account of my life?

As the Lakota say in the Sacred Pipe Ceremony, "Mitakuye oyasin," these are my relations.

She Comes Along Carrying Spears

Speared by this vicious wind,
   how long did she hold the sheep
   before her veins cracked,
   and her eyes turned to crystal stones?

When it went dark for her,
   was it too soon,
   or not soon enough?
And did she feel the beauty
   and the harmony of it
   when her thoughts turned
   to icy splinters?

The singer will surely chant,
"May there be beauty and harmony
   ahead of us to the east,
   behind us to the west,
   on both sides of us as we travel,
   above us and below us as we go;
may we go onward harmoniously,
may it be finished in beauty."

We will all put pollen
   on our heads,
   here and there on ourselves—
      on our legs, which used to walk with her;
      on our arms, which used to hold her;
      on our tongue, which used to talk with her—
   and we'll all throw the pollen in front of us
   to make the road new.

But the way is no longer beautiful,
   and the going not harmonious;
our road will stream forever
   with flags of black hair
   on the surface of the snow,
and we will be watched to the very end
   by eyes of ice,
and our songs will be cut
   by the freezing wind.

There will be ice and snow
   ahead of us to the east,
ice and snow
   behind us to the west,
ice and snow
   on both sides of us as we travel,
ice and snow
   above us and below us
   and in us,
   as we go along.

It is not finished in beauty,
it is not finished in beauty,
it is not finished;
it is never finished.

Prologue
The Snail's Clues

As you can see from the lengthy dedication, *The Anguish of Snails* is more than a book about Native American folklore in the West: It is a work of obligation to those from whom I have learned about everyday Native American life and custom—many of them members of my own family and the Navajo family who so readily adopted me in 1955 when I was a lost nineteen-year-old uranium prospector who came down with pneumonia in their canyon. It is also a work of obligation to my colleagues in folklore and anthropology, many of whom, I believe, have inadvertently distanced themselves from the richness of the Native cultures they study in the name of objective research. This book, then, is an expression of personal responsibility and gratitude to those who saved my life—bodily, spiritually, culturally, and professionally—as well as a professional commentary on the validity and necessity of subjective involvement in the analytical discussion of cultures.

For these reasons, the book contains more than a little emotion and personal bias and demonstrates a less than standard reverence for academic circumspection. I admit these things freely in advance, and I ask scholarly readers in particular to spare me the automatic sermon on objective empiricism. Or spare me at least until we have had a chance to discuss more thoroughly the extent to which scholarly objectivity and emotional distance have really benefitted our attempts to understand the people we so comfortably scrutinize in our writings (where we publish as they perish). My fieldwork experiences have probably not been much different from those of many scholars who have discovered that culturally shaped expressions often defy objective analysis; in fact, we all run into unexpected events which totally change the picture we think we see, which almost derail the project, which confuse or disappoint us. In my case, these unpredictable, uncontrollable moments became so central to my view of the Navajos that they became the bases of things I never would have learned otherwise—or even suspected. And they became the foundation of my conviction that cultural involvement has more substance than has cultural distance.

For example, I learned a lot about the Navajos' funeral customs because of their preference that non-Navajos carry out most of the burial work. For me, it wasn't research that entailed burying three, sometimes four people a week during harsh winter months, and I was troubled when the survivors tried to cheer me up by reminding me that white people enjoy watching people die—a remarkable idea they got from watching our movies. When I took an apparently dying woman to a reservation hospital and discovered the entire staff was away on a two-hour "coffee break," I found it impossible to play the part of the disinterested bystander. When desperate Navajo friends moved to town so they could feed their children better and were told they could expect to get state welfare assistance just as soon as they joined the local church, it was difficult for me to stay aloof from the political and sociological realities of living in a small religious town. And I found Navajo generosity beyond the reach of conventional understanding when families were willing to share their last bit of food with me, not admitting the slightest concern about where the next piece of fry bread or mutton might come from. My responses at the time were quite personal: they included anger, thankfulness, debt, wonderment—all subversively subjective attitudes which remain central to my thinking about the Navajos to this day.

Nonetheless, whenever I—and other scholars similarly inclined—have used these personal perspectives to resolve ethical issues according to Native preference rather than benefit scholar propriety (say, by withdrawing or destroying dangerous or sensitive texts or choosing to avoid problematic themes), colleagues have issued sharp rebukes and reminded us that we are not Natives and should not romantically make believe we are. On one occasion, after I presented a paper explaining why I did not intend to probe more deeply into the witchcraft level of Navajo Coyote stories, a prominent folklorist took me to task for being subjectively "soft" on Indians and thereby betraying my fellow folklorists. "You're not a Navajo," he gratuitously reminded me. "You're not subject to *their* beliefs and fears about witchcraft. You're a scholar and an educated person, and you have the scholarly obligation to delve as deeply as you can into their beliefs, describe them dispassionately and fairly [!], and tell the rest of us what you've learned. Otherwise, why do it at all?" My petulant reply, fueled by a bruised ego, was that I valued my standing among Navajos a whole lot more than my reputation among scholars.

But this was a petty thing to say, and it was, after all, beside the point of either engagement or objectivity. I don't have any special standing among Navajos in general, and I do indeed value my reputation among folklorists. The point is that I do not believe the researcher should have to choose between these two considerations to do good work. The real issues here are the authenticity of the research and the expressions being studied, as well as sensitivity to the people who produce them.

For me, interpretive openness, including my *subjective* sense of commitment to the topic, is as important as empirical observation to the content and the meaning of this book; indeed, without the complex human connections I have enjoyed with Native people, I simply would not have had the interest—or the intelligence—to take their vernacular expressions seriously. After nearly fifty years of working closely with Native people, you may expect I have developed some insights, perspectives, and opinions based on personal experience. I think I have, and I tend to use them, often in preference to things I have read. To my mind, a subjective approach does not preclude being careful and objective in a discussion; rather, it offers a special vantage point born of experience and engagement and should produce a richer analytical frame of reference. There is—or can be—immense utility in deep involvement.

To be sure, the engaged stance of any sensitive observer unavoidably conditions what is seen and heard, affects any interpretation, and colors any description; the reader thus needs to know that my analytical perspective was initially shaped by accidental experience, not by training, education, vocation, or even volition. My academic training has been primarily in medieval languages and literature; my vocation is a professor of literature with an interest in oral literature, especially ballads. I became an unwitting folklorist years ago in the process of trying to account for the amazing stories and rich customs I encountered when I accidentally fell off the turnip truck of the uranium rush and landed among the Navajos. Perhaps some of my readers have had a far better education for such an encounter than I had: I was totally unprepared for the many years of fascination and frustration that lay ahead. In becoming a participant/observer in Navajo folklore, I ate their food, collected their stories, and had my life saved by them on at least two occasions. You could say that I incurred a debt and make small payments on it by trying to use Navajo—and other Native—folklore to dispel stereotypes and misinformation about Native peoples and their cultures.

Please notice that I said "debt" and not "guilt." Guilt is a pointless luxury that allows us to feel chastised and then timidly virtuous without having to acknowledge why some interaction with another culture went wrong or having to account for why something struck us as unaccountably magnificent or eloquent. Inherited guilt simply encourages us to act embarrassed by the terrible acts of our ancestors by continuing to apologize abjectly for their behavior. But let's get real: We white folks of today did not steal the land; we weren't participants in the Sand Creek Massacre, or those at Bear River, the Washita, or Wounded Knee; we didn't hand Ira Hayes that last fatal drink of whiskey; we didn't invent church missions of spiritual and cultural destruction; and we didn't enfranchise the Bureau of Indian Affairs.

At the same time, we can't shrug all these issues off, for we have paid for many of them with our tithings and taxes. And we have certainly become the willing owner-inheritors of the vast land treasure of Native peoples, most of it obtained through less than honorable means by our forebears: How far back can I trace the title for the land my house sits on? Maybe 120 years at the most. If there were no statutes of limitation, I might well be charged with receiving or buying stolen property. On the other hand, despite the seamy behavior of our illustrious pioneers, think of the vast riches *freely* shared by Native peoples in the form of foods that now feed much of the world: corn, tomatoes, peppers, squashes, beans, and potatoes, to name a few. And the several hundred medicines listed in our pharmacopoeia, including many whose complexity surprises us. And the Native languages that were used as unbreakable codes in World War II and function today as tools of discovery in mathematics, physics, biology, and space navigation. Indeed, we are the beneficiaries of remarkable Native gifts, and our indebtedness will not be paid by expressing vague guilt that our grandfathers so assiduously stole most of the land (or as an Indian-activist bumper sticker of the 1970s put it, "We gave an inch; you took three thousand miles").

Neither will the debt be absolved by the many fraudulent books and seminars promising to share Native secrets learned after great difficulty and personal sacrifice from anonymous (or, at best, untraceable) Indian gurus in the trackless deserts and jungles. Shamanic tours of the Andes; weekend sweat lodges for seekers of spiritual experiences; the sacred pipe for beginners; traditional tribal stories for healing, therapy, and profit; peyote high tea for your intergalactic traveling pleasure: All of these show as much respect for the complexity and depth of Native cultures as a Eucharist-wafer-and-wine-spiritual-enrichment-workshop for non-Catholics at the Pink Cactus Saloon demonstrates respect for, or insight into, Christian theology.

From the painful distortions and garish colors of Charles Storm's *Seven Arrows* to the popular, but fictional (and misleading) books of Carlos Castaneda, from the pitiful *Hanta Yo!* to the gentle fraud of *The Education of Little Tree*—all of them strangely far more popular than the various authoritative works which have routinely debunked them—to the many vapid and error-ridden Aquarian guides to Native wisdom, we have chosen kitsch over substance, fiction and wishful thinking over reliable description, white stereotypes over Native perspectives, baloney over truth. In doing so, we have practically enfranchised a generation or two of non-Indian opportunists who claim to give us exclusive guided tours through the sacred and mysterious philosophical innards of the Indian, but most tragically, we have successfully—and with utmost irony—avoided listening to Native people themselves.

As I write this in 2002, a private organization in Utah is advertising a three-day weekend retreat to help you "find yourself and your sacred path." For a mere $350 (which includes special meals for vegetarians and tipis "for a touch of the past"), you are coached on breathing, taught to walk on glowing coals ("aids in focus and clarity"), and provided with an overnight vision quest and three sweat lodge ceremonies. Although such activities are abhorrent to most Indians and have been dubbed "the white shaman syndrome" by many Native American critics, they have become a bonanza for entrepreneurs of weekend spiritualism. But they don't offer much insight or information about Natives and their cultures.

Even in the comparatively more reliable arenas of ethnography, anthropology, and literature, interested readers have become accustomed to seeing the Indian through a veil dimly, presented by someone else—usually a non-Native specialist with an academic degree, a reputation to maintain, and an agenda to fulfill. More people have read John Neihardt's carefully selective *Black Elk Speaks*—not a fraudulent book, I hasten to say, but one more reflective of Neihardt's than of Black Elk's choices—than are familiar with *The Sacred Pipe*, Black Elk's own account of Lakota religion and ritual dictated to Joseph Epes Brown with rich commentary.

Admittedly, *The Anguish of Snails* is not above suspicion, for it is mediated and controlled by someone who is not culturally Native American. I am of course aware that some people who can claim even less Indian "blood" than I do are busily going around the country doing "the Indian thing" for a living. I hope (too optimistically, I'm sure) that at least some of them were brought up by Indian grandmas who taught them what they know. I was not so raised, and I do not subscribe to the notion that Indian DNA carries any built-in cultural depth or ability to articulate complex cultural meanings. What I do believe is that our cultural indebtedness to Native people can be partly addressed by paying serious attention to the kinds of expressions that are *appropriate* for us to see, hear, and respond to. This kind of serious attention and propriety requires respect, not adulation; it requires us to share, not intrude and plunder; it requires us to listen for Native voices, not trumpet our own assumptions.

Therefore, I am not going to claim that Native sages like Yellowman, Little Wagon, Tom Yellowtail, Andy Natonabah, Agnes Vanderburg, Jimmy Descheeny, Tully Benally, or Pete Catches enlisted me as a dedicated apprentice and taught me all their shamanistic secrets—which I am now licensed to pass on to you less fortunate, but spiritually deserving, mortals for the price of this book. No: I want to propose a somewhat more radical and less fashionable set of ideas, beginning with the assertion that Indians are by and large not inscrutable, silent, unapproachable people who spend most of their time in secret shamanic rituals. I want to suggest that—far from needing a passionate guide in a baggy shirt and ponytail— you will have little difficulty learning about Indians and their culture if you simply listen to *their* voices and watch *their* performances, *their* expressions—their freely shared folklore—in the routine of their normal lives. Somewhere nearby, right now, Indian people are making fry bread, telling jokes, singing social songs called "forty-nines," and either dancing pow-wow or getting ready to do so. You and I could be there, included warmly in these events. The question is, why aren't we? Why do we insist on staying at home reading someone else's unverifiable account of Native sacred rituals in the jungles of Manitoba rather than trying to get acquainted with neighboring Native people in their everyday lives? Is it a kind of fear? A grinding of that old inherited guilt? Ignorance? Racial anxiety? Is it just too much work?

To be fair, many non-Native people don't know how to make the initial approach; they are afraid that their sudden appearance on the Indian scene may be intrusive. And so it may be if someone blunders into a ritual ceremony uninvited or unannounced. Yet even here, the outsiders' fears are exaggerated, for most Native ceremonies are not secret, and very few are only for Indians. Some are, of course, so obviously some basic and reliable information is useful. And in all cases, normal sensitivity and respect are required. A hint: Someone will tell you if you're in the wrong place. But don't worry about it; in fact, for the most part, the places where you may easily meet Indian people are the same places where you meet each other: at home and at social gatherings.

I once asked some white teachers on the Navajo reservation how often they visited the homes of their students, which were, admittedly, scattered at great distances away from the school and reachable only over bone-shattering, washboard roads. "Oh, we've tried," I was assured soberly by several speaking all at once, "but you know, they really don't like visitors. In fact, when we do drive up to their hogans, they drop everything and run inside and slam the door. So we got the message; we don't want to intrude where we're not wanted." Since these were teachers who had been there about ten years, I was amazed by how little they had learned about Navajos, impeded as they were by their conviction that the Navajos didn't want normal contact. They were oblivious to a cultural fact they could have learned at any time by asking their students, but they had overlooked it because they didn't believe it was there. The Indian side of the story was clarified by Navajo parents in this area, as well as elsewhere on the reservation, who asked me, "Why do white people act like that? They drive up to our place, just like they want to visit. Then, as soon as we get inside and take our places and get ready to have company, they just drive away! Are they trying to make fun of us?"

Now, the teachers wanted to visit the parents, and Navajos do love to have company, so what was happening here? *Neither* group recognized the normal, customary, everyday visiting habits of the other, and the result was that both groups had their stereotypes strengthened by the experience. But this is a case of everyday culturally conditioned behavior, which can be learned and discussed without a shamanic internship. Knowing a little about the other group's normal folk customs would have served the situation far better than the superficial political correctness by which the visitors elected not to "intrude"—thus allowing both sides to use their own cultural interpretation to perpetuate the gulf separating them.

This is only one example admittedly, but it suggests that our folk belief about the "distant Indian" may well illustrate what Alan Dundes calls *projective inversion*, an outlook that blames the other person (in this case, the other culture) for bothersome behavior that really is more reflective of our own attitudes. We interpret some gestures—avoidance of eye contact or lengthy silences—as intentional signs of conversation avoidance, and we judge this "aloofness" or "inscrutability" as a sign of intransigence, of distancing, of deeply confirmed Otherness: empirical proofs that these people are just as unreachable as we expected. By interpreting their normal behavior as a willful gesture, we project the fault for the distancing onto them, which allows us to maintain the gulf with a clear conscience. In this instance, the whites *saw* Navajos avoiding contact. The Navajos in their hogan, assuming the white visitors were going to act superior and be in too much of a rush for a normal visit, *saw* their sudden departure as a demonstration of impatience, which many Navajos equate with ill will.

This kind of thinking occurs most readily when we are threatened, or when we do not know very much about another culture, when we rationalize other people's expressions in our own terms for our convenience and peace of mind. And it happens most easily when we listen primarily to our voices, not theirs. As this example shows, misunderstanding can and does occur on both sides of the cultural doorway; the big difference is that, while we are not obliged to listen very often or seriously to Indians, they are forced to hear us talking about ourselves all the time. But fortunately there's much more to a culture than talk: There's a whole range of cultural expression in the form of everyday custom—folklore.

Assuming that a great bulk of Native American folk expression is available to us, and that, indeed, much of it is performed directly for us, or at least for the mixed culture we are part of; acknowledging, at the same time, that not everyone knows—as those teachers did not know— that the door is usually open and there is a system of good sense and order through which we may feel welcome to visit, I would like this book to present some significant articulations of Native cultural values that are already in our world, ready to be seen and responded to. I want to do this in the way I would introduce you to my Navajo family if I could take you to their hogan—not by sneaking into a healing ritual unannounced on the one hand, or by barging in noisily with the expectation that the Indians are waiting to entertain on the other—but the way Barry Lopez guides his readers along the banks of the McKenzie River in *River Notes: The Dance of Herons* (1979). He walks us quietly and considerately along the banks, pointing out the indications of life forms inhabiting that zone and suggesting that there is a link between the evidence and ourselves, a connection between nature's "data" and the sensitive interpreter, an observable, experiential basis for learning not how we are *other* than the river's denizens but *related* to them: "Snail shell—made out of the same thing as your fingernail. Here, tap it—Or a rattlesnake's rattles. Roll it around in your hand. Imagine the clues in just this. Counting the rings would tell you something, but no one is sure what. Perhaps all that is recorded is the anguish of snails."

Let's go along this cultural riverbank together, paying attention to what we actually see and hear that may offer us common ground for speculation, discovery, insight. We won't pretend to pry into the secret lives of snails, but we will try to account for the patterns in their shells: In our case, the patterns include the traditional Native dances, foods, stories, arts, and medicines that are the purposeful records, the time-tested articulations of shared emotions and values, of living, ongoing cultures. "Imagine the clues in just this."

I

Cultural Patterns in Native American Folklore

An Introduction

> *The only problem I've ever had with white people has been
> unrequited love.*
>
> —Vic Charlo, grandson of Flathead Chief Charlo

SO THE SNAIL SHELL is our governing metaphor in the following chapters. We can see that the ongoing responses of the living snail have been recorded in the structure of the shell over time, forming patterns with which we want to become more fully acquainted. We believe that the markings before our eyes have meaning, and we want to explore the clues. We start here, not with the snail's sensitive innards. As outsiders, we may not initially understand what the many-patterned expressions of Indians "mean," either, but we can be certain that they mean something, and whatever it is must be important because it constitutes a substantive, out-ward-facing record of feelings and values Native people have shared with each other and with us over time.

Even if "all that is recorded" is *only* the anguish of snails, isn't that more than enough to suggest the way a physical object can excite a mix-ture of ideas in the human mind? Like T. S. Eliot's *objective correlative*, an external object or metaphor provides the touchstone for complex systems of abstract meaning within us and our cultures. In our model, it represents a whole class of abstracts having to do with snail-ness, let's say, just as the Native expressions we will examine represent not simply the unique ideas of one talented artist but the ongoing concerns of many sharing artists within whole cultures.

The premise of this book is that we may use the "clues" provided by Native American tales, songs, dances, architecture, and other arts—provi-sionally, of course—as if they were snail shells, as objects that have mean-ings beyond their physical existence but nonetheless are readable through their details of style and substance. These objects will not be treated as mere cultural items but as fossil records of real responses to living contexts;

as physically crafted, culturally situated, and shared human articulations of irritation, injury, pain, growth, healing, nurturance, and even (sure, go ahead, reach for it) love, phrased in concrete metaphors that at once establish emotional and physical kinship with us and trigger our recognition of other systems of belief, custom, and worldview.

Like the articulations of all cultures, Native American expressions exist for a number of reasons, and few of them are secret or mysterious: They provide entertainment and dramatize ritual and social order; they record and maintain cultural values, providing moral examples, giving instruction, and imparting culturally important information; they express and embody artistic values; they preserve historical records with an eye for culturally significant detail. In our scrutiny of any culture, we easily run the risk of seeing mainly the shell and believing that it is only a shell; thus, we may hastily assume that a narrative is "just a story." But if a snail's shell is not just a shell, if it is an accumulated record of the "agonies" experienced by snails, then its full meaning cannot be captured merely by analyzing its calcium content but will be implied by the style and context of the record, and will lurk quietly in the field of implication, waiting to be brought into focus by an eye willing to read and "unpack" the suggestions of the patterns.

This does not imply that such a pattern is intentionally difficult to understand, or that we need to read meaning *into* the shell, however. Quite the opposite: it requires us to read *out* of the shell as text, and to accomplish this task, we need to be open to what the clues mean in the cultural contexts which shaped that shell. While our insights will be conditioned by what we bring with us into the effort, we must try as much as possible to include as much knowledge as we can of the Native contexts. In other words, we should not apply our own fantasies to this job of perception; neither should we take the lazy way out and say it's just anybody's guess. Nor will we start with the "hidden-meaning premise" usually expressed in the question, "What do you think this *really* means?" Instead, we will ask, "What's being acted out, or dramatized, or made concrete here?"

Attend a Native powwow and you will see that no one is trying to hide anything; rather, something is being performed and projected to you and everyone else, even though it is not explicit. So what, then, is being performed, and how does it mean something to those who do it? You can see it happening, but its significance must be extrapolated from the way the event is actualized in its cultural context. The feathers and beadwork and dance steps and music can be treated as objective correlatives of a set of cultural assumptions, just as the events in a story, the shape of a dwelling, or the items of traditional food can be profitably viewed as *icons* of cultural meaning. Their significance is seldom overt or explained in the text itself, but they come to life or are epitomized in the cultural performance.

Of course, on one level we sensibly hesitate to make a serious parallel between snails and cultures, partly because they are not really analogous and partly because we're not altogether sure that a snail feels anything in our sense of the word, let alone that a snail produces its shell as a reflection of anguish for others to read. And we also know that in the cold light of denotation, it probably can't be said that a culture has feelings or values that *it* records through the vernacular expressions of its members. Agreed, these propositions are good examples of *pathetic fallacy*—attributing feelings to something which doesn't feel. But that's what metaphors and figures of speech are for: they make connections that may not otherwise come to mind, just as the tortured markings on an abalone shell stressed by sponges and bored by clams, or the pearl in an oyster shell, or the twisted limbs of a tree constantly assailed by the wind can suggest some of the most delicate human experiences expressed in non-human terms. From an oyster's perspective, if there is such a thing, a pearl results from an act of creation that emanates from a pain that won't go away—in itself an apt description of what a good poem, or song, or story can do for us. From the human perspective, a pearl is an item on which to exercise judgments about beauty, shape, rarity, possibilities of human adornment, or monetary value. Are these judgments wrong because we're not oysters and thus have no right to an opinion about them?

We do not have to think like an oyster (or dance with snails) to read their artistic output; neither do we have to limit our understanding of them by noting only their genus and species. And while we cannot presume to know what an oyster or a snail or a tree thinks, or even if they do, we have a sumptuous advantage in the case of our Native American neighbors: they do think, and they have produced several thousand years' worth of accumulated feelings and values that are eloquently communicated in their intentional folk performances. And they have been creating their arts in our presence and in response to our appearance for more than five hundred years. There are plenty of these deliberate pearls and snail shells for us to examine.

In addition to establishing the idea of approaching our subject respectfully by reading—and experiencing—those clues obvious on the outside, there is another reason for using the snail-shell metaphor, and that is its circularity. If we can characterize the organization of European American cultures as lineal, we can as definitely describe the organization of Native American culture as circular. Circles abound in Native architecture, narrative, ritual, art, dance, and gesture; circular imagery pervades this book.

And while almost any circle would do to symbolize Native concepts of inclusion, balance, symmetry, and relationship, the snail shell—which spirals and builds upon itself in an interrelated, connected, self-referential, growing way—is a perfect metaphor for the ways the subjects of the chapters in this book depend and build upon, reflect, and interrelate with each other.

While most of this book focuses on everyday expressions of impressive beauty and deep meaning, many other levels of Native culture would admittedly be interesting to talk about. Indeed, those who have spent considerable time with Native American people have seen and probably taken part in esoteric events, and they may well have experienced things that seem almost unbelievable—or at least difficult to categorize using their own cultural logic. It is often this esoteric and exotic range of experiences that inquirers choose when they seek to use Native insights as a way of escaping the apparent confines of their own culture. But think for a moment: these kinds of odd and enlightening experiences are available among any group of people. Spend ten years in an immigrant community, or among the Chinese, the Germans, the Japanese, the East Indians, or the Balinese, and you will certainly have tales to tell of unique, dumbfounding—even traumatic—events. Why the American Indian should have become today's leading source of special enlightenment, inscrutable wisdom, and inexplicable wonder is an interesting and important question; perhaps some of the examples in this book will provide insight into that puzzle.

But extraordinary events and striking phenomena—while fascinating—are rarely the most representative elements of a living culture. Besides, it is often the naïve outsider who finds such events striking because he or she does not understand the cultural logic which imbues the event with normalcy. For example, back in the 1950s, when non-Hopi visitors were still welcome to observe seasonal rituals like the Snake Dance, in which dancers hold live rattlesnakes in their mouths, I witnessed the anticipated concluding rainstorms on three different occasions. I found those events very striking and was moved to tears every time. My Hopi friends smiled confidently and acted the way you and I do when our car starts on a very cold morning: relieved, satisfied, but not teary and dumbfounded.

Part of the job of this book is to discuss some of the most interesting aspects of cultural logic and explore the many ways Native American societies have constructed their sense of logic and ritual in relation to the world around them. But according to our metaphorical plan, we are not going to focus on the surprising and awesome; rather, we will look at the expressions of everyday life and the customs that animate the generalized values and worldview assumptions of Native Americans, for these common cultural goods most accurately illustrate the baseline of any culture. Folklore, the study of traditional, culturally situated expressions in their normal performative contexts, like anthropology and social history, is especially equipped to discuss these matters precisely because it is predicated on the importance of the ongoing, shared, vernacular voice.

Like snail shells with consciousness of kind and volition built in, the expressions of folklore are directed toward others, in the process engaging those others as cultural participants—either audiences or coperformers. Traditional foods require many hands to make them and many mouths to eat them, and seldom is nutrition alone the main reason for their creation. Similarly, jokes, dances, traditional housing (even the decoration of commercially built housing), and songs are ways of expressing, perpetuating, and making palpable—experiential—the complex abstractions of cultural values and assumptions. It's difficult to *explain* what makes ethnic foods, for example, important to weddings or birthdays; but when you, as an insider, see and taste those foods, you *experience* a powerful sense of kinship quite independent from analytical commentary. Insofar as folklore is the performance of what closely related groups have felt and believed and assumed over the years, we may fairly use the term *anguish*—despite its initial melodramatic impact—to represent the depth and intensity of the accumulated emotional load articulated in traditional contexts. Moreover, since the performance of arts, crafts, foods, stories, songs, and dances requires not only intellectual competence but physical and emotional commitment in the form of body movement, breathing, use of vocal cords, tasting, and hearing, the resultant "texts" are redolent with ongoing human feeling. Indeed, folklore could not exist without it.

I have chosen the categories of folklore for this book with several considerations in mind; foremost is the fact that they are all available to non-Indians without the necessity for us to intrude. The first chapters focus on traditional forms, patterned formulations of complex, shared value systems: visual art and architecture, dance, oral narrative. Later chapters deal with cultural attitudes and worldviews expressed through humor and in stories and customs detailing the excitement of scientific and geographical discovery.

In our discussion of Native visual arts, we will look not only at decorative tours de force—which they certainly are—but also visible constellations of meaning. We will discuss the way color, pattern, imagery, medium, and context visually suggest important elements of Native life relating to gender, status, tribal affiliation, and worldview. Perhaps to the surprise of some, we will discover how many Native artistic expressions have incorporated and coopted materials and designs from the encroaching Euro-American world—often producing a sensitive commentary on the relationship between Native and non-Native.

Traditional Native architecture varies widely from tribe to tribe, distinctly expressing a spatial model of human relationships within the natural world. The overall preference for round dwellings where a family or extended family live together in one space is not simply due to the lack of lumber or the absence of a decent regard for privacy but physically evokes a system which views the group—not the individual—as the basic unit and therefore shapes the immediate living space to reflect (and require) constant interaction among closely associated members. We will find that the patterns in architecture, visual arts, and narrative, along with the social assumptions that underlie eating and dancing, grow out of and reflect each other, providing rich networks of cultural experience for Native Americans who participate in these folk expressions.

Folk narratives are extremely valuable for understanding cultural assumptions because their ongoing existence is predicated on the ability— and the interest—of the audience not only to understand what is being dramatized but to pass it on to others who are interested in hearing it. Such narratives arise and are transmitted without the aid of print and are continually reshaped, polished, and reexamined by their tellers; the fact that they have survived indicates that they are considered memorable, they make cultural sense, and they are entertaining on one or more levels. A printed book or a written letter can exist long after its contents have immediate interest for anybody; when an orally transmitted story ceases to make sense or be interesting, however, people simply quit telling it, and it is no longer there. The survival of an orally transmitted story is in itself a testimony to its ongoing validity as an expression of cultural meaning in dramatic terms. A narrative is a sequence of related events, acted out by characters who experience an important complication and then witness its resolution. Of course, most narratives must be interesting and entertaining, or else why keep telling them? On the other hand, many stories, including some sacred narratives, impact us through wonder, awe, or fear, so we may say that mere entertainment is not always the principal reason a story is told, just as nutrition is not the main reason ethnic foods are eaten. But, just as food must offer real nourishment, a story has to be sensible, coherent, and somehow logical to the listeners, or its point is lost.

Beyond entertainment, we will see that the actions of the characters in Native stories usually reveal a broad range of cultural evaluations; whether an actor in a story is a person, animal, rock, or plant, if it does or says something the tribe sees as foolish or dangerous, it will get its come-uppance. Thus, stories not only entertain but also embody Native behavioral and ethical values. Yet they almost never comment overtly on the values that shape the fortunes of the characters; instead, the characters act, and the results offer us insight into the value system through nuances of vicarious experience and empathy rather than open lecturing. We will look at Native narratives as tightly distilled dramatizations of cultural ideas and will not ask, "What does this story explain?" but rather, "What does this story dramatize?"—a quite different question altogether. Although Native narratives are dynamic arrangements of cultural meaning, not just simple entertainment, entertainment is itself culturally situated and must be considered.

In traditional dance, we will look at the way formulaic, culturally defined kinetic movement embodies (in the fullest sense) human concerns, ranging from connections with the earth and its living animals and plants to social and religious patterns that can only be experienced fully as a person goes through the steps. Our focus will not be on religious ritual dancing, much of which requires the kind of insider knowledge and years of personal involvement which we don't pretend to possess. Most—certainly not all—ritual dancing can indeed be witnessed by respectful outsiders, and its patterns are very much like those we will discuss with powwows and other social dances. But we have agreed—I hope—to look primarily at the folk expressions most openly available to outsiders, so in the case of dance, we will follow our Native friends to social gatherings rather than church. Don't be disappointed: there's as much to learn at a powwow as a Sun Dance, and we're not as likely to blunder in our approach or interpretation. And we won't be so likely to delude ourselves into believing we have achieved fast-food spiritual enlightenment, either.

Each tale, each dance, each traditional food, each dwelling is full of cultural meaning because its articulation has been subjected to a cumulative process which changes, discards, or sloughs off the transitory, the trivial, and the inessential. Like the snail shell, the part which survives expresses the aggregate "feel" of the *group* because, in the long process of distillation, it has lost the marks of the original contributors and has compacted the talents and values of the many performers who have repeatedly contributed their expressions to the group's ongoing and ever-developing aesthetics.

However, such expressions, even in their dynamic multiform and interactive richness, do not give us any final Truth about Native American cultures. They do verify that many tribal groups did not "vanish" but persevered and continue to function as cohesive, living cultures.

For those tribes that are still flourishing, for those whose cultures have been partly demolished, and even those whose worlds were devastated, the expressions of folklore provide us with the best and most articulate records of perspectives that we cannot do without precisely because they embody the relatively unmediated cultural voices of the peoples who have shaped the realities of life in the Western Hemisphere. In this book, they emerge as the hallmarks of accumulated values, attitudes, and world-views—the living matrices from which cultural constructions like humor, art, exploration, and scientific discovery proceed.

Like all cultures, Native American tribes exhibit a wide spectrum of expressive customs at all levels of society—from the exceedingly formal and demanding systems of highly trained specialists (it can take a Navajo singer from five to twenty years to learn one ceremony—and a good singer usually knows several) to the informal gestures and anecdotes of everyday interaction, which everyone readily picks up from infancy. As with all cultures, the Native American languages are complex and varied, and answer the demands of their users fully; of the several hundred languages—not dialects—once extant in North America, an estimated 150 are still in daily use. Nobody knows how many of the languages in Central and South America have been eradicated by the European invasion and the ongoing "development" of agricultural lands by fire, but certainly hundreds remain today.

Native cultures are organized in ways that may seem startlingly different from those of the later invaders and immigrants, yet—as I've suggested—they possess the same kinds of human features: language, music, art, religion, shelter, and food acquisition and preparation. In other words, while they are different—and often even different from each other—we shouldn't expect them to be odd, deficient, or opaque. They are functioning cultures that have developed in this hemisphere over a tenure estimated by some at more than thirty thousand years.

While Native Americans never developed the intense bureaucratic and aristocratic systems that have marked some European and Asian societies, they created extremely complex political and religious structures of their own, many of which seem quite advanced to us. Among the Iroquois, for example, men have primarily been elected as leaders, while the women chiefly have done the voting. While Native peoples did not evolve a machine-based technology—complete with marketing plans—they did of course develop techniques sufficient to fulfill their needs. Beyond that, most tribes encouraged an impressive range of visual arts among virtually all members of their society. Without laboratories, they discovered and consistently used medicines on which we still rely.

Without colleges of agriculture, they developed a kind of grass into a grain humanity depends upon—corn—that now feeds people and animals around the world. They articulated few—if any—engineering theories, but some tribes developed portable housing while others built huge complexes like Pueblo Bonito in Chaco Canyon, whose 500-plus-room edifice, deserted by 1400, is thought to have been the largest apartment building anywhere in the world until the late 1800s, when massive hotels were erected in Europe.

Surely, the cultures of North America are in their own ways as subtle as any in the world. These are not "backward" or "primitive" people—unless one equates primitive with the absence of bureaucracy or the technological inability to destroy vast numbers of fellow human beings. Moreover, the artistic and literary works of these cultures are as stunning as those found anywhere in the world—and may strike us as even more impressive because they were produced and perpetuated without royal patronage, university instruction, church encouragement, art studios, publication media, or a field of critical theory. But before we make a heroic case of the Native Americans—as if they had somehow triumphed over their unfortunate illiteracy and lack of proper schooling—let's take a brief, and no doubt superficial, look at the main elements that constitute any culture so that we don't make the mistake of believing there is any one "normal" set of criteria expected of one.

The term *culture* is itself a concrete reference to a set of related abstractions, and consequently the term is easier to describe than define. To begin with, the English word comes from the Latin *cultus*, "cultivation [of the earth]," and reflects the notion that plowing the soil improves the land. Leaving aside for now the more recent discovery that plowing is not the best thing to do to the land, which comes up again in our discussion of Native agriculture, let's just note the implication, the connotation, that culture originally had something to do with making things better or more productive. And certainly, because of the difficulties of raising food in northern Europe in earlier days—especially in contrast to obtaining it by hunting and raiding—the image of plowing must have had a powerful effect on people: It envisions cooperation, it suggests the steady investment of labor in the production of food, it implies a relatively sedentary life—all of which no doubt were central in the establishment of stable communities. Hence, it is no accident that we talk about both the soil and ourselves being cultivated and that we define culture as that constellation of social operations which encompasses the traditions, beliefs, institutions, arts, and behaviors that bind us together to maintain that stable, identifiable, productive, ongoing, cooperative system which assures our survival.

But the trick is, of course, that the conditions that stabilize one group of people may destabilize another, so we must recognize—for one important example—that the idea of perfectability, or at least the urge toward making things better than they are, is itself a constructed assumption that rides along with the word culture and encourages us to look at other groups of people as if they are less or more cultivated than we are, depending on how far along they are in bettering themselves or exploiting the earth's resources.

In other words, even in the presumably neutral terms we want to use may lurk a set of our own built-in cultural values. On the issue of cultivating the soil, for example, most tribes immediately rejected the idea of plowing, abhorring the notion of cutting open the earth because that was both symbolically and physically destructive. This, of course, was viewed as backward behavior by white settlers, who thought the Indians were lazy and uninterested in using the land. Believing that "rain follows the plow," whites churned up as much land as they could get their machinery into and eventually created a dust bowl. This perfectly sensible cultural idea was so powerful and "right" that people practiced it wherever they went, overlooking local customs and environmental realities with the passion of the righteous. The millions of bison who once thundered across the plains never did nearly as much long-term ecological damage as a few thousand plows and could have supplied meat practically forever, but they were expunged.

It is easy to imagine, then, that Native terms for what we call culture are not rooted in metaphors of the way early farmers learned to survive on the cold, dark fields of northern Europe; nonetheless, Native peoples had—and still do—behaviors, institutions, beliefs, and expressions which characterize and maintain their identity, and we need a term to describe this system. We're stuck with culture for now, but remember not to assume all cultures have the same construction.

A helpful and mercifully succinct description is given by folklorist David Hufford, who holds that culture exists to nurture and convey any shared system of values; and—only partly in jest—Elliott Oring adds that folklore is that part of culture that lives happily ever after. Well, what kinds of values are these? and where do they come from? and why are they so important that it takes the whole network of a human society to pass them on? And why do some of these values continue to be performed on the vernacular level in everyday life in the genres we call folklore?

Culture is an ongoing accumulation of interactive, interdependent human experiences and expressions that grow out of and articulate such factors as a) the general biological needs and inherited patterns of human life; b) the psychological patterns shared by humans; c) the psychological patterns and peculiarities of particular individuals; d) the intersection of human populations with their environments; e) a "spiritual" longing that seeks to reconcile the palpable world with powers and processes that seem to lie beyond empirical observation; and f) the organization of these factors into the normal patterns of a particular community.

As these factors are construed, understood, and valued through shared assumptions and worldviews, they develop a kind of cultural normalcy in accord with the perceived realities of the group. It is important to note that these realities may be viewed as practical necessities and may therefore possess logical explanations, but most of them are nonetheless understandings *about* reality, not necessarily *of* it. The white settlers *believed* they had to plow to produce crops, and so they did. The Blackfeet *believed* they had to do the Buffalo Dance to assure the annual return of the buffalo, and so they did. There's a sense of "Of course! What else would you do?" about these matters. People didn't suspect that following the optimistic route of the plow would actually lead to destruction of the land. People didn't expect that another group would come along and fracture forever the delicate ritual balance between humans and their animal relatives, the bison.

So it is well to remember, no matter whose culture we are discussing, that even though biological, psychological, and environmental factors seem like antiseptic functions of nature, they are almost always interpreted in the evaluative framework of culture, and the medium for this ongoing interpretation is folklore. Satisfying our biological needs may certainly assure the continuation of our species, but the subject is usually phrased in abstractions like courtship, marriage, sin, chastity, and sexual orientation. Inherited characteristics are described in the light of positive and negative family values ("You sure got your mother's family's nose," or "You act just like your father"), in terms expressing societal expectations about beauty or size, or as ethnic and racial evaluations about hair, color, or build which may be positive within a group but seen as negative by outsiders. Long before they actually met Europeans, the Chinese and Japanese commonly depicted ghosts and demons as white skinned, blue eyed, and red haired because such characteristics were so unthinkable in their normal world. Even today, one common Chinese word for foreigner translates as "ghost."

The generally shared psychological patterns studied by Carl Jung and his followers are often tagged with the unfortunate label "archetype" because of their alleged universal meanings, and for this reason, many scholars dismiss the idea of inherited images as too nebulous. But a total rejection of Jung's concepts seems hasty and ill conceived, for there is a lot of evidence for the existence of imagery that reaches beyond the experience or recollection of single individuals. If we can inherit superficial features like the family nose and hair color, why not more subtle qualities stored in the brain? If birds and turtles can inherit complex and accurate maps that are not the result of instruction or example and are far more precise and discerning than gross instincts, why can't humans conceivably inherit patterns, perhaps even from ancient times? Joseph Campbell and other scholars offer rich examples of this possibility, and even if it is true—and it is—that Campbell and his followers in their zeal happen to focus on the examples that illustrate their premise, handily downplaying or ignoring examples that don't match up, nonetheless the examples they cite are really provocative. But of course the notion of universal archetypes, like the theory of deep-structure language, cannot be proven so much as inferred.

Thus, while there may well be a universal archetype of Mother or Water or the Sun, and while all of us may certainly have both an anima (female side) and animus (male side) in our psychological makeup, the massive evidence about culture generated by years of anthropological and folkloristic fieldwork has pretty well established that these elements are differently organized and articulated—as they are even in everyday language—by the cultures where they appear. The sun is male in one culture, female in another; the hero goes out and conquers in one society, while in another, he stays home and attends to business; water is destructive in one culture, sacred in another, sensuous and seductive in yet another. In some cultures, there are two genders; in others, three; the Navajos distinguish seven or eight genders. The same themes and images are there all right, but rather than assuming they have a universal value, we usually expect them to be different every time we encounter them. But this doesn't mean they do not exist as inherited symbols of deeply rooted meaning; on the contrary, their existence testifies to the ability of a culture to interpret and reconstruct something *meaningful* from inherited materials.

As Freud and others have demonstrated, the individual's psychological state reflects not only the unique patterns formed in a particular psyche by upbringing, nurture, trauma, sickness, and disappointment but also parallels the psychological states of others closely enough to allow generalizations. These, in turn, become the bases for understanding, diagnosing, and treating psychological conditions. But even when these conditions seem unique to the person—a case of psychosis or manic-depressive behavior—we know that they also reflect a life shaped by a community of behaviors. A child reared in a middle-class home in the United States will likely be raised as an individual with rights and responsibilities, with his or her own room; one brought up in Japan will be given the sense that the group is more important than the individual and personal privacy is a form of egotism. A Native American child reared traditionally is virtually never alone, and this provides a living sense of being part of a larger and more important group—a sense amplified by living in a one-room dwelling and having some kinds of competition suppressed.

Personal psychology in these contexts is naturally interpreted—and even experienced—in terms of the culture's assumptions about normality. For example, many Hmong immigrants to America have died of shock in their sleep from a culturally constructed psychological condition our culture has only recently defined ("sudden unexpected nocturnal death syndrome," or SUNDS). Hispanic people suffering from *susto*, a kind of shock, are easily diagnosed as psychotic by Anglo-American doctors who don't recognize the culturally defined symptoms. Some Japanese individuals suffer from a depression caused by fear of embarrassing other people—an idea that hardly makes sense in Western culture but is a real Japanese phenomenon nonetheless. Hopis recognize several different kinds of individual depression, including petulance and broken heart. What is crucial in all these examples (and hundreds more like them) is our slow recognition that even in the most private recesses of an individual's mind, processes are shaped and interpreted by the particular culture.

The same can be said, of course, about human interaction with the environment. While, on the one hand, we can look at environmental processes with relatively scientific objectivity, we normally have certain cultural agendas in mind. A culture that assumes it is superior to nature—whether by virtue of biblical decree or dint of advanced intelligence—makes an easy assumption that nature can—and ought to—be controlled if not dominated. From the taming of the frontier to the eager protection of threatened species, from the suppression of forest fires to the exploitation of natural resources, the technical and scientific talents of Euro-Americans are most often directed at controlling the outcome of the environmental equation, dominating the choices of survival rather than abiding by the outcome of natural processes as other cultures normally do.

Most Native Americans come from cultural backgrounds where people assume nature has a delicate balance which cannot be controlled but with which one must be in harmony; most often this is viewed as a ritual or spiritual harmony that does not relate logically to whether one litters or recycles. For many Anglo-Americans, deer are a harvestable natural resource; to many Native American cultures, deer are relatives who are willing under normal circumstances to do what relatives do: share food with their kin. I do not make this contrast to suggest that one system is more right or moral than the other but to point out that someone who considers the earth a relative or a sacred symbol of universal motherhood and nurturance is going to make decisions and interpretations that are quite different from those of a person who thinks that the earth is a magnificent collection of resources assembled by geologic chance or a generous Father in heaven as a piggy bank for his children.

In *Forests: The Shadow of Civilization*, Robert Pogue Harrison demonstrates brilliantly that forests are not simply stands of trees but have become symbolic ways of expressing human relationships to nature and marking the outer edge of civilization. In the typical northern European folktale, the forest is the setting for danger, evil, and the unexpected. In the English and Scottish ballads, the forest is the scene for murders, seductions, attacks, and rapes. My own research on water folklore has convinced me that here, too, an apparently independent substance has been interpreted/translated into clashing cultural realities by Mormon ranchers, Hispanic farmers, and Native Americans in distinctive ways that have little to do with the objective nature of H_2O. How do all these cultural paradigms come about? I see no great evidence that they flow from the leading thinkers and scientists of any era; to the contrary, as Norwood Russell Hanson so well reveals, scientists are keyed by their cultures to look for certain things they already believe to be there. I think there is ample proof that in every culture the cultural constellation predates and shapes the field of discovery, a topic that will receive more attention later in this book.

Utilizing local attitudes about region and environment, biological need, psychological states, religion, occupation, gender, family, ethnicity, age and death, every ongoing group of people discovers and refines a dynamic system of reference to which individuals relate and by which they judge themselves and others. Insofar as this system becomes socialized into the everyday lives of its members and gets passed on, the group may be said to "have" a culture.

Because of the distinctive mix which characterizes each culture, however, even geographically neighboring groups may be vastly different. The neighboring Navajos and Hopis, for example, while they both have an essentially matriarchal family organization, nonetheless have entirely different worldviews about time, space, movement, and land tenure. And the contrasts are even greater when we compare European with Native American cultures: The heavy European use of nouns and straight lines is monumentally different from the Navajo preference for verbs and circles. In Navajo, which has 356,200 conjugations for the verb "to go," movement is the central leitmotif; in the European languages, where nouns are central, the key subjects are things, place, ownership. We even refer to ideas as things: "Let's get things straight."

Although the roots of these cultural ideas are biological, psychological, situational, and ecological, the way each group assembles, understands, and codes these factors is markedly different. For this reason, the term *cultural construction* gives us a way to discuss cultures without expecting all of them to be alike. It is difficult to say whether people construct their culture or it constructs them; it's probably both, in an interactive way. But the term calls our attention to the fact that, while the building materials may be similar, the edifices and their meanings diverge—even among groups that may seem at first to be similar. Folklore, in the aggregate, is made up of the vernacular performances that embody these cultural concepts.

We will look at the folk expressions of Native Americans in the West, then, not only because they are open to our scrutiny but also because they represent a relatively unfiltered articulation of everyday cultural codes, compared with the more highly trained and focused utterances and priestly traditions of specially educated orators, ritual leaders, and healer-doctors. We begin with Native visual arts because their construction, their meaningful arrangements of pattern and color, and their concrete articulation of culturally significant ideas make them one of the most readily accessible, intellectually congenial arenas for actually experiencing—albeit vicariously—the anguish of snails.

Notes

The Blackfoot Buffalo Dance was described by George Bird Grinnell in *Blackfoot Lodge Tales* (New York: Charles Scribner's Sons, 1917), 104–7, 220–24, 229–30. A summary of the Buffalo Dance story is given by Joseph Campbell in *The Masks of God: Primitive Mythology* (New York: Viking Press, 1959), 282–86. Its main feature is the marrying of a Blackfoot woman to a bison chief, thus establishing the reciprocal family logic by which the buffalo provide their flesh for food and the Blackfeet supply the restorative dance and prayer. Peter Nabokov presents fascinating historical testimony on the interactive relationship between Natives and bison in the Yellowstone area, which even extended to Natives corralling and protecting small groups of the animals when it became evident that the whites were bent on total destruction. When the government finally decided to preserve the species, many bison were bought from the Native people who had protected them (see Peter Nabokov, *A Forest of Time: American Indian Ways of History* [Cambridge: Cambridge University Press, 2002], 60–63).

Comments from David Hufford and Elliott Oring come from, respectively, David Hufford, private correspondence December 2, 2000; Elliott Oring, private correspondence, June 15, 2001.

Various aspects of the culturally informed "constructions" of health and healing can be found in Erika Brady, ed., *Healing Logics: Culture and Medicine in Modern Health Belief Systems* (Logan: Utah State University Press, 2001) and in Bonnie Blair O'Connor's *Healing Traditions: Alternative Medicine and the Health Professions* (Philadelphia: University of Pennsylvania Press, 1995). Both of these works provide extensive and thorough bibliographies. Shelley R. Adler discusses the SUNDS phenomenon in "Terror in Transition: Hmong Folk Belief in America" in Barbara Walker, ed., *Out of the Ordinary: Folklore and the Supernatural* (Logan: Utah State University Press, 1995), 180–202.

Robert Pogue Harrison's *Forests: The Shadow of Civilization* (Chicago: University of Chicago Press, 1992) is a brilliant exposition of the culturally constructed notion of what a forest is. Norwood Russell Hanson shows how central cultural worldview is even to the supposedly objective processes of scientific discovery in his *Patterns of Discovery: An Inquiry into the Conceptual Foundations of Science* (Cambridge: Cambridge University Press, 1958). His observations (along with those of several others) are integral to my chapter, "Folklore and Cultural Worldview," in *The Dynamics of Folklore* (Logan: Utah State University Press, 1996), 263–313. One of the best discussions of the relationship between cultural worldview and language is Gary Witherspoon's *Language and Art in the Navajo Universe* (Ann Arbor: University of Michigan Press, 1977). To my knowledge, Witherspoon was the first person to use a computer to determine the number of conjugations for the Navajo verb "to go."

2

Visual Patterns of Performance

Arts

> *When I began making baskets, I could feel the fingers of those long-ago women touching my fingers.*
>
> —Deni Hockema, Coquelle basketmaker

ON AUGUST 12, 1868, just-retired Secretary of State William H. Seward (who had earlier urged Congress to buy Alaska from the Russians, a deal later labeled "Seward's folly"), visited Sitka, then the capital. In his brief speech, he praised the beauties and resources of Alaska, predicted the territory would one day become a state, and then resumed his voyage. Standard biographies of Seward do not mention what the makeup of his Sitka audience was, but oral history, buttressed by a local Native art form, provides us a much fuller picture of this apparently trivial event. Tlingit chiefs, clan leaders, family heads, and shamans came out to receive Seward in colorful ceremonies during which they gave him important artistic and ritual objects like drums, carved wood, and blankets. According to later Tlingit accounts, Seward received all these wonderful presents without comment and offered no gifts in return.

After his departure, several of the insulted Tlingits commissioned the carving and erection of a "shame pole" to commemorate the event. At the top of an otherwise plain pole balanced an ornately carved chest or box, which one could imagine to be chock full of potential gifts; sitting on the chest, symbolically keeping the box from being opened to share its contents, perched a white man with beard, top hat, and frock coat. Now, some 130 years after the insult and long after the pole disintegrated—as most totem poles do—this eloquent artistic statement is still remembered sarcastically by elderly Tlingits, as well as by southeast Alaska history buffs, Native and non-Native alike, who recount and savor numerous stories of being snubbed by officials from the Lower Forty-eight.

The Seward shame pole may fairly be called "folk art" because it represents not the unique vision or tastes of a particular carver but the shared opinions and mutual requirements of the entire community of everyday folks who prompted it. As a striking piece of wood carving, it would have been recognized in any art-museum collection as an odd totem pole by modern non-Natives; in fact, it did not represent anyone's totem (natural ancestor); quite to the contrary, it parodied someone who was perceived as *resisting* the establishment of reciprocal family relationships—the system which drives the Tlingit world. Of course, the total absence of important family and clan crests on the pole proclaimed the lack of connection between Seward and the Tlingits. One assumes poor ex-Secretary of State Seward was innocently ignorant of these details.

Without the story and its historical and cultural context, we would have no way to "read" the Seward shame pole; and now that the pole itself has rotted away, the story, itself an artistic text, becomes more valuable, for it's the only remaining reference to that community art piece and its eloquent expression of cultural disgust. Other carved poles feature non-Natives at the top: the old Lincoln Pole, which once stood on Tongass Island (and now resides in the Alaska State Museum in Juneau), apparently used the figure of Lincoln, arms akimbo, to represent a powerful white man; a more recently carved pole in Sitka honors—or at least memorializes—the strong Russian influence in that area (fig. 1), where today, at the church which houses the Russian Orthodox bishop of North America, you can hear a Tlingit choir singing the *liturgia* in four-part harmony.

So then, how do we know if a pole is meant to honor, memorialize, or shame someone? We have to become acquainted with the tribal culture, its customs, and its values, for the "meanings" emanate from the living cultural contexts, not the isolated art work itself. And to make matters more complex (but also more interesting), poles are not always read the same way. While Northwest tribes generally read poles from top to bottom, the most important figure is not necessarily the one at the very top but the biggest or most prominent one. The Lincoln Pole, for example, has a huge carving of Raven at the bottom, topped by a smooth pole of about thirty or forty feet, with a rather spindly Lincoln standing at the top. Not surprisingly, the Tlingits do not call this the Lincoln Pole but the Proud Raven Pole, indicating that members of the Raven Clan were claiming something basic and powerful about their first encounters with the whites and were not implying in any way that that white guy was "top man on their totem pole." But this observation raises the possibility that some poles may be read from bottom to top, or at least that a particular sequence is not mandatory. Clearly, to go any deeper would require us to master a lot of tribal convention and custom, much of which we may simply not have access to.

Fig. 1. Trader Legend Pole that signifies the importance of Russian whites to totem-pole makers; Sitka National Historical Park, Sitka, Alaska. Photo by the author.

Fig. 2. Bicentennial Pole carved by Duane Pasco,
a non-Native American from Washington State;
Sitka National Historical Park, Sitka, Alaska.
Photo by the author.

Yet, even without extensive esoteric knowledge, we can still register the richness of artistic nuance in such stories as the following. A persistent legend (a story told as true by someone who nonetheless was not an eyewitness) in the Sitka area accounts for the meaning of a pole commissioned by Sitka National Historical Park and erected next to park headquarters during the U. S. Bicentennial (fig. 2). The pole was carved by Duane Pasco, a non-Native American, who, according to the story, meant it to read from the bottom up: A figure representing the older, traditional generation (holding a halibut hook and a shaman's rattle) gives rise to—and provides a foundation for—the newer generation, which, building on gifts from the whites (writing, the cross, the rifle), emerges on top holding both a traditional carved "talking stick" and what looks like a large scroll of paper. Some local Tlingits, who felt snubbed that the contract for crafting a pole for their own tribal area did not go to one of them, suggested that the pole was carved "upside down" in Tsimshian style and should be read from the top down in normal (i.e., Tlingit) fashion: The modern Native youth, trying to live precariously in two worlds at once (signified by a thin carved stick and a flourescent light bulb), is supported by the hegemonic forces of white society (literacy, religion, and increased power to kill) and thinks he is at the top of the world, but the weight of his success, and that of the whites, is being borne by the patient, but now trampled, elder, who is trying to retain the old ways despite the heavy burden placed on him.

Such a detailed decoding of the Bicentennial Pole sounds more like a political statement than a traditional reading, yet it stands as an example of how evocative traditional art can be: the meanings reside in, and are continually reexamined by, the knowledgeable culture. The fact that most of the poles in the Sitka totem park are in Haida style (which reads from the bottom up but raised no objections from local Tlingits) suggests further that what's really topsy-turvy here is the presence of a prominent white creation (with all the attendant white notions about Indianness) in the midst of a rich display of local Native art.

The carved poles of the Northwest are excellent examples of the Native folk arts we will discuss here (although they are only one genre out of an amazing variety of artistic achievements among the Northwest peoples): They articulate community taste and worldview; they are designed for public display (though many of them also had ritual uses); they are made from materials which themselves have cultural significance; and their meaning derives from their cultural contexts since the work of art suggestively phrases a set of culturally recognizable propositions and dramatizes them for an appreciative audience.

Fig. 3. A male hogan made with desert sand and vertical poles; Monument Valley, Utah. Photo by the author.

In this sense, all folk arts are performances. Whether the statement is in weaving, in beadwork, in carved wood, in dance, in song, in the design and construction of living spaces, in food, or in humor, it constitutes the artist's attempt to employ communally understood, culturally charged codes to dramatize the group's values and elicit recognition from the audience. We are obviously not dealing with folk art as it is often mislabeled by some in the museum community: naïve, untutored, "primitive," or outsider art produced by artistically gifted people who have no formal training. Indeed, Native American artists have had plenty of training, but it is the kind that comes from cultural immersion, not isolation in a studio.

As our snail-shell metaphor suggests, I am proposing that the meaningful patterning in Native folk expression, along with the traditional processes through which Native Americans produce these patterns, offer them—and us—powerful icons of their shared assumptions about order, balance, symmetry, human and natural relationships, worldview, and, obviously, beauty. The development of the Navajo hogan over the past five hundred to six hundred years provides a striking example of the dynamic intersection of visual design and lived culture. The earliest identifiable Navajo dwellings are shaped much like the northern Plains tipi: a tripod of forked poles supports numerous other poles and branches to form a cone-shaped structure which—apparently—was covered with hides or, in warmer weather, more brush. Similar structures are still used by the

Fig. 4. A female hogan made with desert sand over horizontal poles; Monument Valley, Utah. Photo by the author.

northern Athabascans and (without the cone shape) by the Yupiks. As the people who eventually became known as Navajos migrated south and began to settle into the Southwest, they started covering their lodges with rocks, clay, and desert mud. The cone-shaped dwelling had an entryway on one side, which you can imagine had previously been made by draping hides on a frame (fig. 3). As the Navajos learned agriculture from their predecessors in the area, the Pueblo peoples, their hogans acquired a new contour (fig. 4): The round floor plan was created by placing upright posts in a circle, and the roof was given a dome shape by corbeling, exactly the same kind of construction technique used in the roofs of Pueblo kivas (figs. 5, 6).

In addition to what this says about intercultural borrowing, the design change actually mirrors a powerful paradigm shift in Navajo world-view, and that's what makes it particularly interesting. As the hogan was changing from a tall, pointy structure to a bigger and more rounded dwelling, the culture was changing from a male-centered system (inherited from their Athabascan hunting and fishing relatives in what is now western Canada and interior Alaska) to a female-centered one (based on that of their new neighbors, the Hopi, Zuni, and other Pueblo farmers). I'm not arguing a Freudian interpretation but a cultural one, for the Navajos actually call the first kind (known to anthropologists as the "forked-pole hogan") the *male hogan*, while the later kind is called the

Fig. 5. Corbeled roof on female hogan interior. Photo by the author.

Fig. 6. Wall and roof of female hogan interior. Photo by the author.

female hogan. When you are inside a female hogan today, you are to imagine that you are in the womb of Changing Woman; her navel is overhead (the smoke hole), and her birth canal (the east-facing door) is the means by which you are reborn every day as you go out into the world. The Navajo mother owns her hogan, and her husband moves in with her (and can be ejected at her discretion). She "owns" her children and most of the livestock; her children trace their lineage through her clan, and only secondarily through their father's.

When you consider that this shift in gender power has occurred during the past five hundred or so years, you can see what a massive difference its perspectives have made in the lives and values of the people we call Navajo. The move from a tipilike, easily erected, male-dominated, hunting-camp structure to a round, permanent, female-oriented birth chamber reflects and emanates from the changes occurring in the Navajo culture. The female hogan offers a wonderful example of our snail-shell metaphor.

And the same principle operates on all levels, from tiny pieces of jewelry to large dances. Ranging from physical representations, where culturally charged mediums and materials (like wood, roots, hides, quills, and beads) are organized and foregrounded by color, design, and familiar patterning, to oral stories and songs, where culturally resonant themes and concerns are organized and "performed," colored and nuanced by word and tone, Native artists—like all artists—use anatomy, voice, familiar material objects, rhythm, and color to render immediate and experiential the abstractions which animate the culture and their shared life.

Fashionable contrasting terms like "high" and "low," or "elite" and "folk," do not help us define or understand this art, largely because they obscure the important living contexts in which all art is situated. Because cultural context plays a more dominant role than the individual's tastes in the aesthetics and production of Native arts, it is more useful to consider not the sophistication and vision of particular artists but rather, the extent to which community values and expectations influence the act, the direction, the function, and thus the meaning of the artistic expressions. Obviously, individual talent and inspiration play important roles in any art, and the impact of a community of receivers is never absent, either. Instead of a value-laden vertical scale, we must envision a spectrum which admits the artist's prominence at one end and the culture's importance at the other, tempered by the corollaries that a) there is always a relationship between the two, b) they are not opposed or contrary but interactive in their value, and c) the particular "mix" between artist and culture constitutes a statement of that culture's idea about the relationship between art and society.

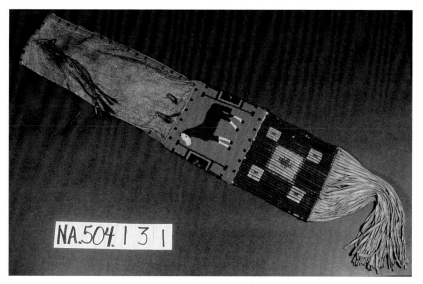

Fig. 7. Sioux pipe bag; the horse is in beadwork, and the lower portion is in the
standard quillwork. Adolph Spohr Collection, gift of Larry Sheerin
(NA.504.131); Buffalo Bill Historical Center, Cody, Wyoming.

Because of the way their culture functions, tribal artists are likely to
be more attentive to culturally transmitted, tested issues than personal
forms of expression—not because they are less capable as artists or less
aware of themselves as individuals, but because in tribal systems the interests and welfare of the group supersede individual demands. "Tribe" does
not denote a backward or primitive society but simply one which believes
it continues to exist because individuals cooperate rather than compete.

But this does not imply that artistic innovation is discouraged by
tribal life; rather, it usually expresses itself through well-established cultural habits and attitudes instead of breaking free from them, as Euro-
American artists might do. When glass beads gradually replaced quillwork
(fig. 7), familiar geometrical patterns were retained and intensified, and
newer patterns developed that maintained cultural themes of balance and
reciprocation while allowing newer images to emerge.

The reality of Native arts, then, encompasses both the careful transmitting of older methods and attitudes and the possibility for modern rein-
terpretation within the larger cultural assumptions of the medium. On the
conservative end of this spectrum, the Santa Clara pottery traditions
exemplified by National Heritage Award winner Margaret Tafoya are not
hers but belong to her family and community: "I was taught to stay with
the traditional clay designs because that was the way it was handed down

to my mother and me. I am thankful for my mother teaching me to make large pieces. I watched her and tried to do like she did. And I did." A year before she died, Jeannie Thlunaut, once the last Chilkat blanket weaver in Alaska, told fifteen younger women she was preparing to teach: "I don't want to be stingy with this. I am giving it to you, and you will carry it on."

Yet transmitting and maintaining traditional approaches does not preclude creativity and innovation. Tom Yellowman, for example, a Navajo potter in Blanding, Utah, combines Anasazi patterns and styles with Plains Indian dream-catcher designs to make a modern intertribal ceramic statement that is true to several traditions while also articulating a contemporary way of being "Indian." Nearby, on the small White Mesa Ute Reservation, flute maker Aldean Ketchum carves traditional love flutes according to the teachings of one-hundred-year-old Billy Mike, his recently deceased mentor; but he now decorates them with small bands of colorful beadwork by his Navajo wife, Wanda, who was taught by her Ute in-laws, who have never beaded love flutes (figs. 8, 9). Aldean's discovery of a cultural and linguistic connection between the Utes and the earlier Anasazi led him to burn in some Pueblo symbols (like the hump-backed flute player) as decorations on his flutes, and he has experimented with ceramic instruments—which have the same dimensions as Billy Mike's wooden flutes—after he found some fragments in Anasazi ruins near his home.

Not far away, in Montezuma Creek, Santo Domingo/Acoma silversmith Willie Tortalita lives with his Navajo wife, Joanne. Willie points out a ceramic water bottle hanging on the wall and explains that its designs (a bear-paw print and a set of deer tracks) represent the powerful forces of nature a hunter needs to keep in mind while far from home. A young man going away to hunt was given a specially made ceramic canteen that not only supplied water but also reminded him of his relationship to nature, ritual obligations, and correct deportment. But this particular canteen hanging on Willie's wall has the animal tracks incised entirely through the clay, not painted on; the vessel will not hold water, as Willie explains, because it now plays an expanded role. The canteen has been intensified from a partly practical, partly suggestive item to a wholly symbolic expression of his family's concern for him since he lives among the Navajos, far from his mother's village.

Such strong symbols of nurturance and family concern are among the most powerful themes for Native artists, who are trying to maintain their traditional cultural values while they live and earn their living in a contemporary setting, surrounded by culturally different and often antagonistic neighbors. Other prominent patterns are circular interaction, centering, reciprocation, reflective bilateral and quadrilateral symmetries,

Fig. 8. Aldean and Wanda Ketchum. Photo by Dave Smith, courtesy of M.J. Thomas Photography, Grand Junction, Colorado.

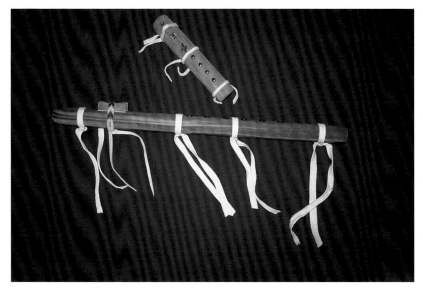

Fig. 9. Flutes by Ute flutemaker Aldean Ketchum; beadwork by his Navajo wife, Wanda. The small flute was given as a joke to the author in response to questions about flutes being intentionally phallic. Photo by the author.

containment and surroundment, and a reciprocity with plants and animals, who, envisioned as relatives, are assumed to owe us the same kind of attention we owe them, the normal situation in tribal family relationships. These images are powerful because they kinetically embody the abstract ways tribal and other ethnically intense cultures view the relationship between the individual and the environment. These concepts are not necessarily purer or more sensitive than those of other cultures; they just portray a distinctive way of seeing the world, society, and the individual.

And these distinctive ways, which we may call *cultural worldview,* are not simply romantic or philosophical flights of fancy: they are based on culturally constructed logic. For example, if we regard plants and animals as our relatives, we will behave differently than if we view them as mere natural resources. Believing that their prayers and ritual buffalo dances would continually restore the bison to life, Plains tribes stampeded them over cliffs in great numbers, taking mostly the fat parts (which were the most nourishing; after all, would your bison relatives want you to starve in the midst of plenty?) and leaving the rest. Mormon pioneers in southern Utah, believing their God would supply them with all the resources they needed, cheerfully denuded the slopes of the Abajo Mountains and gave thanks for the increased water runoff each spring (after calling you to settle in the desert, wouldn't God want you to have more water?). These are both perfectly rational attitudes based on the shared values and assumptions (worldviews) of two different cultures, and the arts of these cultures express the same ideas visually: the bison continues to appear as the *center* of life's powers in Plains art, and in Mormon art, the pioneers are shown, triumphant, at the far *end* of their linear trail, lifting their hats and shouting, "Hosannah!"

In contrast to Native Americans' preference for the surrounding circle, so-called Western cultures employ the straight line and square to suggest the predominant sense of cultural order. From town squares, city blocks (and rectangular cities—especially in the West) to pictures in square frames, calendars, and figures of speech ("Let's get things squared away, straightened out"), the straight line is a major way European American culture expresses itself. People traveling this straight line from alpha to omega are seen as individuals, separate beings having individual rights and responsibilities, people having the capability—indeed, the obligation—to think and act independently (as long as they do not endanger their society). They are often believed to have an individual soul which will be rewarded or punished for its own deeds, or an individual personality which can be dealt with, when necessary, in private by a specialist. They look out mostly for Number One, try to keep up with (or surpass) the Joneses, and compete strenuously for upward mobility. Individuals are admired for planning ahead and achieving their personal potential, and criticized for resting on their laurels. Since personal accomplishment is highly prized, artists in this culture usually follow their own path, often operating, as do philosophers and theologians, far in advance of everyday tastes. In a lineal, individual-oriented society, being "out in front," "cutting edge," "avant-garde," or "pioneering" is usually seen as daring, energetic, even heroic. Artists are said to own their own works and usually copyright them; they (or an agent) promote themselves and their unique vision.

Such values do not necessarily indicate egotism running rampant in Western society or artistic disdain for fellow human beings, as any contemporary artist will quickly point out. Nor do I want to suggest that Native artists are shy, retiring, or unaware of their own talents. Each kind of artist expresses the abstractions of his or her culture; thus, our issue is not ideal quality but a recognition of the way art articulates the culture out of whose living contexts it proceeds. Obviously, now that most contemporary Native artists are resident in, surrounded by, and often trained by Western culture, no clear line of demarcation exists between the two orientations as far as modern art is concerned.

In addition, not surprisingly, since we have pushed ourselves into the Native consciousness for the past five hundred years, much of the traditional art is already addressed to us, aimed at us, and performed in front of us (in many cases because of us). It reflects our presence as well as tribal con-sciousness. So our considerations are not just another charitable exercise in understanding "the other" but an attempt to recognize our own presence in the picture, a picture that, despite this ironic inclusiveness, is nonetheless constructed and understood from a different set of assumptions than our own. We are starting with the visual arts because here we can become famil-iar with the basic patterns and formulations we will encounter in the other expressive forms. These texts, these performances are visible parallels to our snail shell, as well as maps to immense cultural territories.

There is remarkable consistency in the way cultural performances provide tangible enactments of nontangible issues. The Navajos, the peo-ple I have worked most closely with over the past forty-five years, share the assumption of most Native tribes that everything is essentially cyclic, cir-cular. The individual artist or craftswoman, instead of standing on a straight ribbon of time leading from past to future, stands in the middle of a vortex of forces exerted in concentric circles; these are represented by her immediate family (and since Navajos are matriarchal, it is *her* family), her extended family, her clan, and the whole ecological system within which she lives and functions. Of course, the Navajos have a good sense of the past, but they see it surrounding them so they can readily consult it for traditional patterns, not fading away behind them. Religious rituals are almost all focused on either retaining or regaining the balance, harmony, and reciprocation necessary to live properly in this surrounding world, and, interestingly enough, the desired condition of harmony is called *hózhǫ́*, most easily translated as "beauty" in English. Imagine the clues in just this: balance, harmony between humans and nature, is equated with esthetics.

Since the Navajos are surrounded by natural harmonies which they must keep in good repair, their principal artistic themes and logical approaches feature circularity, enclosure, mutual reciprocation. So, in the case of the simple cedar-berry necklaces which were once very common (and are still found here and there) in Navajo country, the idea is to sur-round the wearer with a dramatization of significant meaning. The cedar seeds (actually mountain juniper) are gathered from the food caches of small ground animals by children after they inspect them to make sure there's already a hole in one end (this means the animals have already taken the meat and will not be deprived of food). These seeds are strung together with colored glass beads, sometimes in simple strands, sometimes in circular designs representing star constellations or wedding baskets (fig. 10). The whole work of art thus represents a cooperation between the trees, the ani-mals, and humans; it surrounds the wearer with a physical reminder of the reciprocations and balances in nature (figs. 11, 12).

Fig. 10. *Gad bináá'* (juniper-seed) necklace in the design of a Navajo wedding basket. Photo by Ron Daines.

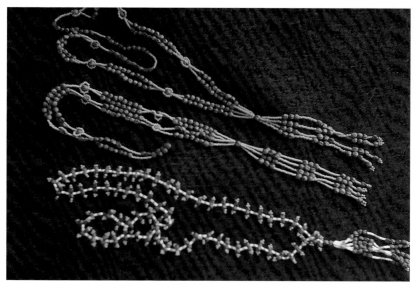

Figs. 11 and 12. Navajo *gad bináá'* necklaces. Colored beads have been added to attract white buyers. Photos by the author.

Navajo rugs are composed on the loom by the weaver using a four-way reciprocal logic that proceeds from the bottom up (figs. 13, 14). Up to the midway point of the warp, whose length is known because it has already been stretched on the loom, the weaver starts at the center; whatever she weaves on the left side is matched, in mirror fashion, on the right since geometrical designs are developed in reciprocation. As she reaches the middle of the warp, she repeats the same moves in reverse, "unbuilding" the identical geometrical designs until the final rug mirrors itself from end to end as well as side to side. However, anyone who has seen a great variety of Navajo rugs already knows that not all of them have geometrical patterns: there are "pictorial" rugs, "eye dazzlers," double-weave pieces, and combinations of geometrical and pictorial designs. But the weaving procedure is similar in all of them.

The rug patterns, said to be based on photographs of Persian rugs shown to late-nineteenth-century weavers by local traders, build on earlier weaving traditions learned from the Pueblo peoples by the Navajos after they arrived in the Southwest about five hundred to six hundred years ago. Athabascans from the far Northwest, they had previously used skins for clothing and floor mats and were constrained by their new environment to learn a great range of life-supporting skills from the earlier inhabitants (including agriculture; the Navajo word for "corn" is still *naadą́ą́'*, literally "enemy food"). By the 1930s, Navajo rugs had become so popular that most weavers produced them for trade, not their own use, and so, of course, they created rugs that would bring the highest prices in goods from the trader—who, in turn, peddled them in faraway places.

What's Navajo about Navajo rugs, according to my weaver friends, is not that they provided a way of avoiding starvation in the terrible years between 1900 and the 1950s but that the method of production requires the weaver to act out the patterns of balance and reciprocation so important to Navajo mental health: The yarn is spun on a spindle which is *rotated* sunwise (so the yarn won't come unraveled); the weaving entails making a *circle* with colored yarn around every strand of the warp during every step; the stereotypical geometrical patterns *can* represent clouds or mountains (as they also do on the Navajo wedding basket; see fig. 15), but they also demonstrate a four-way reciprocation that echoes the four surrounding sacred mountains, the four principal directions, and the base-four repetition in most Navajo ritual.

On a still larger scale, weaving is seen as one symbolic aspect of human interaction with the surrounding world. When John Adair and Sol Worth conducted their famous experiment where they trained Navajos how to use movie cameras but did not tell them what to photograph or how, they were

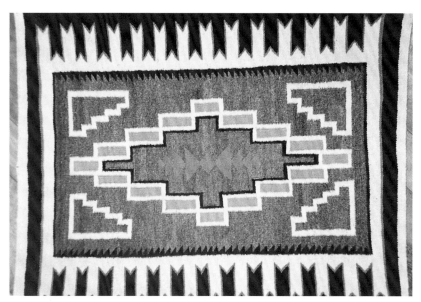

Figs. 13 and 14. Two rugs by Helen Yellowman; Blanding, Utah, ca. 1975. Photos by the author.

Fig. 15. Navajo wedding basket. These baskets were originally woven by Ute or
Paiute women, but now they are produced widely by Navajos.
Photo by Ron Daines.

surprised (and pleased) when one woman produced a film called *Navajo
Weaver*. The half-hour film had lengthy scenes of kids herding sheep,
women carding wool, women looking for plants and herbs, men shearing,
and women spinning, but only a few scenes where anyone was actually
weaving, and only a few quick shots of finished rugs. Moreover, these elements of the process were presented in no particular order: while we might
expect to go sequentially from herding to shearing to carding to spinning to
dying to weaving, the Navajo filmmaker felt no logical need to fulfill such
a lineal agenda. As a result, the film strikes an Anglo audience as far from
documentary, while Navajos see it as entirely normal because in their yearly
round of activities, some people are always out herding and looking for
herbal dyes, while someone else may still be spinning yarn from last year at
the same time that others are carding this year's batch; another person may
be dying a two-year collection of wool for a particular rug she has in mind,
while still someone else is outside helping the men do the shearing.

For the Navajos, weaving arises from everyday life (though everyone
is not a weaver), and the rugs dramatize that way of life, expressing the
culturally understood interaction of people and nature in the search for
vegetable and mineral dyes, the care for animals demonstrated by herding
and shearing (Navajos call sheep "the mothers of our children" because
tending them teaches children many of their responsibilities), and the

Fig. 16. Helen Yellowman, the author's Navajo sister. Photo by the author.

movement of people across a familiar landscape (the Navajo worldview and language, which—remember—has 356,200 conjugations for the verb "to go," seem to have been vastly influenced by their long migration from the Northwest). The final product, the rug itself, perhaps bought in a gift shop in Santa Fe and eventually displayed on the floor of a rustic ranch house or ski chalet in Jackson Hole, is the least Navajo part of this artistic process. But the actual weaving is considered so expressive of Navajo cultural values promoting harmony and balance that the weaver must guard against distractions, emotional excess, and closed-mindedness. For example, the so-called spirit line (*ch'įdii bitiin*, literally "evil spirit's road"), often believed by whites to be a way to "let the evil out of the rug," is usually explained by Navajos as a positive sign that the weaver's mental image of the emerging pattern was not totally closed. A few years ago, while my adopted sister, Helen Yellowman (figs. 16, 17), was teaching some younger women how to weave, one of them yelled, got up from the floor in frustration, ripped the rug off its loom, and threw it in the corner. Helen quietly gathered her weaving things together, went home, and didn't weave again for several years because of the emotional impact.

Navajo moccasins provide another example of surroundment, as do baby carriers. Both of these items are usually made by men from sacred deerhide, that is, a hide from an unwounded deer. To get such a hide, someone must catch a deer, smother it with corn pollen, and remove the hide in a ritually prescribed way. Although this doesn't require actually

Fig. 17. Helen Yellowman weaving at Utah State Fair, ca. 1975. Photo by Van E. Porter.

outrunning the deer, it entails jogging along behind him, sometimes for much of a day, until the animal is exhausted. According to my friend Yellowman, there are several reasons for this procedure, but his favorite is that it recognizes the difference between food and clothing. Deer, regarded as relatives, are willing to supply us with food. We offer them prayers, and they offer us their bodies, which we obtain by shooting them.

Fig. 18. Navajo moccasins made of deerskin and cowhide by Hugh Yellowman. Photo by Ron Daines.

But clothing goes a step further toward providing for our comfort and requires us to acknowledge a very personal reciprocation, which is carried out by corn pollen, regarded as a sacred substance which ensures life, articulation, and good health. The deer whose hide is to be used is caught, embraced by the hunter, and translated—so to speak—into a sacred animal by the corn pollen.

Not many people get their hides this way today, but the concept still exists. When you put on a new pair of moccasins that have been made for you, they are still slightly damp, and they conform to your feet as they dry out. They become an outer form of your feet (inner and outer forms are important in Navajo religion, but we need not explore them here), as contrasted with deer meat, which goes inside your body. The words for "foot" and "moccasin" are identical in Navajo: *ké* (fig. 18).

For all the traditional nuances, the art of moccasin making, like other arts, is open to dynamic change mirroring developments in Navajo life. Since the turn of the century, Navajo moccasins have had cowhide soles, obviously an innovation made possible by recent acquaintance with cattle. When I asked Yellowman if he had an explanation for the change (thinking there might be some new Navajo theory about human/animal relationships), he gave me a quick look to see if I was joking. Then, after a long pause, he said, as if the answer was obvious, "Cowhide is thicker. It lasts longer when you walk on it."

Fig. 19. Yazzie and Herbert Yellowman, of Blanding, Utah, carrying their daughter Lorraine in a cradleboard, 1954. Photo by the author.

Just as moccasins embrace and surround your feet, the cradleboard surrounds and holds your baby (fig. 19). Navajos and other tribes believe that the baby feels more secure when it's wrapped; babies go to sleep more readily, and they seem generally more at ease because they feel they're being held most of the time. In addition, if the parents are working or traveling, the baby can be slung from a saddle horn, strapped against the seat of a car, carried on the shoulder or the back, or hung from a tree branch. The bow (made of wood by the Navajos but constructed of reeds, woven twigs, or beaded leather by other tribes) allows a blanket to shade the baby's face from the sun or provide privacy for nursing (fig. 20). If the cradleboard falls forward, the bow hits the ground first, protecting the baby from injury. And for many tribes, the bow symbolically represents the rainbow, commonly a sign of fertility, connection between earth and sky, and good health (fig. 21).

Beyond these physical and spiritual elements of surroundment by sacred deerskin, protective bow, and the arms of family members, there is a larger issue of natural and visual surroundment: A baby in a cradleboard experiences the world from an entirely different perspective than a baby in a crib, for the cradleboard, virtually always upright when the baby is awake, allows views very similar to those of adults: out and around in a context usually full of familiar people—in contrast to a baby, alone in its own room, staring up at a flat ceiling. Such differences in early life experience are

Fig. 20. Ute Mountain cradleboard by Shirley Denetsosie. Photo by Herridge and Associates, courtesy of the Utah Arts Council.

Fig. 21. Northern Ute Virginia Duncan with a cradleboard she made, Roosevelt, Utah, 1997. Photo by Craig Miller, courtesy of the Utah Arts Council.

powerful but subtle ways of training young people in the perspectives of their culture.

A close look at a Native art form with the guidance of a sympathetic artist helps us see the role art plays in maintaining culture and reveals limitations in our understanding of what art is and how it functions. During the early 1970s, I helped bring a Klamath/Hupa basketmaker, Mrs. Elvira Matt, to the University of Oregon campus, where we had arranged for her to conduct a two-week workshop for a number of local craftspeople interested in Native arts. Instead of launching into basketmaking directly, however, she spent the first few days teaching her students how to sing a number of Native songs. She then took them into the nearby forests to gather materials for the baskets they would make, but this operation also lasted more than a day, for it turned out that she expected each participant to sing certain songs to specific plants which were being harvested. And after they brought the materials (grasses, tree roots, willow branches) back to the classroom, they were to hum some of these songs as they softened, split, and cleaned the materials by running them through their mouths. Toward the end of the two-week session, they finally began to construct the most rudimentary baskets and felt a mix of minor accomplishment and major frustration as the workshop came to a close. The participants thanked Mrs. Matt for the rich cultural experience, but one person couldn't help observing in a friendly way that everyone had anticipated making baskets rather than learning songs. Mrs. Matt sat silent for a bit, as if puzzled about how to explain the obvious. Finally, she said, "Well, after all, you know, a basket is a song that's become visible."

Well, after all, you know, most—if not all—visual art can be described as abstract ideas that have become visible. But what about the difference in genres: How can we say that a basket is a song? Let's look at this assertion as a chance to understand a principle that was so self-evident to Mrs. Matt that she had to grope for a rational explanation. It is not sufficient to ask only, *can* a song become a basket? or, *can* a basket be understood as a song? We must inquire first, from the Native point of view expressed by Mrs. Matt, what is a basket, and what is a song, and in what ways can they be understood as appropriate parts of the same metaphor? Extensive ethnographic work with Klamath and Hupa basketmakers would certainly supply richer answers to these questions, but Mrs. Matt's comment, combined with its two-week context of gathering plant materials and learning songs, becomes a meaningful constellation which is susceptible of deconstruction and discussion. What are some of the clear—though unstated—underlying assumptions of that two-week workshop and its closing metaphor?

In terms of time and effort, it seems clear that singing (learning the songs), singing (while gathering the plants), and singing (while preparing and cleaning the materials) was more central to Mrs. Matt's agenda than the physical act of weaving the baskets. When making a basket, then, is singing more important than weaving? Given the tremendous variety of practical uses for baskets, plus the amazing richness of patterns and decorations, probably not. More likely, Mrs. Matt was underscoring the appropriate cultural preparation for making baskets, and this—as she showed the students—is a process far more complex than merely knowing where to find the raw materials: it entails establishing a cultural and personal relationship with the materials through the medium of song.

So what kind of songs did she teach them? They were mostly prayers of thanks to reciprocate for the implied permission to use carefully selected roots, stems, and branches from plants which were to remain living, and expressions of gratitude for the plants' cooperation. Songs like this are elegant demonstrations of that assumed Native sensitivity to nature that many have made into an idealistic cliché. Like most stereotypes, there is indeed some substance in it, but the problem is that such clichés relieve us of the inclination to look further for even more valid (and usually more complex) cultural assumptions and customs beneath the surface. Although we needn't say a blessing over a meal for it to nourish and strengthen our bodies, those who do are signaling who they are and where they stand culturally.

Just so with the prayers of basketmakers. I have met some who believe the plants are listening and responding in their way, and others who simply feel it would be arrogant or crude just to go into the woods and take the materials without performing, either in front of others or alone, some structured expression of their utter dependence on the plants that supply them with what they need. There may be many reasons for this custom, which is widespread among basketmakers in the West, but certainly one must be the fact that baskets relate humans directly to a food supply (gathered, dried, hauled, stored, cooked, or presented in baskets) and are associated with prayers, viewed in terms of family relationships, and connected to a world of ritual practice (where the basket takes on an even more intensified meaning). The same mouth that shapes the materials also sings the songs, utters the prayers, and eats the food.

Clearly, basketmaking is a process where the human and natural worlds intersect so powerfully that a view based only on the craft or the practicalities (not implying that these are in any way simple) will not reveal the cultural logic that underlies baskets. This logic provides us with perspective, and not with a new and better stereotype, for not all basketmakers use prayer songs the same way or for the same reasons, and some do not pray at all. We are discussing a culturally constructed idea that relates many artists to their materials, not an inflexible "rule" of Native behavior.

An important contribution of such songs is that they remind us to look not only forward (from the basketmaker toward the potential materials and the eventual basket) but also back (from the basketmaker toward the traditions that inform her art and ritual). Songs of this sort are sometimes personally composed (working, of course, within tribal conventions), sometimes learned from another artist, but in either case, the tradition out of which such compositions grow connects the current basketmaker with long-standing tribal custom. So one effect of singing a prayer song is to reexperience an important cultural connection that ties the singer to previous generations of basketmakers. In the case where the song itself has been passed down, say from mother to daughter through time, the singing also prompts a personal (remembrance), physical (vocal cords, breath, ears), and emotional (shared events, love) reexperiencing of significant people in the basketmaker's life. In light of all these considerations, it's easy to see that a serious basketmaker would never neglect singing the appropriate songs.

Yet it's possible for an artist to decline singing for other cultural or personal reasons. I asked Selina Peratrovich, an elderly Haida basketmaker from Ketchikan, Alaska, if she was passing her traditions on to her family. After telling me that she would never give up speaking to the plants and animals that give her materials, she admitted she was not going to be able to teach the basket arts to her grandchildren because they didn't know the proper songs and prayers. Why didn't they? Because they didn't know the Haida language to express these prayers and songs. Why not teach them the language then? I asked. She fixed me with a fierce stare and said, "Listen: When I was a girl in a government school, we were physically punished for speaking our language. I don't want my grandchildren to go through that, and since I can't guarantee that it won't happen to them, I'd rather just save them from it. That's more important to me than baskets."

Belle Deacon, a well-known Athabascan birch-bark basketmaker who lives in Grayling, Alaska, told me that she sings to the birch out of respect, not just spiritual obligation: "[We] always respect the birch bark. . . . Where you go, you respect the trees because they make big canoes out of it. . . . It's based on respect for the birch because the birch tree—you can make sutures out of it, sleds, and lots of good out of it." So songs of respect, praise, and thanks—when they are offered—are vocal expressions of the dynamic interactions that make basketmaking a deep and culturally coherent process.

And songs are not the only way for a basketmaker to reciprocate for gifts from the natural world: Mary Black, a Yupik basketmaker from Kongiganak, Alaska, told me, "We don't need to sing to the grasses; we just leave some small gift, like maybe a little berry."

Deni Hockema, a Coos/Coquelle woman on the southern Oregon coast, has been researching the basket-weaving customs and styles of her people, using the old baskets (now protected in the new tribal cultural center), coupled with what few oral traditions she can obtain from older people in the tribe, augmented by recent studies by basket specialists. At first, she thought her research would be simply a matter of learning and retrieval, but she soon discovered that the experience had a strong emotional element—strengthened, no doubt, by the massacres, internment, and general predation experienced by her people during the last century, which led to the almost total loss of cultural expressive forms. As she began touching the knots in the old baskets, she could feel the fingers of the long-dead weavers and hear their voices. It was a traumatic experience for her, and she cannot weave baskets today, or even talk about them, without getting tears in her eyes.

While we usually see only the final artifact, our snail shell, it is well to remember that such emotions, personal thoughts, prayers, and songs, all mediated by cultural settings, are the motivating factors, the anguish of our snail. And we are indeed lucky when a Native artist is willing to share them with us—especially if we don't wish to intrude on their thoughts or demand their explanations. Beyond the thoughts, feelings, and abstract beliefs, we may also anticipate that the grasses, roots, wool, beads, quills, leather, and paints that are brought into the artist's orbit and shaped into physical expressions of cultural ideas are further enriched by their inherent qualities, which become part of the total meaning. Selina Peratrovich told me that when she uses her baskets of spruce roots and cedar bark to carry or serve food, she remembers the way the roots nurture the tree and, beyond that, how the tree provides wood for boats and masks, a haven for birds, and a shelter for people. When Navajos make juniper-seed necklaces (*gad bináá'*), they may not articulate the fact openly, but they can hardly avoid thinking of how the seeds were supplied by the tree, gathered and stored by small ground animals, and finally collected and strung together by people—a simple, but effective, acknowledgment of important relationships in the Navajo world. Navajo wedding baskets feature visual designs representing clouds, mountains, circularity, and a vaginal passage, but in addition to these visible patterns is the obvious fact that the same *chiiłchin* plant (desert sumac), whose branches are split by teeth and fingers into three strands, also produces a bitter orange berry that Navajos grind into a paste which supplies vitamin C.

When we attended Huckleberry Feast one summer at the Warm Springs Reservation in central Oregon, my family and I were impressed by the emotional entry of about twenty women into the huge long house, each one carrying two large, breast-shaped baskets full of mountain huckleberries they had gathered. One by one, they carefully dumped out the berries onto handwoven reed mats covering the center of the floor. Then they all reverently laid their right hands on top of the pile and, with almost beatific smiles, circulated among the happy crowd, shaking everyone's hands. I asked our Warm Springs host, Matilda Mitchell, what the handshakes were all about, and she said, "Well, those huckleberries don't have any hands of their own. How else can they greet us when they come back every year with our women?" And then, of course, I asked the next obvious question: "Why are those baskets shaped like breasts?" I couldn't tell whether Mrs. Mitchell was suppressing embarrassment or laughter (probably the latter), but she finally got herself together and said, looking in my wife's direction, "The women feed our families, don't we?" One could hardly ask for a more appropriate dramatization of female nurturing of relatives than this close interaction between basket art, annual custom, and tribally rendered human reality.

Ignorance of such complex nuances of the basket art can surely result in a cultural and aesthetic loss for us all, but there are practical, academic, and legal ramifications as well. Think of all the museums where Native arts are displayed without adequate explanation or tribal identification (sometimes, since such objects are often gifts from collectors, the museum simply doesn't know where something came from). But ponder the question: "Should this item even be on public display?" In the wonderful Texas Memorial Museum on the campus of the University of Texas in Austin is a Pomo basket decorated with tiny red woodpecker scalps, quail topknots, other colored feathers, and beads. The label in the museum reads only, "Pomo feather basket," and a color photograph in the museum guidebook has the same caption, accompanied by a succinct comment on the facing page about the Pomo use of feathers on their baskets.

But surely the feathers and their designs have some kind of meaning for the Pomo, and I would know virtually nothing about it if I had not encountered Mabel McKay, an elderly Pomo basketmaker who attended the Pacific Rim conference on basketmaking in 1981 at the University of Alaska Museum. After showing everyone her baskets and demonstrating her way of using materials, she admitted that she had brought other examples of her art but had decided there were too many people for her to show them. Later, after a lengthy conversation about Native values, she glared me in the eye and said, "Well, if you think you're strong enough, come with me," and led the way to a back room where the basketmakers' personal belongings were stored. I assumed she wanted me to help carry something or open a box for her, so I followed willingly. She pulled a dark cloth bag from her suitcase, looked all around to make sure no one else would see, and secretively let me look into the bag. There was a basket, about seven or eight inches in diameter, covered inside and out with patterns of redheaded woodpecker scalps, quail topknots, and beads. "It's a medicine basket," she explained, "and it's very powerful. I can't let just anyone look at it, or they might get sick. You feeling okay? You need to go back?" I felt okay, and I also felt flattered that she trusted me to look at her basket. I asked the dumb question, "Do you put medicines in the basket, then?" and was chastened by her gruff reply: "It *is* medicine!" Very much like its maker (who is probably the last dreamer/healer among the Pomos), the basket certainly had its own power.

Years later, when I encountered that Pomo feather basket in the Texas Memorial Museum, I didn't feel so okay, and I wondered what Mabel McKay would think if she could see that icon of her tribe's most serious ideas about health, healing, and power hanging in an antiseptic glass case, far from home. Should it even be there on display? On the other hand, how will anyone in the world ever know about the absolutely beautiful feather art of the Pomos if we never see any examples? Was the basket given willingly by an Indian who had "decommissioned" it? Or was it given to the museum by a generous donor who got it "somewhere," not knowing that he was meddling with someone's cultural patrimony? Questions like these are difficult to answer, but they remain important nonetheless. Since my aim in this book is not to intrude in artistic arenas that are not freely available, I only describe the basket, without supplying a picture (I did not ask to photograph Mrs. McKay's basket anyway, and she probably wouldn't have given permission if I had). Not everything has to be seen to be believed. Later on at the Alaska basketmakers' symposium, I did notice that when Mabel McKay's picture was taken for the exhibition catalog, she included a much smaller feather basket (carefully turned upside down) among the samples arrayed around her. That was her choice.

Thus far, my discussion has focused mainly on baskets, perhaps giving the impression that they are the most common or significant of Native arts in the West—and in the case of some of the desert tribes, they are indeed the primary artistic expressions. But I have begun with baskets for another reason: Since they are essentially woven objects, they provide us with an excellent example of the complex meanings of the word *text*, a term used by folklorists to indicate any traditional expression under discussion and thus a word used often in this book. It comes not—as one might guess—from a Latin word for reading or writing but from the word *textus*, "that which is woven." It is cognate with words like "textile" and "texture" and thus references not only an understandable item but one that is "readable" because it was shaped by someone—in the case of folklore texts, that shaping includes all the cultural nuances of process, material, pattern, and value that we have discussed with baskets. There is more to say about baskets later on, especially a dynamic flowering of Navajo basketry that began in southern Utah just a few years ago. But at this point, I want to bring other artistic texts into our discussion: woven, molded, carved, beaded, sewn, created objects which—like baskets—are concrete embodiments of cultural abstractions, performed by knowledgeable, culturally embedded artists for a nonrestricted audience that includes their families, neighbors, other Natives, and total strangers. We are interested not only in the texts but the dynamics that testify to their constant and ongoing contemporaneity.

In the play between the traditional forces of convention and the dynamic forces of talented artists, I see, in addition to signs of practical adaptability (the cowhide sole of the Navajo moccasin, the substitution of canvas for buffalo hide on Plains tipis), a delightful audacity and openness to experimentation. Not only do Navajo pictorial rugs now feature such items as school buses, pickups, and dinosaurs, a rug depicting the first moon landing, woven by Cecilia Yazzie, was on exhibition recently at the Museum of American Indian Art in Santa Fe, while another by Anita Hathale, owned by the Autry Museum of Western Heritage, shows Comet Hale-Bopp. A beaded wristband made for me by Ellen DeGross, a Tututni from southwestern Oregon, is said to archive an old basket pattern which can't be made anymore because the materials are unavailable (fig. 22).

Beads, a relatively recent arrival among white trade goods, use a new medium to express (for the artist and the wearer) the fact that white suppression of forest fires has deprived basketmakers of their old medium, the shoots of bear grass that emerge after a fire. A watchband with beaded rosettes bigger than the watch (fig. 23) and a beaded pen (fig. 24), as well as a beaded cap (fig. 25), tennis ball (fig. 26), fisherman's hat (fig. 27), and sneakers (fig. 28), demonstrate cooptation of white designs by Native artists; these little masterpieces turn our attention away from the practical considerations of the white world toward the cultural performances of Native artists. We sometimes focus on all the Native arts that were lost during the devastating invasions of this continent (and that loss was considerable, no doubt about it), but we should not overlook the lively, audacious, and creative ways the Native artistic voice dynamically persists in the visual arts.

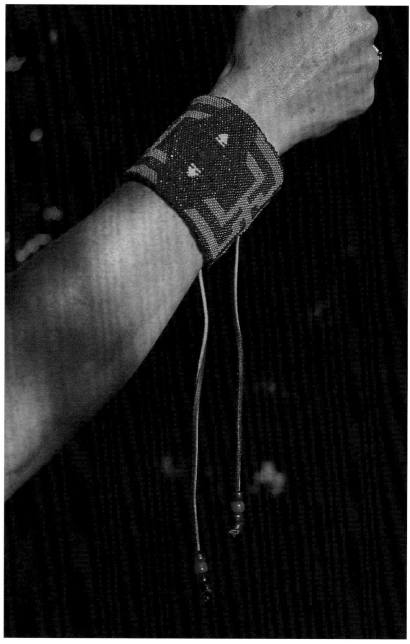

Fig. 22. A beadwork wristband fashioned for the author by Tututni basketmaker Ellen DeGross from an original basket design. Photo by Ron Daines.

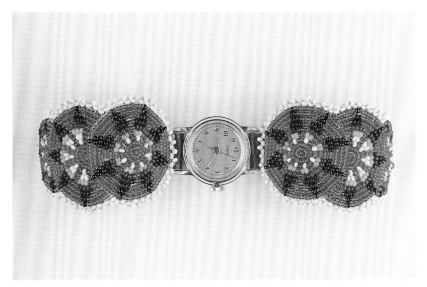

Fig. 23. Watchband by Apache artist Polly Davis. Gift of Jo and Warren Buxton (NA.202.846); Buffalo Bill Historical Center, Cody, Wyoming.

Fig. 24. A pen beaded by female Flathead beadmaker Willie Wright. Photo by Ron Daines.

Fig. 25. Beaded baseball cap by a Sioux artist. Buffalo Bill Historical Center, Cody, Wyoming (NA.202.394).

Fig. 26. Beaded tennis ball; Rocky Boy Reservation, Montana. Buffalo Bill Historical Center, Cody, Wyoming (NA.507.89).

Fig. 27. Beaded Sioux hat, ca. 1895. Buffalo Bill Historical Center, Cody, Wyoming (NA.202.90).

Fig. 28. Beaded sneakers by a Sioux artist. Buffalo Bill Historical Center, Cody, Wyoming (NA.507.89).

Mary Holiday Black, a Navajo basketmaker from deep in Monument Valley (and a recipient of the National Endowment of the Arts [NEA] National Heritage Award), is one of the best weavers of Navajo wedding baskets, which are used in practically every ceremony and given away to singers (medicine men) as part of their honorarium for curing rituals (fig. 29). She and her family also use the basic form and style of the wedding basket as a departure point for new, creative designs incorporating Pueblo symbols, star constellations, and other figures from southwestern Native art and everyday life. Recently, Mary's daughter, Lorraine, wove me a basket which shows a hogan (in three dimensions), surrounded by the typical items of everyday Navajo life (figs. 30, 31). One of the most striking elements of this renaissance in Navajo baskets is that, while their makers still follow the older traditions of materials, dyes, methods, and composition and produce the typical wedding basket—which remains central to Navajo daily and ritual life—the newer baskets are often works of art for display rather than artistic expressions of Navajo traditional concepts (figs. 32–37). Bringing the tradition full circle is a basket made by Kee Bitsinni, which seems to be a solid example of the wedding-basket design but on closer examination turns out to have a hole in the center, which prevents it from being used, as in normal practice, to carry cornmeal flour or hold yucca seeds or items being blessed in a Beautyway ceremony (fig. 38).

In a similar development, Bill Weatherford, a Creek craftsman, made a sacred pipe to commemorate my reunion with my Navajo daughter after many years (figs. 39, 40). He knew that Vanessa had been given the name Wanbli Ota Wi (Many Eagles Woman) by a Sioux family after she had danced a four-year Sun Dance vow on their reservation in South Dakota. He also knew that one of her daughters was named Chaunopa, the Lakota word for the sacred pipe. But he had no way of knowing that I had been given the name Wanbli Chanopa (Eagle Pipe) by Frank White Buffalo Woman some years before. Weatherford showed up at Vanessa's place on the Navajo Reservation and excitedly gave her the pipe: "Its name is Wanbli Chanopa," he explained. This kind of simultaneity is not rare in Indian country, but a sacred pipe made of an elk antler (instead of having a wooden stem) is a rarity; in other respects, though, the pipe has the standard accoutrements: catlinite (pipestone) bowl, feathers, beads.

But it turns out this pipe is a work of display art by default: So far, no pipe carrier I have shown it to will do a ceremony with it since that would require pushing the eagle's beak and face into the dirt (in the ceremony, which is not secret or closed to non-Indians, one end of the pipe is lifted up in the four directions as a parallel to erecting a Sun Dance pole). Since

Fig. 29. Mary Holiday Black holding one of her Navajo baskets; Halchita, Utah,1994. Photo by Carol Edison, courtesy of the Utah Arts Council.

Fig. 30. *Left:* Navajo hogan basket woven by Lorraine Black; *right:* wedding basket by Lorraine's mother, Mary Holiday Black, a National Endowment for the Arts National Heritage Award recipient. Photo by Ron Daines.

the eagle is an artistic representation of sacred forces, pushing it into the ground would be a sign of disrespect at the very least, while pushing the end of a wooden pipe stem into the ground would solidly parallel setting up a ritual tree. Again, it's not the item so much as the culturally shared ideas behind it that control its meaning, usage, and definition.

In larger scope, the same can be said of Native dwellings, a subject that's far too broad to deal with here. Native people have structured the spaces where they live with pretty much the same cultural logic that shapes other pieces of visual art: the Navajo hogan, the Plains tipi, the Eskimo *iglu,* and various grass houses, brush shelters, wickiups, and wigwams are essentially circular, arranged to enclose and surround, designed to include a family group in one space. Even the plank houses of the Northwest or the long Quonset lodges of the northeastern tribes, though usually rectangular, accommodated family groups organized in circles within them. The various Pueblo groups in the Southwest built rectangular apartment houses (or groups of houses) but still envisioned their tribal structure and clan systems as circular. Consult virtually any study of the Pueblo Indians and notice the way the circle predominates in their worldview—even when not in the shape of buildings. Lakota pipe carrier Black Elk expressed the concept much the same way most tribes articulate it:

Fig. 31. Lorraine Black holding one of her Navajo baskets; Mexican Hat, Utah.
Photo by Carol Edison, courtesy of the Utah Arts Council.

Fig. 32. This turtle basket is one of the few examples of basketry done by a man, Peter Holiday, also a relative of Lorraine and Mary Holiday Black. Photo by Ron Daines.

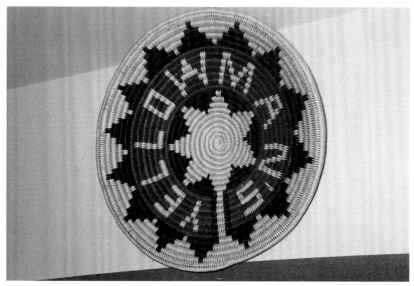

Fig. 33. A traditional Navajo wedding-basket design that incorporates the Yellowman name. This basket hangs near the ceiling in Nelson Yellowman's home. Photo by the author.

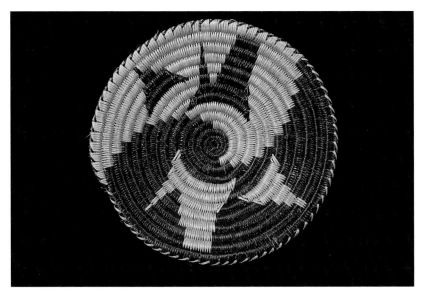

Fig. 34. Navajo basket by Bonnie Bitsinni. Photo by Carol Edison, courtesy of the Utah Arts Council.

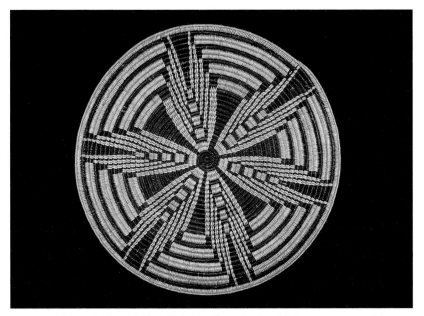

Fig. 35. Navajo basket by Elsie Holiday. Photo by Carol Edison, courtesy of the Utah Arts Council.

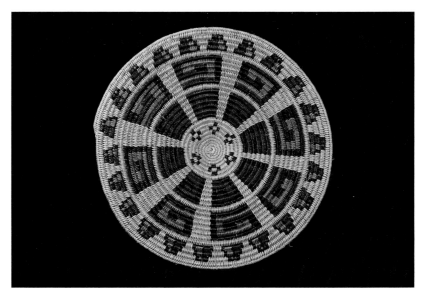

Fig. 36. Navajo basket by Christine Edison. Photo by Carol Edison, courtesy of the Utah Arts Council.

Fig. 37. A Navajo wedding-basket design made into an antimacassar in the Nelson Yellowman home. Photo by the author.

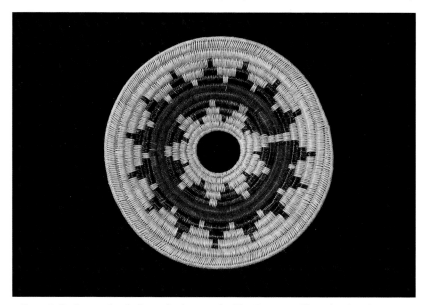

Fig. 38. Basket with a hole in the bottom by Kee Bitsinni. Photo by Carol Edison, courtesy of the Utah Arts Council.

> You have noticed that everything an Indian does is in a circle, and that is because the Power of the World always works in circles, and everything tries to be round. . . . The sky is round, and I have heard that the earth is round like a ball, and so are the stars. The wind, in its greatest power, whirls. Birds make their nests in circles. . . . The sun comes forth and goes down again in a circle. The moon does the same, and both are round. . . . Our tepees were round like the nests of birds, and these were always set in a circle, the nation's hoop. . . . But the *wasichus* have put us in these square boxes.

From the Native perspective, we *wasichus* (whites), who are sometimes called *gussik* (from cossack?) by the Yupik in the far North, have put lots of things in our square boxes, ranging from the presumed riches in Seward's steamer trunk, to the many real treasures stored in dry museums, to ideas held hostage by European American preconceptions. Some years ago, traveling by bush plane with my friend Dennis DeGross, who was organizing medical facilities in remote Alaskan villages, I dropped (almost literally) into Mountain Village on the Yukon River. I was using his trip to discover areas where traditional Native artists might be eligible to apply for grants under the aegis of the Folk Arts Program of the NEA. When I asked Andrew Brown, the Yupik mayor of Mountain Village, if

Figs. 39 and 40. A sacred pipe by Bill Weatherford carved in the likeness of an eagle's beak (out of an elk antler). The pipe bowl and mouthpiece are pipestone. It cannot be used because the face of the eagle cannot be pushed into the ground the way pipes are customarily handled in the ceremony. Photos by Ron Daines.

there might be an opportunity to speak to the local folks about the importance of their Native arts, he looked at first startled, then puzzled, then said with a grin, "We're having a town meeting tonight, and you could talk to us after business is over. We always look forward to having visitors, and besides, everybody around here likes a good laugh!"

Shortly before the meeting, Mayor Brown came over to me and said, "Oh, by the way, we have a practice of doing all our business in Yupik, so that means you'll have to give your speech one sentence at a time, and I'll translate it for everybody. Then I'll translate their questions back for you." As a compulsive talker, I was a bit unnerved but went ahead phrase by phrase and was relieved to see that the room full of smiling, nodding listeners seemed impressed by everything I was saying.

When I asked for questions, there was a long silence, during which people kept nodding and smiling at me. At long last, a man in the back of the room stood up, waited a respectful minute or so, and then said something in Yupik. The people nodded and smiled. Andrew Brown translated, "We're wondering when will those people in Washington make up their minds?" I said I wouldn't want to make any bets on that but then asked what in particular he meant by the question in regard to Native arts. He said,

> Well, years ago, our folks used to carve ivory, and they taught a lot of it to us. Of course, in the old days, people just did it for recreation. They'd make animals, monsters, funny figures, even tools, but then usually throw them away. The white teachers and missionaries told us that was wasteful, that we ought to do it for income. So some people began carving for the tourists, and it brought in some money, but not everybody was a good carver, and some people couldn't make a living at it. Then some guy from Washington came to Mountain Village and told us we should start doing something useful; give up our old ways; start a small factory or something. I think he wanted us to make rubber boots or something like that. He told us the old ways are disappearing, and we'd better try to live in the modern world. We should send our kids away so they could get an education or a real job somewhere. So I guess we lost our enthusiasm for our old ways—what you call our arts.

The audience grinned and nodded. He continued,

> Now you come and tell us that the people in Washington want us to practice our old arts again. We don't know what to say. You seem like a nice enough person, but what if we get interested in all this? What if some other guy comes from Washington in a couple of years and wants

Fig. 41. Bears carved from found wood by Yupik Eskimo Waskey Walters. Photo by the author.

us to start up a dental-floss factory? We always try to be agreeable, you know, but when are those guys over there going to make up their minds?

I had no answer for him. And I still don't. But in a way, he had a deeper answer for me: Seeing that I was dejected by his response, he came up to me after the meeting and invited me (in English) to visit his home the next day. "I'm Waskey Walters. You can recognize my place," he said, "because it's got a dead rat stuck under the mudroom door." I was in for two surprises that next day: I learned first of all that everyone in Mountain Village speaks English perfectly (they just do their business in Yupik so they can keep control of their affairs). And when I entered the small Walters home the next day, I discovered that traditional art was far from dead in the far North: I found every surface of his place crammed with small wood carvings he had done and was still doing (figs. 41–48). He said, "I just get pieces of driftwood off the riverbank, and then I look them over for a while and decide what's in there. And then I cut away

Fig. 42. A shaman walrus mask made from found wood by Yupik Eskimo Waskey Walters. Photo by the author.

everything else except what's in there." I didn't venture to inform him that his phrase has been attributed to virtually every major sculptor in history; it meant enough to me that he said it. I learned that his father had been an ivory carver and his son—now off at school somewhere in

Figs. 43 and 44. Two fanciful views of human beings carved from found wood by Yupik Eskimo Waskey Walters. Photos by the author.

Fig. 45. Shaman carved from found wood by Yupik Eskimo Waskey Walters. Photo by the author.

Fig. 46. Assorted creatures carved by Waskey Walters. Photo by the author.

Fig. 47. A carving (about three inches tall) of a man bringing his kayak onto the beach by Yupik Eskimo Waskey Walters. Photo by the author.

Fig. 48. Figures at an Eskimo dance carved from found wood by Waskey Walters. Photo by the author.

the Lower Forty-eight—was carving soapstone and argillite. And they all carved the same things: animals, monsters, spirits, tools, models of boats, "just things we discover there in the wood or the stone."

As I left, Waskey said, "Now don't go telling people I use a Dremel tool in my carving. Nobody would believe that it's right for a Native to do that. But I think any good workman uses the best tools he can find, don't you?" I said I did and got away while I could still talk. As I made my way down the muddy street, he called after me, "See, we don't need Washington for everything!"

One thing our snail teaches us is that the humor and patience of Native artists is vastly underrated, and that fact, in turn, must be largely due to the resiliency and dynamism of Native arts.

Notes

If there's one aspect of Native American expressive culture with which non-Natives are already familiar, it's undoubtably art. We have admired it, bought it, stolen it, and copied it; we have studied it and put it on exhibit; we have loaded our museums and our mantels with it. And we've commodified it for resale in the popular marketplace: high-end Navajo "squaw dresses" offered in exclusive women's catalogs; generic kachina dolls made in China for western souvenir stores; the once-serious Lakota dream catchers touted in nearly every New Age shop as a "Native mandala"; the hump-backed flute player (identified oddly by white folks as Kokopelli, a Hopi kachina) pressed into service as a logo, a lawn ornament, a key chain, a house decoration. Ekkehart Malotki's *Kokopelli: The Making of an Icon* (Lincoln: University of Nebraska Press, 2000) explores this fascinating topic with the skill of a lifelong expert on Hopi language and culture, but one assumes it will not have much of an effect on the very lucrative Kokopelli industry. But in spite of our egregious misuse of some Native images, Native arts generally have attained a status we might not have expected even fifty years ago. Major exhibitions across the country and in Europe have showcased Native artists' stunning use of color and design, where a hundred years ago our predecessors were noticing the fortuitous attractiveness of practical, primitive "crafts."

But even though Native arts are known, loved, and collected, books about them are hard to find outside the library—mostly because the necessary illustrations make them too expensive to keep in print. I'll mention a few good ones out of the many that have been published, trusting that the reader can find them (and others) in local libraries. One caveat: try to find the books (for example, the catalogs of major museum exhibitions are usually high quality) that are produced by people—Native or non-Native—who have real credentials in art, art history, folklore, anthropology, museology, and Native studies. They do not use made-up names like Noble Wolf, Silver Feather, Warm Summer Rain, Night Flower, or Coyote Moon.

Among the many books which try to present the whole sweep of Native art in North America are Diana Fane, Ira Jacknis, and Lise M. Breen, eds., *Objects of Myth and Memory: American Indian Art at the Brooklyn Museum* (Seattle: University of Washington Press, 1991) and David W. Penney, *Native Arts of North America* (Paris: Terrail, 1998).

It has often been said that the Pacific Northwest tribes were surrounded by so much food that they were able to apply most of their daily endeavors to art, dance, and ritual, an impression well supported by their amazing artistic output. Bill Holm's *Spirit and Ancestor* (Seattle: University of Washington Press, 1987) deals with the spectacular arts of several Pacific Northwest coastal tribes, while Robin K. Wright's *A Time of Gathering: Native Heritage in Washington State* (Seattle: University of Washington Press, 1991) focuses on a horizontal strip of Native arts ranging from the Pacific coast to the inland plateau. The hide work and beading arts of inland Alaska and western Canada are the focus of Kate C. Duncan's *Northern Athapaskan Art: A Beadwork Tradition* (Seattle: University of Washington Press, 1989). A larger perspective is provided by Aldona Jonaitis in *From the Land of the Totem Poles: The Northwest Coast Indian Art Collection at the American Museum of Natural History* (Seattle: University of Washington Press, 1988). Still more inclusive are William W. Fitzhugh and Aron Crowell, eds., *Crossroads of Continents: Cultures of Siberia and Alaska* (Washington, D.C.: Smithsonian Institution, 1988) and Suzi Jones, ed., *Pacific Basket Makers: A Living Tradition* (Fairbanks: University of Alaska, 1982); the latter is the catalog of a circum-Pacific basketmakers' conference and exhibition.

The relatively small but amazing collection of the Sheldon Jackson Museum in Sitka, Alaska, is worth going there to see. These items are surveyed and discussed in Peter L. Corey, ed., *Faces, Voices, and Dreams* (Juneau: Division of Alaska State Museums, 1987). Corey, the indefatigable curator of collections at the Sheldon Jackson Museum, has been extremely helpful over the years as I sought to understand Alaska's many tribal cultures; his elucidation of the Bicentennial Pole in Sitka is one example.

When the Rainbow Touches Down, by Tryntje Van Ness Seymour (Phoenix: The Heard Museum, 1988), focuses on the art of the Southwest, providing not only selected photographs but rich and extensive comments on the tribal backgrounds and the artists. Southwest Native artists have not only maintained traditional themes and media but have also sparked new developments, ranging from large-scale oil paintings to folk art (contemporary—often self-parodic—works in carved stone, cloth, ceramics, and weaving). For one example, see Chuck and Jan Rosenak, *Navajo Folk Art* (Flagstaff, Arizona: Northland Publishing, 1994). Another work which covers southwestern art from ancient pottery to modern painting is Duane Anderson, ed., *Legacy: Southwest Indian Art at the School of American Research* (Santa Fe: School of American Research Press, 1999).

Particularly focused on basketry in the region are Larry Dalrymple's *Indian Basketmakers of the Southwest* (Santa Fe: Museum of New Mexico Press, 2000) and Carol A. Edison, *Willow Stories: Utah Navajo Baskets* (Salt Lake City: Utah Arts Council, 1996), which features the work of Mary Holiday Black, a Navajo matriarch (and the only Utahn to receive the NEA's National Heritage Award) and her extended family and neighbors, who have been carrying on a startling renaissance of basketry. I am indebted to Carol Edison for her photographs of their impressive work in this chapter.

The Ute courting flutes of Aldean Ketchum are traditionally made to have a distinctive sound by which the young woman being courted could recognize her favorite candidate and decide whether to meet him privately. When I asked Aldean if the flutes were also intentionally phallic, he blushed and said he'd rather not discuss it. But when he visited us a few months later, he brought the smaller flute shown in fig. 8 and said, "I made this one just for you!"

Settlers in Monticello, having denuded the nearby Abajo Mountains, praised God for the increased water runoff, which—for a time—aided their irrigation project. See Charles Peterson, *Look to the Mountains* (Provo: Brigham Young University Press, 1975), especially pp. 120–21. I discuss juniper-seed necklaces at greater length in *The Dynamics of Folklore* (Logan: Utah State University Press, 1996), 278–85. John Adair and Sol Worth describe their Navajo film project in *Through Navajo Eyes: An Exploration in Film Communication and Anthropology* (Bloomington: Indiana University Press, 1975).

Pictures of basketmakers Selina Peratrovich, Belle Deacon, and Mary Black—along with several of their baskets—are in Suzi Jones's *Pacific Basket Makers*. Further stories and comments by and about Pomo basketmaker Mabel McKay appear in Greg Sarris, *Keeping Slug Woman Alive* (Berkeley: University of California Press, 1993). Mabel's photo is on page 18 of *Pacific Basket Makers*.

The Warm Springs Huckleberry Feast appears in a 1997 documentary made by the Forestry Media Center at Oregon State University. Entitled *The Huckleberry Story: Building a Bridge between Culture and Science*, its coverage of the sacred is intertwined with the secular.

For more on National Heritage Award winners (both Native and non-Native) and their eloquent remarks on the cultural importance of their arts, see Steve Siporin, ed., *American Folk Masters: The National Heritage Fellows* (New York: Harry N. Abrams, 1992).

Black Elk's complaint about square houses can be found in John G. Neihardt, ed., *Black Elk Speaks: Being the Life Story of a Holy Man of the Oglala Sioux* (1932; reprint, Lincoln: University of Nebraska Press, 1961), 198–200. For an excellent survey of Native architecture, see Peter Nabokov and Robert Easton, *Native American Architecture* (New York and Oxford: Oxford University Press, 1989). On Navajo hogan development, see Stephen C. Jett and Virginia E. Spencer, *Navajo Architecture: Forms, History, Distributions* (Tucson: University of Arizona Press, 1981).

3

Kinetic Patterns of Performance

Dance

> *When I dance with all my regalia on—animal skins, feathers, shells,*
> *ermine furs—(it's not a costume, you know), I feel like all the living*
> *beings of the world are with me. There are the wingeds, the four-*
> *leggeds, the ocean beings, and the fur-bearers; when you dance*
> *surrounded by them, it makes you feel majestic. Dancing without*
> *regalia is just empty.*
>
> —Vanessa Brown, Navajo powwow dancer

> *A powwow is like dancing to your heartbeat with all your friends.*
> —Jimmy Boy Dial, an eastern Indian
> powwow dancer, quoted in the *New*
> *York Times*

WHY DO PEOPLE DANCE? Obviously, it's a form of artistic expression, but that begs the question: Why do we do it? What does it accomplish that we could not do for ourselves some other way? And why do different cultures understand dance in different ways? There must be a lot of possibilities but let me suggest one: Dance, as a conscious organization of human body movements, is a kind of kinetic "italics"; everyday movements of the arms, legs, head, and torso are extended, foregrounded, exaggerated, and reorganized to mean something beyond mere practical human motion. Though some forms of modern dance encourage dancers to move in special ways for artistic impact, traditional dance can be described as normal human movement made meaningful more by its culturally driven organization and nuance than the individual dancer's interpretation. Just as visual art allows us to create concrete objects to articulate complex cultural values, just as stories and songs allow the expression of cultural ideas in the patterns of oral performance, so dance allows us to dramatize, to act out, to *embody* a set of ideas or values which otherwise would remain unarticulated.

Dance can be viewed, some would say, as a form of language where the grammar is made of movements: it allows us to put our body where our mind is, so to speak, and of course the process is guided, constructed, and understood by cultural norms. In the Middle East and much of Europe, dance is a form of joyful exuberance, a way of embodying a culture's celebration; note the idea expressed in Ecclesiastes 3: 4: "A time to weep, and a time to laugh; a time to mourn, and a time to dance," suggesting that dancing is a communal expression opposite to mourning. In northern Europe, dances were often celebrations of plenty—as at harvest times.

As you might expect, dances among American Indians incorporate the same wide range of values and concerns suggested by the vast variety among the cultures themselves. So—for our inquiry and insight—let's ask not, "*Why* are they dancing?" or "What are they dancing *about?*" but rather, "*What* are they dancing?" That is to say, what is embodied in a particular dance while people are performing it? What do the accumulated patterns "say" to us? Here's how John (Fire) Lame Deer accounts for the development of the Lakota Sun Dance:

> Huddling in their poor shelters in the darkness of winter, freezing and hungry, hibernating almost like animals, how joyfully, thankfully they must have greeted the life-giving sun, let it warm their frozen bones as spring returned. I can imagine one of them on a sudden impulse getting up to dance for the sun, using his body like a prayer, and all the others joining him one by one. So they made this dance, and slowly, generation after generation, added more meaning to it, added to its awesomeness.

We notice that Lame Deer does not talk about the "steps" of the dance, or the details of its music and rhythms, or the way exceptional dancers may extend the meaning with their own notion of graceful motion. He concentrates first on the way the dance embodies a personal, then a communal response to the sun.

One of many Arctic stories about dance is a Yupik myth told by Ceril Chanar of Toksook Bay, Alaska, during the filming of Leonard Kamerling and Sarah Elder's wonderful *Drums of Winter:*

> Two men entered open water in kayaks. They had only a drum and a spear. They approached an enemy village saying, "We fight our enemies and we die, yet still we continue to fight. But our spears are meant only for killing animals." They began to beat the drum, and women came down to the shore, dancing. The two men asked to

enter the dance house to hold a peace council with the villagers. Afterwards the men went home and said to their village, "There will be no more war." Now the people fight only with dancing.

Another version of the story, collected by Ann Fienup-Riordan, describes the two hunter-warriors as being on a mission of revenge against a neighboring village. But they decide to break their spears in half and use them to beat a rhythm on the sides of their kayaks. The village women come down to the shore and begin to dance, standing in front of their men as if protecting them. Other anthropologists might point out that, according to older Eskimo custom, the men probably would have been invited to spend the night with the wives of prominent village leaders, a practice once used to create relatives, people who were no longer a danger to the village. But the myth doesn't mention that likely historical possibility; rather, dancing together becomes the mythic embodiment of coexisting, and the older threat of competitive warfare is replaced by the newer social practice of competitive dancing. The story dramatizes the idea that this cultural shift required men and women who saw a culturally structured way out of a culturally situated dilemma.

Eskimo dance today (by *Eskimo,* I mean the circum-Arctic peoples who are more accurately known by the names of their languages: Yupik, Aleut, Alutiiq [Sugpiaq], and Inupiaq) continues to exist despite years of suppression and ridicule by missionaries (who considered it evil and tried to forbid it), teachers (who thought it was backward and discouraged it), and government officials (who thought it was unhealthy and tried to limit it). Dancers usually congregate in the communal men's sweat house, called a *qasig,* or, more recently, in the school gymnasium. Large hoop drums (a drumhead of skin, gut, or plastic stretched over a hoop) are warmed up, singing slowly begins, and eventually one dance after another is performed in the middle of the floor by groups of friends or families who have been practicing (fig. 49). Men often dance in a kneeling position, mimicking motions made while rowing or hunting in a boat by strenuously moving their arms, upper torso, neck, and head in time to the heavy beat of the drumming and singing. Women often dance standing up, bending rhythmically at the knees and waving their dance fans at arms' length.

Dancing may accompany a potlatch (giveaway), or memorialize friendships forged between two villages, or continue the ongoing friendly dance rivalry among villages, or celebrate special cultural events. In 1996, for example, Ann Fienup-Riordan organized an exhibit of thirty-six carved Eskimo dance masks (an art form that had also been the target of missionaries and teachers) to tour museums in small villages in Alaska;

Fig. 49. Father René Astruc, a Belgian priest, dancing with Eskimos. He has been a supporter of Eskimo dance as a form of prayer for fifty years. Photo by the author.

the Native response was intensely emotional, and every location welcomed the masks with local dances (fig. 50). The exhibit title, "Our Way of Making Prayer," reflects the Yupik term for mask making and indicates that the relatively neat line between Western concepts of sacred and secular does not work in the Arctic, where social and religious events overlap warmly. It's clear also that the fields of visual art (the masks) and dance are interactive, not separated by generic boundaries. If anything, the two art forms enrich each other. And both dances and masks are now viewed as cultural treasures that were almost wiped out. Interviewed at a dance held when the exhibit visited Toksook (which is five hundred miles from any highway), Aassanaaq "Ossie" Kairaiuak remarked, "These things were lost to us for a long time. But they're coming back now. They're not going to be lost again" (fig. 51).

Although we will not deal in great detail with dances that are primarily sacred, it is worth pointing out that, like the Yupik dance, most ritual Native dances are not exclusively sacred or secular. They represent an overlap, an interchange, an intersection between the forces of the sacred world and the components of everyday life, whose elements are perceived as interrelated dimensions, not existing at opposite ends of a scale. When a Hopi

Fig. 50. The dance in Bethel, Alaska, honoring the
tour of Yupik masks, which had been kept in museums
until this time. Photo by the author.

member of the Long-Hair Kachina Society, for example, puts on the large
kachina mask (which covers his head and shoulders) and grasps in his teeth
the small cotton thread which unites him with the spirit of the kachina, he
becomes a combination of this world and the sacred one, serving as a link
between the two by literally embodying both at the same time.

Ironically enough, considering the stubborn stereotypes of non-
Natives, even sacred dances like the Hopi Kachina, the Navajo Yé'ii
Bicheii, or the Zuni Shalako are technically not secret ceremonies
closed to non-Indians. The Hopi Rain Dance (usually called the Snake
Dance), for example, is done to bring about rain for the entire earth, so
it would be inappropriate and illogical to bar outsiders. But, unfortu-
nately, since the 1930s, when this dance became a tourist attraction, so
many visitors have ignored the Hopi ban on photographs and recordings
that today it is indeed difficult to attend. Once, in the 1950s, as a Hopi
friend and I were watching the dance, a white stranger near us kept slip-
ping a camera from under his jacket, even though we told him photos
were prohibited. Suddenly, without warning, a muscular brown arm

Fig. 51. A dance celebrating the Yupik masks on tour from museums. Photo courtesy of the *Anchorage News*.

reached over his shoulder from behind, seized the camera, and silently sent it in a beautiful silvery arc over the edge of the mesa. By the 1960s, Hopis had learned that secretly recorded tapes of their singing were being played over loudspeakers in downtown Phoenix to advertise bus outings for white visitors to attend the ceremony. And a group of white enthusiasts calling themselves the "Smoki Indians" were putting on costumed demonstrations of the "snake dance" for tourists "to honor" the Hopi. No wonder Hopi members of the activist American Indian Movement started to block cars and buses of white tourists trying to reach Hopi villages during the 1970s.

Especially in the case of sacred dances, there are particular places where the dancing should be done, particular people who are trained and responsible for performing the dance properly, particular times (computed by complex examination of star constellations) when the dance should take place, and a particular cultural matrix in which the performance of the dance means something to the people who do it. Thus, even though most of these dances are not secret, they are done only by practiced people, while the rest of us watch. And they do have religious overtones for the local people which, while not exclusive, nonetheless involve beliefs and assumptions that the outsider may not know.

On the other hand, the modern social dances most often associated with the intertribal powwow phenomenon can be danced by anyone who is willing to get the proper regalia together, learn the dance steps and customs, and act appropriately during the event. Even without regalia, you and I are free to join and enjoy the round dances although we cannot step into a Navajo Yé'ii Bicheii or a Hopi Kachina Dance. So, without ignoring the importance of dance generally to Native people, I'll focus on the contemporary function of the intertribal social dance called "powwow" as an expressive form based on Native dance logic and patterning.

How old is the powwow tradition? We don't know. Utah historian Will Bagley gives an account of a visit by several hundred Sioux to Utah's Ute tribe in 1886. They had ridden their skinny ponies more than nine hundred miles from the Pine Ridge Reservation in South Dakota, mostly to trade pipestone for better horses. In addition, they no doubt discussed the Ghost Dance, which the Utes had been practicing since 1870, because the Sioux were dancing it by 1890; shortly afterward the Wounded Knee Massacre brought it to an abrupt halt, at least in the Dakotas. The visit was celebrated by a great gathering of several thousand Indians in the Uinta Valley, where people feasted on beef, delivered grand orations, and danced together. The three hundred dancers included at least a hundred Sioux; they wore paint on their faces and dressed in feathers, beadwork, and bandoliers of sleigh bells. According to the local Indian agent and his officers, who were invited to the event, the first dance lasted twenty minutes. So it sounds to me as if the intertribal dancing now known as powwow was already well developed more than 120 years ago.

The contemporary intertribal powwow, an increasingly popular vernacular dance among Native Americans, has not been given much attention by scholars, even though it has become one the most common articulations of "Indianness" today. Indeed, for many Americans, Jonathan Wacks's film *Powwow Highway* may provide the first (and only?) exposure to a cultural phenomenon occurring around them practically all the time. Perhaps the powwow's very contemporaneity, its dynamism and rapid spread in recent years, and its participants' unhesitating use of modern designs and colors run so contrary to white stereotypes and assumptions about the Vanishing American and are so opposed to the way non-Natives think Indians ought to behave that some people see the powwow as a cheap mishmash of leftover ideas no longer taken seriously in the Native American world. Some may think the older, "purer" customs have died out and see little left beyond a modern nostalgia for a vanished way of life perpetuated in exercises which lack their original depth and meaning.

This myopic view has allowed us to ignore one of the most rapidly growing expressions of ethnic awareness and identity anywhere in the world today and overlook an important concept about the transmission of cultural values: An idea may be phrased in a number of ways and will probably survive more successfully if it is continually reassessed and translated into newer, more functional modes of expression. The Navajos, for example, whose principal cultural and linguistic "leitmotiv" is *movement*, were happy to encounter the horse, for it made moving faster and more efficient; they were even happier to get pickup trucks, for—far from abandoning older cultural ideas—they could maintain and intensify an essentially Navajo idea about mobility in a newer context. Does the powwow offer some parallel intensification which accounts for its increasing popularity? Is there something about the idea of dance per se that articulates or embodies something important for Native Americans today? Does the intertribal nature of the powwow indicate a reassessment of older tribal allegiances in relation to modern Indian identity?

I think the powwow phenomenon can be viewed as a decodable kinetic statement about the realities of life for ethnically aware Native Americans, as well as a tableau of intense cultural meaning. The dynamic relationship between tribal and intertribal concerns, as well as between intertribal and mainstream (immigrant, in the view of many American Indians) cultures, is articulated by the powwow in the spatial and temporal arrangements of activities, in the similarities and differences between tribal customs, in the specific styles of dance and their continually developing meanings, in the roles of men and women, in the delicate balance between cooperation and competition, and in the overlapping of the secular and sacred.

The powwow in its current form is an outgrowth of earlier social dances done by almost all tribes for their friends and allies. The difference today is that these dances involve members of all tribes, not just allies. That is, they express common interests now felt by virtually all Indians, many of whom see themselves as surrounded by a hostile and domineering culture. The intertribal connections initiated and nurtured by powwow dancing are politically as well as ethnically important for Native Americans, for powwows often offer a social occasion where Native Americans can discuss political and legal ways to survive in the modern world. The value of intertribally shared interests—in contrast to historical tribal differences that might have divided them—is expressed vividly in the powwow. But politics can be discussed without dancing, after all. Thus, even though the political issues discussed at powwows are modern, using the dance to symbolize reciprocation and cooperation testifies to the continuing performance of older modes of expression.

The term *powwow* seems to come from one of the Algonquian languages (northeastern America), where it originally meant a "medicine man" or "conjurer." The term was borrowed by white Europeans to refer also to a meeting where curing took place. Eventually it was used by the whites to denote virtually any gathering of Indians, especially where singing or dancing was central. Indians have borrowed back this term (and several others used in the powwow, like "war dance") from English usage.

Today a powwow is primarily a social gathering where Indian people from several tribes dance together, using a few basic patterns that all the tribes recognize. The music is highly stylized, and the dancing goes on most of the afternoon and evening, with the dancers resting occasionally while particular groups (younger men or older women, for example) compete for prizes. From time to time, the hosts or a visiting group demonstrate a particular dance from their own tribe while other participants watch. Visitors are welcome, but non-Indians are sometimes asked to pay an entrance fee to help underwrite the event and the prizes.

Although powwows today are similar in many details, each has its own characteristics. Student powwows often include honor dances and awards for leaders and recent graduates; tribally based powwows honor local leaders, veterans, or old-timers. But the ethnically weighty matters taken up in dance and social form by the powwow are much alike the country over. The regularity and system with which certain events and activities occur at virtually all powwows—rural or urban, indoor or outdoor, whatever their size and tribal affiliations—are testimony to the existence of a growing body of tradition, custom, observance, belief, propriety, and awareness which have superseded the specific tribal customs that once underscored the differences (often the open enmities) among the participating tribes. The emergence of this larger body of custom and observance, which overarches and to a large extent subordinates older differences, is an indication that specific tribal identity is being reassessed by many Native Americans and being replaced by a powerful synthesis of related traditions that can articulate contemporary Indianness without obliterating tribal and family identities.

Powwows on or near reservations pull Indian people home from wherever they may be working or living, while urban powwows call people from the reservations to join their city cousins in a non-Native place (a school gymnasium, a rodeo arena) which has been converted to a gathering place for reestablishing family and social ties. An outdoor event often features a large encampment with tipis, wall tents, modern campers, and mobile homes. An urban, indoor event, on the other hand, requires participants to locate housing and purchase meals.

Crow Fair in Montana is so large that thousands of Native Americans spread themselves over many acres in family camps (fig. 52); in a parallel

Fig. 52. Crow Fair, 1979. Photo by Michael Crummett, courtesy of the American Folklife Center.

to older times, a crier (nowadays with a public address system mounted on a pickup trick) circulates announcements and camp rules and lets people know which dances are coming up in the large central arena where most of the action takes place. The area is full of traders' stalls (people selling raw materials, such as beads and supplies for Native artists who create powwow outfits), booths selling books about Indians and tapes of Indian music, booths where Indians sell and trade other items, and stands where churches and veterans' groups sell burgers, fry bread, and cotton candy. Other powwows may offer a hall where teenagers can gather and dance to more mainstream music if they wish, or a covered pavilion where several energetic stick games (a form of Native gambling) are constantly in progress, or small rooms where card games are played.

But the arrangement is not haphazard, for most powwows look like concentric circles when viewed from above: In the center is a dancing arena, then a circle of booths and stands (some of them mounted in mobile homes or campers for easy transport to the next powwow), then a larger and more amorphous circle of tents, tipis, and other campers. The pattern is essentially the same as it was two hundred years ago in villages of the Plains Indians, though the details have changed considerably.

For urban, indoor powwows, the pattern is still recognizable, though it takes form in another framework. Within the confines of a cavernous field house, the gym floor is the dance arena, surrounded (as is the dancing area at outdoor events) by a circle of seated participants and observers. Outside that circle, usually in the hallway surrounding the basketball court, is a ring of concession tables, traders' stalls, and book and tape booths. And around that—in the gridded, anonymous town—is an imagined circle of homes whose owners have agreed to let Indian visitors stay for a couple of nights.

Even though the room may be rectangular, the dancing area in all cases is our now-familiar circle, the normal pattern of nature. In the center of the area, or arranged around the perimeter, from one to five (sometimes more) drums are situated. The dancing takes place around them, with the prevailing motion usually clockwise or sunwise. Each drum (the term includes the drum and the group of singers gathered around it) alternates with the others in singing, although a particular drum may be asked to perform out of sequence for an honor dance.

Aside from planning sessions and fund-raising, the first stage of the powwow unfolds as the area slowly fills with people in dance regalia, and singers and drummers gather around their drums. Several drums have probably been invited, but perhaps some couldn't make it; other drums may show up unannounced. A drum group from the local area may be honored by the planning committee by being asked to serve as host drum. But people have often not decided ahead of time exactly who will drum, and a drum will not begin until the proper number of singers has come forward (the number varies in different tribes). When a "critical mass" has gathered, the people around a drum begin to sing and practice, and it is not until two or three of the drums have warmed up a few songs that people move onto the floor and begin dancing. When it is clear that there are enough drums to allow a sequence of dances, the master of ceremonies announces the opening processional, usually called the Grand Entry. This opening moment arrives naturally as an aspect of the process, not in response to the clock, and it indicates vividly the temporal assumptions of Indian life: things begin and end when the participants are ready.

Most powwows start and end on "Indian time"; that is, in spite of detailed planning, both indoor and outdoor powwows unfold according to general Native American attitudes about time in relation to event. Rather than starting exactly at the advertised moment of 7:30 P.M., a powwow actually gets under way much earlier as people from out of town arrive, meet each other, get their outfits together, wait for the drums to gather, and get a bite to eat. At 6:00 P.M. a few people are on the gym floor, talking, and a drum or two is setting up and trying a song. By 8:00 P.M. the Grand Entry may or may not have occurred, depending on whether everyone who is expected to be in it has shown up. By 9:00 P.M. the opening

Fig. 53. The honor guard for the Grand Entry at the Flathead powwow. Indian people are saluting the Indian flag, the feathered staff at the far right, which commemorates all Indians who have died in American wars, whether they fought against or with the whites. Photo by the author.

number is over, and the floor is crowded with dancers; by midnight there may still be a few diehards, but most of the people have left to find their host families or a stick game. It is difficult to time any of this by the clock, for these actions are responsive to the internal dynamics of the event far more than the arbitrary measurement of elapsed time. Since the timing is internal, the event is more like a flower blooming than an airplane departing the gate; the schedule is created, so to speak, by the passengers, not the airline. It is clear that powwow dancing itself is the kinetic centerpiece of a culturally structured and expressive event.

The Grand Entry is led by war veterans, usually carrying the national flags of the United States and Canada, plus the state flag and perhaps the tribal flag, along with the Indian warriors' flag, actually a staff festooned with eagle feathers honoring Indian people who have died in warfare (fig. 53). Many Indians are veterans of World War II, the Korean War, and Vietnam, and many of them belong to official veterans' groups. But it is made very clear during this processional that the warriors' flag represents Indians who have fallen in *all* wars, a pointed reference to the many people who died fighting European invaders. The tableau of the American, Canadian, and warriors' flags in procession around the dance floor may initially strike us as ironic politically, but it is a reminder of the ways

American Indians have survived culturally by uniting many of their interests with those of the countries which surround them. The procession also symbolizes the syncretic, inclusive, centripetal force of the pow-wow itself.

After the opening Grand Entry or Flag Song, there is often an invocation or pipe ceremony, then an "intertribal war dance"; this is not a dance that has anything to do with war but one whose steps are celebratory (which led early white observers to assume that it was a dance connected with battle). The first half-dozen dances are all of the intertribal war-dance variety and are often described as "warm-up dances" because they draw everyone into the festivities and help the drummers get into good voice.

Drummers are expected to know their songs thoroughly. Not everyone is allowed to approach the drum, and definitely not anyone under the influence of drugs or alcohol. Since menstruating women supposedly have powerful influences on drums (which are thought by many tribes to be alive), they usually do not sing around the drum or dance, but they do attend the powwow as spectators. Each drum receives payment to cover transportation expenses, but if one drum is asked to sing an honoring song during the powwow, the family of the honoree donates an additional gift of money. While these sums are usually quite modest, for an honoring dance—particularly for someone recently deceased—the amount can be as much as a hundred dollars. The gift is almost always announced publicly as well. Singers usually spend the entire powwow gathered at or near their drum, but several drums make it possible to rest singers' voices between songs, so drummers often get up and join in other dances, especially toward the end of the evening. Whenever a round dance is announced, where all spectators and participants are invited to take part, two or three of the drummers move through the crowds gesturing at people with their drumsticks to come and dance. As the evening goes on, the drummers sing louder and louder, and there is a tremendous strain on their voices; they may chew and swallow traditional Indian medicinal plants, such as yarrow root, to protect their throats.

Although there are demonstrations of particular tribal dances during pauses in the powwow schedule, the bulk of dancing done by participants falls into two overall categories: war dances and round dances. In the former, dancers move alone according to their own variation of accepted powwow style (although often friends dance near each other); everyone who wants to dance is on the floor, but there is no attempt to dance alike except that everyone is moving to the same drumbeat. The round dances, on the other hand, place everyone in the same (or concentric) circles, and they all must use the same step, usually a side step in trochaic meter.

The result is several hundred people surging sunwise around the arena in unison and one pattern.

In war dances, the two principal styles are marked by clothing as well as execution. The "straight" or traditional dancers wear more conservative clothing (often suggested by their name, the prominent animal or bird in their outfit, or even the theme of their vision quest); the "fancy" dancers wear more modern adaptations of earlier styles, featuring more color, more feathers, more fringe, more moving parts. Fancy dancing tends to be faster and more energetic, and the moving parts of the dancers' outfits accentuate their athleticism.

Men dance energetically, and most of them have noisemakers attached to their legs: sleigh bells, various kinds of shells, even large cowbells (fig. 54). The men's role in the war dances is to maintain and accentuate the steady pulse of the drum, which holds all the people together. The women, on the other hand, dance very lightly, seeming to float over the ground, for their role is to symbolize the dignity and delicacy of the woman's position in nature. But in both cases, the basic orientation is to the earth, and even in athletic specialty dances like the Hoop Dance, there aren't any of the magnificent upward leaps of the European ballet style that suggest flight or escape from the earth.

Most of the women dance a style of war dance that is traditional, both in outfit and dance step. Some of the younger women, however, do a fancy dance called the Shawl Dance, where the dancers wear large shawls with long fringes that wave back and forth as the women twist and turn (fig. 55). The shawls of the 1800s were buffalo hides; later, woolen blankets were used, and nowadays fringed polyester is popular. The footwork is spectacular, and the dance is so athletic that hardly anyone over the age of twenty does it. Similarly energetic, the Jingle Dance has become increasingly popular among young women; the dance takes its name from the hundreds of snuff-can lids rolled into cone shapes and sewn on the dancers' dresses. (fig. 56). The demand for snuff-can lids has so exceeded the supply in recent years that you can often find cast-metal "jingles" for sale in those little stalls surrounding the powwow.

Fancy dancing derives mostly from the Plains Indian tradition but is done by members of virtually all tribes attending a powwow. It is especially common in competitive events because of the demanding footwork. Lately, however, the straight-dance style has become popular again, and in larger powwows today, traditional dancers have increased to the point where there are often more of them in contests than fancy dancers.

During the final stages of competitive fancy dancing, the drummers try to trick the dancers by stopping suddenly in the middle of a song. The

Fig. 54. A dancer at an outdoor powwow at Ft. Belknap, Montana, 1979. Photo by Michael Crummett, courtesy of the American Folklife Center.

Fig. 55. An unidentified young woman waits for traditional-style powwow dancing, 1979. Photo by Michael Crummett, courtesy of the American Folklife Center.

Fig. 56. Kahealani Johnson waiting to dance in her jingle dress covered in rolled snuff-can lids formed into bugles; Bluff, Utah, 2001. Photo by the author.

drum, however, can stop only at certain traditional places, at the ends of particular musical phrases. Normally the song goes on at this point, but the drum has the option of stopping momentarily and then starting again. When the drumming and singing stop, the best dancers—who know the song and its characteristics and are paying close attention while they dance—are also ready to stop on the same beat. Any dancer who takes another step attracts attention by the sound of his bells. Through such trick stops, the less proficient, or less attentive, dancers are eliminated from competition, and only the best fancy dancers remain. Obviously, even though part of the competition judging is based on how energetically and proficiently a dancer performs the steps, only those who know the songs and traditions thoroughly can remain in competition until the end. Thus, the knowledge and application of tradition is valued as highly as the competition itself.

In addition, those who win the top prizes (which range from fifty to fifteen hundred dollars) almost always share their money with their competitors and the drums. This redistribution of prize money is a standard element of Indian attitudes about competition and selfishness: anyone who gains riches or power by his own means and does not share them with his family and friends is considered antisocial by many tribes, in some cases even a witch. Thus, the tendency is not to keep money and goods but redistribute one's belongings as far as possible. The powwow provides a functional modern context where this may be done openly.

Both the intertribal nature and secular function of the powwow are illustrated by the clothing worn. One seldom if ever hears the term "costume" from Indian people (the terms "regalia" and "outfit" are more common); powwow clothing is seen as something to dress up in, a demonstration of personal and Native identity, not mere entertainment for others. Even then, the public, social nature of the dance is indicated by the fact that outfits avoid tribal-specific regalia one would expect at a religious observance. For example, a Navajo who dances in a ritual Yé'ii Bicheii dance would never wear his mask and ritual sash to a powwow; rather, when he enters a fancy dance competition, he wears an assemblage of feathered wings and bustles which would seem totally outlandish to his Athabascan ancestors (and, admittedly, overkill even to the well-feathered Plains Indians who originated the motif). In feathers, bells, shells, hot colors, satin gym trunks, and perhaps sunglasses to boot, he looks unlike any Indian of two hundred years ago but very much like thousands of other powwow dancers today. Whether the men are dressed in fancy dance feathers or in deerhide and a Hudson's Bay blanket, their outfits function as a recognizable badge of intentional involvement.

On the other hand, the adult women's clothing at a powwow is often what they would wear at home on any special Native occasion. Many Indian people feel that this consistency is the embodiment of the dignity, grace, and power of women. That is to say, women do not have to wear special clothing for a powwow because they take their own tribal dignity with them wherever they go. Indeed, in many tribes it is the women who continue to pass on language, religious belief, and other cultural instruction to the younger generation, especially since it is the custom among many tribes for the grandmother to raise the children.

Whatever the style of the outfit, straight or fancy, creating the clothing (often made as gifts by friends, relatives, or lovers) is based on beliefs and assumptions about its symbolic function. Outfits should include something from the "wingeds" (because birds are two legged like humans, they are considered close relatives), especially the feathers of an eagle (figs. 57, 58). The "four-leggeds," who supply us with food and provide hides for moccasins and dresses, are also represented in the outfit, along with decorations made by human hands and supplied by creatures from the waters in the form of shells. Sometimes the "fur bearers," those four-leggeds who supply their pelts for decoration, receive special attention. In addition to animal references, powwow regalia also reflects the plant world in many subtle ways: Dancers may carry sweet-grass or sage bundles in their pouches or use juniper or other seeds along with glass beads in wristbands, headbands, and necklaces, and many dancers smudge themselves and their regalia with sage or sweet-grass smoke before entering the dance arena.

The total outfit is said to honor all that gives life on earth, all that provides humans with food, warmth, and sacred power. By wearing symbolic clothes, the dancers become one with all the living beings who share the world with them as their relatives. As people create their regalia for the powwow, they tell stories and share comments about the symbolism with younger people, who usually participate in the process. Thus, the outfits worn at the powwow provide an occasion for the material and oral articulation and transmission of traditional values associated with—and expressed in—the dance.

Because the various parts of a powwow outfit may be very special, dancers have developed a complex way of dealing with the loss, destruction, or deterioration of regalia. The one most obvious to a powwow spectator is the Lost Item or Lost Feather Dance. Anytime a part of a dancer's outfit drops to the floor, its return to the owner is ritualized. Of course, minor items such as a bell or a pair of glasses may simply be turned in or reported to the master of ceremonies, but something like an eagle feather calls for an ornate and serious ceremony. Naturally, there are regional and

Figs. 57 and 58. The front (top) and back (bottom) of a beaded fancy dance bag by a Salish artist. Simplot Collection, gift of J. R. Simplot (NA.203.825); Buffalo Bill Historical Center, Cody, Wyoming.

tribal variations of this ritual, but typically in the West, the Whipman (or the "Head Man Dancer")—one of the chosen officials on the floor— immediately goes to the spot and stands by the feather to make sure no one dances on it. After the conclusion of that dance, the lost feather is announced, and a Lost Feather Dance is quickly arranged. Usually four male dancers (who must be war veterans) surround the feather and dance around it and up to it almost as if they are hunting an animal. Just before they reach the feather, the changing beat of the drum calls them back to the perimeter of their circle, and the hunting starts again. Finally, after some minutes of dancing, one of the dancers (sometimes the person who actually noticed the feather first but a war veteran in any case) dances up to the feather, picks it up, and holds it over his head with a triumphant whoop; then all dancers circle the area sunwise. The owner is asked to come forward and claim the feather, then narrate a story about how it was first obtained and what relationship it bears to the dancer's outfit or char-acter. The owner may sing a song or play a drum to honor the person who recovered the precious feather. In some powwows, all lost objects are dealt with this way, partly to show publicly that a missing item was not stolen or misused and partly because it calls the loss to the attention of the owner, who, in a large crowd, may not have noticed part of his outfit falling or heard an announcement over the loudspeaker.

One duty of the powwow hosts, beyond supplying the arena and housing, is to provide occasions for the expression of tribal identity (including their own) in a way that does not place undue attention on any particular one. For example, the local hosts of a powwow, if it is being held in Indian country, may begin the event with one of their own spe-cial dances to welcome participants. Every eight or ten years at the Arlee Powwow, the Flathead people do their Snake Dance, a long processional that begins far out in the tipi village surrounding the dance area, moves single file through the tipis, and eventually arrives at the powwow grounds. Only Flatheads take part in this dance, which is said to derive from a time when a Flathead who had been bitten by a snake was cured when the whole tribe did the snake's dance. Occasionally this dance is done to celebrate the relationship between Flathead Indians and the snakes (whose appearance and disappearance during the year are also cal-endar signs indicating when certain stories may be told). Since the pro-cession visits every tipi in the encampment, the dance demonstrates Flathead hospitality and promotes new acquaintances (and one Flathead friend confides, "It's a great way to scope out the visiting girls").

But since the hosts do not want to dominate the event, they also try to find out which visitors would like to present a specialty dance representing their own tribal affiliation. For example, a young man visiting from Pueblo country may be invited to do a southwestern Hoop Dance, or a group of teenage girls from Oregon's Warm Springs Reservation may be asked to do their Butterfly Dance. The floor is cleared of all other dancers, and the girls dance a very slow step, their blankets wrapped around their shoulders and heads, their bodies bent over, representing the cocoon of a butterfly; later, when the dance's rhythm becomes more energetic, the girls launch into a much more active step. They throw their arms and blankets back, using the blankets as if they are wings, and whirl in large circles, celebrating the movement from cocoon to butterfly and also, of course, symbolizing the progression of a young girl to womanhood.

One year at the University of Oregon's student powwow, the Tolowa Indians of northern California were invited to do their Deer Dance, where the dancers simply stand in a line and bend at the knees while small deer hooves attached to their costumes click together in rhythm. The dance, formerly part of a religious ritual, is done today as an exhibition, and only the Tolowa do it. The women in the group danced topless the first night, resulting in a large crowd of non-Indian spectators on the second night. But the Tolowas, not wishing to sensationalize their contribution, added bras to their outfits (both males and females). This immediate adjustment in the interests of harmony at the powwow is characteristic of the participants' attitudes. The Butterfly Dance is done almost every year at the University of Oregon's Native American Student Union Powwow, but to my knowledge the Tolowa Deer Dance has never been repeated because of its unfortunate effect on white people.

But planned humor is another matter. At Montana's Arlee Powwow, almost every year sees another enactment of the Wanna-be Initiation Dance, a gentle satire of outsiders. The announcer—often Bearhead Swaney or Colonel Doug Allard—asks all Indian people to vacate the center of the arena so that non-Indian visitors can be honored by induction into the Wanna-be Society. Hippies in beads, German and Japanese tourists festooned with cameras, elderly California matrons heavy with Navajo jewelry, and grandpas on vacation in Hawaiian shirts and sandals are all dragged into the arena and given basic instructions on how to stamp their feet in time to the drums. Then, as they dance in puzzled embarrassment, they are told they are now participants in the Wanna-be Dance, the special ritual for those who "wanna be" Indians.

At powwows around the Northwest, several elderly ladies from Warm Springs Reservation in Oregon volunteer to put on an Old Women's Dance. It starts with the apparently ancient women hobbling around the arena on their canes, stumbling and sometimes bumping into each other.

Then one pretends to take offense and swings her cane at one of the others, who in turn ducks and tries to strike back. Then follows a melee where the old ladies try to hit each other across the shins or on the side of the head, all the while jumping over each other's blows, ducking, and swinging their canes, all in time to the relentless drums. The battle lasts until everyone is laughing too hard to swing anymore.

Sometimes the master of ceremonies asks if anyone is willing to lead the Oklahoma Two-Step. To a heavy, rapid drum beat, the lead couple, holding hands, runs around the arena, followed by other dancers, also in couples. The lead couple may stop and dance in place, may jump up and down, may run backward, may split off with the men and women going in different directions to come together at another part of the pavilion. All participants must follow the actions of the lead couple, and usually the dance dissolves in laughter as people begin tripping over each other and falling on the ground.

One of the most difficult aspects of Indian life today is competition, for it is heavily promoted in schools and business, but in nearly every tribe, it carries a negative connotation and is usually associated with moral decay, selfishness, and even witchcraft. In some tribes, competition may be expressed in play or games but not everyday life. Even in games, serious personal competitiveness is politely avoided (a Navajo grandmother watching a basketball game on television asked me, "Why don't they give each of those teams a ball so they won't have to fight over that one all the time?"). The powwow allows for a mediation between the competitive urges of mainstream society and the cooperative tendencies of Native culture. Thus, while serious personal competition in and of itself is considered offensive, competitive demonstration of one's abilities at culturally meaningful occasions, carried out in a culturally structured context, is a positive sign of belonging to, and accepting, one's own value system. Moreover, winning a powwow competition brings cash prizes, which, in turn, allows good dancers to afford the continuous travel to powwows. Most Native dancers, then, have learned to view the dance competition as similar to other games that take place at the same event, such as gambling, stick games, and even courtship. As a game, the competition is permissible and enhances excitement and attendance. In a way, this aspect of the powwow is reminiscent of rodeos or contemporary square-dance contests among Euro-Americans: mastery of older, culturally important traditions which are not "for sale" is demonstrated in a social atmosphere which actually promotes the importance of holding onto them.

The bigger the prizes, the more likely a powwow will attract the best dancers; if everyone expects the finest dancers, the powwow draws more people, both Indian and non-Indian. The Indians expect to see (and participate with) leading exponents of a cultural art form deeply significant to them; the non-Indians, while they do not share the deeper cultural values supporting the powwow symbolism and deportment, nonetheless understand competition and enjoy the event for that and its exotic and exciting colors and rhythms. The larger the crowd, the better the powwow committee can pay its bills and plan a bigger event for the coming year.

But even though some aspect of competition is now an unavoidable element of the powwow experience, the competitors themselves are evaluated by Indian standards and not the applause of the crowd. The women's dancing, for example, is judged by other Native American women, who look for certain highly valued abilities that relate to Indian custom, including authenticity of dress, delicacy and style of footwork, and knowledge of the dance tune (indicated by stopping precisely when the singing stops). What is rewarded is not personal flair (as in modern ice-skating contests) but cultural competence and traditional know-how. Similarly, in the men's traditional dancing, the dancers are judged on their knowledge of the songs, the authenticity of regalia, and the forcefulness with which they dramatize the vision of the animal or process they are symbolizing. These judging criteria encourage younger dancers who aspire to do the traditional dance steps to learn the traditions thoroughly before they dare compete. In August of 2001, at the Northern Navajo Fair in Bluff, Utah, one of the best male dancers appeared numerous times without his headdress, which cost him points in his cumulative score; it turned out he had won numerous contests and wanted to insure that others would have a better chance of winning this one. From the Indian point of view, then, strengthening tradition rather than competing for money, trophies, or personal acclaim is the central feature of the powwow. And thus, a potentially corrosive situation (competition) is converted to a positive demonstration of tribal and intertribal values.

How is it, however, that *dance* plays this all-important role for Native Americans? Other ethnic groups use food, language, music, clothing, or liturgy, and dance does not function so complexly even for those who find it an important medium of expression (for example, the Greeks in America). Nor does dance provide such an all-encompassing metaphor for cultural reality for other groups. Perhaps the Native American attitude toward dance itself offers us part of the answer, even though every tribe has its own point of view on the subject. As our discussion implies, and as you can learn by asking almost any Native American who knows about dancing, both ritual and social dances in Native American cultures mean far more than ritual gesture, entertainment, or artistically motivated motion.

Dance is a dynamic dimension that one enters intentionally, a kinetic model of personal involvement by which one places his or her body into the active, ongoing processes of cultural life (sort of like raising one's hand at an auction). In the words of Vanessa Brown, a Navajo who is a consummate powwow dancer, "When we dance, we experience the rhythms of nature, like our heartbeats, like seasons, like gestation periods. When we dance with other people, we use our bodies like living gestures that relate us to those other people who are there, and to all the other people everywhere" (fig. 59). Whether or not this is a common attitude among the various tribes whose members are powwow dancers, it is clear that powwows have developed into an abiding and deeply emotional model for those who participate in its process. The following examples illustrate this idea more fully.

During any powwow, several honoring dances may call attention to the survivors of calamities, the anniversary of some well-known person's death, the services and values of old people, or graduates of local high schools and colleges. During an honoring dance, one drum plays a slow war dance, and the person or persons being honored dance sunwise around the floor all alone. On the second time around, close friends and family members may join in behind, and as the dance continues, all dancers fall into place until the entire pavilion becomes a parade. At Crow Fair in 1979, such a dance honored Tom Yellowtail, leader of the Crow Sun Dance. At Arlee the same year, the dance welcomed back a young man who had been unjustly jailed. At Oregon's Native American Student Union (NASU) Powwow in 1983, Vanessa Brown asked everyone to join in her celebration of reunion with the family she had lost touch with for thirty years.

Dancing with people as a symbol of supporting them, agreeing with them, or honoring them extends to other important events in the lives of Indian people. For example, at the Umatilla Reservation in northeastern Oregon, I saw a special dance where a young son who had come of age and was about to go off to school danced around the arena with his father. On the fourth time around, they danced down the middle until they reached the halfway point; then they turned and danced in opposite directions. At this point, both dancers and their families were in tears, for the dance symbolized the separation of father and son as he moved away from the reservation area.

Similarly, when middle-aged people move back to their reservation from the cities, as is often the case, they may request the master of ceremonies at a powwow to ask people for "permission" for them to return. Actually, they need no permission, but they want the emotional and cultural support of their people. Such a couple, along with their children,

Fig. 59. The author and his daughter Vanessa Brown at an outdoor pow-wow in Bluff, Utah, in August 2001.

may then do a round dance alone around the entire arena, side by side. Then, one by one, other members of their families, friends, and even people who don't know them move out and join the dancing until the entire arena is full of concentric circles. Usually at this point, the family who has asked to be reabsorbed into the tribal system is visibly moved by the powerful symbolic significance of this dancing gesture of inclusion. Especially in cases like this, dance clearly becomes a kinetic model of community patterning, an enactment of what community is, in the Native view.

For this reason, after a recent death, it is customary for relatives *not* to participate in powwow dancing or even attend. But after a year has gone by, a memorial dance may be held, often at a powwow, where the deceased person is praised and relatives dance in commemoration. Often a younger person in the family dances in some of the traditional clothing that belonged to the deceased, while other items are displayed in a processional.

As concentric circles of round dancers move around the floor, people sometimes shake hands with others passing in the other line, whooping loudly as they do. On occasions like this, the whooping or yelling is often directed especially at a non-Indian who seems to be dancing for the first time. If the person smiles and whoops back, all present respond by whooping, but if the outsider seems embarrassed and looks away in confusion, another Indian reaches out and tries to shake hands. The idea is not to embarrass visitors but urge them to become participants, enclose them within the same circle. Most visitors find this a heartwarming custom, especially if they had fears about spending the evening among "stoic, uncommunicative" Natives.

Dance for American Indians evokes experiential engagement, integration, and reintegration. In the fullest sense of the term, dance *embodies* or enacts cultural attitudes which cannot readily be articulated today in other ways. Just as the Hopi kachina dancer becomes part of the sacred forces of nature by interacting with sacred processes through the medium of dance, actually participating in and embodying the fertile powers which nurture the people; just as a Navajo Yé'ii Bicheii dancer, by putting on his mask and sash and dancing, actually embodies the powers of healing which help the sick patient recover, so the dancers of a secular round dance form a living constellation of the integrated group with which they seek connection. Today Native American communities are beset with pressures, including competition, that in the tribal view lead to disintegration, dissolution, depression, alienation, and separation. Whatever their tribal differences were in the past, their contemporary reality embodies commonly perceived and experienced corrosive trauma. One of their only ways of dealing with this shock is selecting features of their various cultures which offer a way of sharing and maintaining what they have.

The powwow, then, gives Native Americans a dynamic arena where the potentially conflicting elements of contemporary life are mediated in an ethnically rich (and therefore nurturing) environment. Polarities such as female/male, insider/outsider, old/young, Indian/non-Indian, host/guest, group/individual, cooperation/competition, tradition/change, straight/fancy, and Christian belief/tribal religion are seen by most American Indians not as diametrically opposed alternatives but overlapping and interactive realities, sometimes exemplified in their beadwork. Viewed as competitive opposites, these qualities can produce friction and disharmony; but integrated and embodied in the gestural commitment of dance, they have the capacity to promote wholeness and well-being even among tribes that were once deadly enemies. The powwow can reintegrate alienated individuals within their larger ethnic community without pretending that it is possible to lead a pristine tribal life unaffected by the disaster of invasion and plunder. In other words, the fact that the powwow differs from older tribal traditions is not a sign of cultural slippage but of selective, intensified ethnic tenacity. This is an activity which promotes pride in being Native while not ignoring the fact that there are other tribes, other values, other religious views; it expresses Indianness without ignoring the confusing framework surrounding that condition.

The powwow provides a living context for young people to learn older patterns and experience a tremendous range of expressions based on worldview assumptions that remain important to Indian people. It takes place in concentric circles of family, tribe, and nature, the artistic representation of which, as we saw in chapter 2, provides not only an idealized model of cultural and ethnic stability and enactment of community for American Indians but also a dramatic way to find and experience a personal place in the Native family. As Nez Perce powwow dancer Steven Reuben claims, "I like to dance for my people to the songs I remember my grandfather singing."

Notes

In rethinking this chapter, I have been greatly aided by conversations with dancer Michiru Onizuka-Kempen. Jimmy Boy Dial is quoted in an article on eastern powwows written by Evelyn Nieves for the *New York Times*, 23 July 1992, National section, p. A-13. *Uksuum Cauyai: The Drums of Winter* (1988) is a brilliant film by Leonard Kamerling and Sarah Elder exploring the dance, music, and spirituality of the Yupik Eskimo people of Emmonak, Alaska. Lame Deer's account of the Lakota Sun Dance appears as chapter 12 of *Lame Deer: Seeker of Visions* by John (Fire) Lame Deer and Richard Erdoes (New York: Simon and Schuster, 1972); the quoted passage is on page 199. Will Bagley's historical account of the 1886 powwow in Utah's Uinta Basin appeared in the *Salt Lake Tribune*, 24 June 2001, p. B-1.

Ann Fienup-Riordan is one of the foremost (and most insightful) commentators on Yupik life and culture. Her description of the dance origin story is in *Eskimo Essays* (New Brunswick: Rutgers University Press, 1990), 138. A newspaper account of the mask exhibition's visit to Eskimo villages (a project developed and nurtured by Fienup-Riordan) appeared in the *Anchorage Daily News*, 28 January 1996, pp. J-1, 4–5. She also edited *Agayuliyararput (Our Way of Making Prayer): Yup'ik Masks and the Stories They Tell*, transcribed and translated by Marie Meade (Seattle and London: Anchorage Museum of History and Art, 1996).

Two descriptive articles appeared in the 1987 issue of *Folklife Annual*, edited by Alan Jabbour and James Hardin (Washington, D.C.: Library of Congress, 1988): "American Indian Powwow" (pp. 46-69), by Barre Toelken and Vanessa Brown, gives a general overview of the powwow phenomenon and is the basis for many of the observations developed in the present essay (another, far-stuffier version appeared as "Ethnic Selection and Intensification in the Native American Powwow" in Steven Stern and John Allan Cicala, eds., *Creative Ethnicity: Symbols and Strategies of Contemporary Ethnic Life* (Logan: Utah State University Press, 1991), 137–56. The author thanks the American Folklife Center for permission to use portions of the original essay here. The other *Folklife Annual* article, "Celebration: Native Events in Eastern Canada" (70–85), by Michael Sam Cronk, Beverly Cavanagh, and Franziska von Rosen, describes analogous celebrations in Canada. A particularly good insider's description of the powwow is George P. Horse Capture's *Pow Wow* (Cody, Wyoming: Buffalo Bill Historical Center, 1989), which contains great illustrations and helpful definitions. A collection of fine powwow dancer portraits, accompanied by their own sentiments about dancing, is Ben Marra's *Powwow: Images along the Red Road* (New York: Harry N. Abrams, 1996). Steven Reuben's photo and comment (quoted at the end of this chapter) appear on page 47. My Lakota son-in-law, Peter DeCory, appears on page 70.

I have visited the Arlee Powwow a number of times. For information about the powwow and its meaning to the inland Salish people, I am indebted to Mrs. Adelaide Matt (an excellent beadworker), Willie Wright, Victor Charlo, Agnes Vanderberg, Johnnie Arlee, Bearhead Swaney, and Betty White. During my twenty years on the faculty of the University of Oregon, I often had the opportunity of helping with the NASU Powwow and occasionally served as its master of ceremonies. Native American students most involved over the years were George Wasson, Dick Wilson, John Wasson, Ed Edmo, Robert Bojorkas, Dennis DeGross, James Florendo, and Larry Calica. Traditional visitors from Warm

Springs Reservation usually included Verbena Green, Matilda and Louis Mitchell, Prosanna Williams, and their families.

Vanessa Brown, my daughter, was born on the Navajo Reservation and raised traditionally in the Shonto area. After attending reservation schools, she married an Ojibwa from Canada and lived for several years on the Roseau River Reserve near Winnipeg. During that time, she entered the powwow circuit and came to know people from a number of Midwest tribes; eventually she announced herself for a Sun Dance and fulfilled a vow of dancing four years in that ritual at the Pine Ridge Reservation in South Dakota, during which time she was given the name Wanbli Ota Wi (Many Eagles Woman). She lives today with her five children in Tuba City, Arizona, where she is active in developing youth programs, providing cultural education, and encouraging Navajo and Hopi participation in powwows. Recently, on the Navajo and Hopi reservations, three of Vanessa's children have begun Sun Dance vows.

Another view of why and how people dance culturally is provided by Jose E. Limon in his richly descriptive *Dancing with the Devil: Society and Cultural Poetics in Mexican-American South Texas* (Madison: University of Wisconsin Press, 1994).

Two particularly interesting and insightful works on dancing were produced by non-Indians. Reginald and Gladys Laubin's *Indian Dances of North America: Their Importance to Indian Life* (Norman: University of Oklahoma Press, 1977) is based on longstanding acquaintance with Plains Indians by a couple who have dedicated their lives to studying Native customs at close range. They have been adopted by elderly Lakota, lived for extended periods of times among several Plains nations, and been invited to dance for Native American audiences of all kinds. Their personal knowledge of Native dances seems encyclopedic. More specifically focused on powwow dances is Adolf Hungry Wolf's *Pow-wow: Dancer's and Craftworker's Handbook* (Skookumchuck, British Columbia: Canadian Caboose Press, 1999), a slender book full of designs and how-to instructions and especially interesting for its wonderful collection of rare historical photographs.

4

Oral Patterns of Performance

Story and Song

> *Everything is made possible through stories.*
> —Hugh Yellowman, Navajo, explaining why stories are told

> *I've been poor most of my life; I've known only one song.*
> —Little Wagon, Navajo, when asked about the importance
> of songs

EARLY IN THE NAVAJO CREATION STORY, First Man and First Woman (who are depicted as gendered holy beings made up of colored light), hear a strange noise on a nearby mountain shrouded by clouds. Apprehensive about what this unknown noise may signify, but feeling a need to investigate, First Man rejects First Woman's advice to avoid the dangers, saying:

Do not be afraid . . .
Nothing will go wrong. For I will surround myself with song.
I will sing as I make my way to the mountain.
I will sing while I am on the mountain.
And I will sing as I return.
I will surround myself with song.
You may be sure that the words of my song will protect me.

What First Man finds on the mountain is a baby girl, crying; it is Changing Woman, the first real personage in Navajo mythic history, and the closest to a full deity of all the sacred people (*yei*) in the Navajo pantheon. He brings her back to First Woman, and the two, totally clueless about what to do with a baby, set about ritualizing her life and physical development by creating proper words and stories.

Much of the Beautyway story and ceremony focuses on the discovery and maturation of Changing Woman, and today, whenever a hogan is blessed, or a wedding is performed, or a young woman celebrates her first menstruation, songs from this extensive ceremony are sung, the words vividly dramatizing for contemporary people their identity with the sacred past. For Navajos, actually uttering words creates the reality of their world: Spoken or sung language is a creative act; hence, people avoid speaking of things they don't want to see appear in the world around them. One of the most terrible things to say out loud (if a Navajo carpenter pounds his thumb with a hammer, for instance) is *shash*, "bear," for—uttered in passion— the word may really summon a bear, and bears are ritually (and factually) difficult to deal with.

Spoken words, especially when enhanced or intensified by repetition, ritual structures, and musical phrases, are the principal means Navajos use to create a sense of order and harmony in the world they inhabit. The medicines administered to a patient in any Navajo healing ceremony are a response to the symptoms being treated, but healing in any deeper sense comes through the power of the words in the ritual. Along with doing sand paintings (which are symmetrical, cyclic, oriented to the universe, and usually four sided), placing the ritual inside a hogan (which is round, oriented to the east, and represents the womb of Changing Woman), and using four-way repetition in the songs (which represents the four directions), Navajo curing ceremonies have the same patterns and assumptions we have been discussing. Most of these rituals are not secret and are not conducted by mysterious shamans but by *hataałii*, literally "singers," who may be either male or female (hence the uselessness of the stereotypical English term "medicine man") and spend about fifteen to twenty years learning the songs, sand paintings, stories, and medications for one ceremony or "way." Most of these singers know several ways, which are healing rituals envisioned as moving along a trail; obviously, even mastering one is an intellectual achievement of some distinction.

By contrast, a *shaman* (the term is based on a Siberian Tungus word, so the second syllable has nothing to do with gender) is defined as a person who has gained control over the processes of life and death—usually by having died and come back to life. Shamans are most active in cultures which depend on a lively interaction between the living and the dead—hunting cultures are the most prominent examples—where the death of animal relatives is explained and mediated, and breaches with the animal world healed, by the magical ability of the shaman to visit the world of dead animals. Such a person would be called a witch by the Navajos and other southwestern tribes, mostly agriculturalists, whose way of viewing reality entails the verbal encouragement of health and fertility for plants and people alike.

Much has been written about these ceremonies, and since our object is to deal with expressions readily available to outsiders, I want only to call special attention to the concept of the creative power in spoken words. When I was a patient in a Beautyway ceremony a few years ago (urged on me by my adoptive Navajo family to promote stability in my life), we reached the part of the story where the Hero Twins, sons of Changing Woman (fathered by the Sun and some drops of water since there were no men yet), are on their way to visit their father, the Sun, who is protected by powerful warriors whose job it is to fight off anyone who approaches. Not only was the story being told—in part through ritual songs—but we were to think of ourselves as actually being there, floating up to the Sun on the same feather that was transporting the Hero Twins, empowered by the words uttered by the singer. As we got closer to the Sun and the battle became fiercer, my Navajo family members began shouting words of encouragement like "Don't give up!" "We're almost there!" "Protect us with your spear!" What I had been doing for an hour during the ceremony was holding over my head a foot-long, chipped stone spearhead, which was in fact getting heavier every second. The singer, Jimmy Descheeny, had also tied a row of stone arrowheads around my head, and I began to realize that these armaments were my means to reach the Sun and assure the safety of those traveling with me; I, the sick one, provided the only protection. After our success, which was celebrated with several fourfold song stanzas, the story described us returning to earth on a lightning bolt. Imaginary, you may say. Sure, in the same way a gripping play or film is imaginary: if it's done right, it becomes a very vivid experience.

Not all tribes believe that spoken language is creative in the same way the Navajos do, but every tribe I know believes that songs and stories are dramatic enactments of reality which go far beyond mere entertainment. A good story is like an affective ritual: it puts you there, makes you experience or reexperience something. And that something is an otherwise-abstract but real idea from your culture, made concrete and experiential through the imagination and knowledge which you bring to the story performance, enhanced by the power of the performer.

Indeed, narrative structure is so central to human thinking that some scientists believe that *story* is the engram of our species. In the same vein, John D. Niles, a scholar of oral literature, has argued that we should be called *Homo narrans* (storytelling man). In the following songs and stories, then, let's take story structure and song nuance seriously and ask, "What does this song or story dramatize or embody?" (not "What does it describe?" or "What does it explain?"). Many Native stories end with a formula like "and that's how the bear got a short tail," leading listeners to assume that such tales are primitive (and childish) ways of accounting for the features of the natural world. But when you ask the storytellers, they don't see the story as an explanation of anything but rather, an enactment of something: A bear is dramatized as lazy, or uncaring, or selfish, or careless; because he fails to act appropriately, he gets his tail caught in the ice, and, persisting in being selfish or egotistical (instead of calling for help), he tears himself loose and leaves his tail stuck there.

When we hear the story, we're reminded of how personally damaging and painful it is—even for someone who is large and powerful—to be lazy, uncaring, selfish, or careless. When we see a bear in the world around us, we notice the short tail and recall the story and our cultural obligations. Once again—this time through a story—the animal becomes (and through oral tradition remains) our mentor. Interpreting the story as a serious explanation of bear physiology is equivalent to seeing "The Three Little Pigs" as a serious report on porcine behavior.

A good example of the dramatic patterning of cultural abstracts through narrative occurs in a story performed by a Lummi (Northwest coast) woman for Jan H. Brunvand, Joseph Campbell, and me while we were speaking at a symposium at Western Washington State University in the late 1960s. None of us had brought a tape recorder, so the following is not verbatim but reconstituted from my notes, not by any means an ideal situation but acceptable because the story itself—even partially recaptured—is quite powerful. The woman spoke in English but said she had grown up hearing the story in Lummi. Because it was a story reflecting her tribe's traditions and not her own ideas, she said we could use it—for it was not secret—as long as we didn't associate her name with it. She didn't give it a title, but I identify it in my mind as "The Five Lummi Sisters." Here is the written version; the separate paragraphs indicate segments of the story, not her performance dynamics.

> Five sisters went out to get huckleberries; each one carried two baskets.
>
> When they got out there where the huckleberries grew, they saw that the bushes were just covered with big huckleberries. There were way more than they could ever pick, so they knew they'd get all they wanted.
>
> The oldest sister said, "Look at all these huckleberries! We can fill our baskets easily." So they held their baskets under the bushes and shook the berries in. Right away they all had their baskets full, so they sat down in the shade to rest.
>
> The oldest sister said, "Look; there are plenty of berries. It's a nice warm day, and we could just eat these berries and fill our baskets again

before we go home." So they ate all the berries they had picked, and then they turned the baskets over and hit them against their legs like this [slapping her hands a few times against her thighs] to knock all the leaves and stems out. And so they went back to the bushes and started picking again. Again their baskets filled right up with no trouble at all.

The second sister said, "Those berries were really good, and look how many more there are. If we don't eat them, the birds will just get them. Why don't we eat these and then get some more before we go home?" So they sat down again and ate all the berries they had picked. Then they beat their baskets against their legs again like this [slapping her thighs a few times] to knock all the leaves and stems out. It took them a little longer to get rid of all those leaves. Then they went back to the bushes and picked some more. Just knocked them off the bushes into their baskets, and they got full baskets again right away.

The third sister said, "Look how many berries are still there! The birds will get them if we don't. Let's eat these we've picked and then fill our baskets again before going home." So they sat down again and ate all the berries. After they rested a while, they got up and slapped the baskets against their legs like this [slaps her thighs a few times] to get the leaves and stems out, and it took even longer this time. Finally, they went back to the bushes and began pushing the berries into their baskets, and their baskets got full right away.

The fourth sister said, "Those berries were so good! I'd like to eat some more. There are still plenty of berries here. Let's sit down and rest and eat these. We can still fill up our baskets again before going home." So they sat down and ate the berries, and afterward they knocked the baskets against their legs again like this [slaps her thighs several times] to get rid of the stems and leaves and little bugs. And it took a long time to clean out the baskets. They went back to the bushes and began picking again. Actually, they didn't even have to pick: the berries just fell off, and right away they had all their baskets full again.

The youngest sister said, "Those berries were warm and sweet, and I'd like to eat some more before we go home. There are still plenty left for us and for the birds." So they sat down again and ate everything they had picked. They got up. They started knocking the baskets against their legs [slaps her thighs continuously through the rest of this sentence], but they couldn't stop, and their arms went higher and higher, and they kept hitting the baskets against their legs, and they couldn't stop until finally, they lifted off the ground, flapping their arms faster and faster, and they flew away.

They became the birds. That's where birds came from. That's all.

Now, if we read that last line as the meaning of the story, we have a conceptual problem because how can a story where the birds already exist and the characters refer to them explain the origin of birds?. So let's start elsewhere: What's dramatized by this story and how? At the same time, it's appropriate to ask, "What does the Lummi audience know that I don't? What do they bring to this dramatic experience that makes the narrative mean something for them?"

What is clear is that between the simple opening and closing sentences is a sequence of five events—all practically the same. Five is the standard dramatic number in Pacific Northwest narratives, just as three is the standard Euro-American number, and four is the most common number in the Southwest. But this is more important than just observing that different cultures prefer different numbers: these are methods of thinking about the relationship among the narrative parts. The one-two-three lineal sequence we are so familiar with in Euro-American jokes, tales, ballads, and even personal anecdotes usually comes to some point on count three (the third little pig is the one who keeps the wolf from the door; the third try is the charm). The Southwest use of four, since it refers to the main directions, almost always suggests surroundment, encirclement, focus; in stories structured in fours, there is no punch line or result, for the device is not envisioned as lineal. Rather, the listeners know that if something is repeated four times, the event is important and may even have ritual significance.

The Northwest five may be patterned after the fingers of the hand, for in many cases (as in the beginning of "The Sun's Myth," discussed next), it suggests completeness, wholeness. Within a story, the device is not used unless the idea repeated five times is important. In a way, it is a kind of oral italics, a means of intensifying. So, while a non-Northwest person may see the repetitions in "The Five Lummi Sisters" as needless redundancy, the Northwest Native understands they are a sign that the action of eating berries and dumping baskets has considerable consequence.

Why would eating and dumping be so important though? Part of the answer can be inferred already by anyone who has eaten a great quantity of berries; eating is fun, but getting rid of the byproducts can be problematic. But the story offers us more than gratuitous advice about diarrhea. In virtually every tribe, food gathered and hunted away from the village should not be consumed until it's brought back to be shared with family and other villagers. Eating gathered food by yourself, away in the woods, is a form of gluttony and viewed by most tribes—unless it's a case of raw survival—as antisocial. When the *oldest* sister, who should be the most knowledgeable in the customs and values of her people, makes the first move to break the code, it makes it easier for the younger ones to follow.

Incrementally, as the human social order breaks down, the girls go out of control and become birds. Why birds? Observe them, and you'll notice that they eat berries, dump the residue, and spend most of their time bringing food back to their nests for their families. For their inattention to social values, the girls become living icons of the social principle of sharing; the birds remind us of the idea as they fly by—the beating of their wings sounds like baskets against girls' thighs.

Another pattern in Native narrative can be called *reciprocative structure*. Some years ago, John Bierhorst suggested that many Native American myths are structured in two parts, one reflecting, expanding, or reciprocating the other. In the following story, also from the Pacific Northwest, the device achieves great power. "The Sun's Myth" was collected in 1891 by Franz Boas, who took it down phonetically from the dictation of Charles Cultee, one of the last three speakers of the Kathlamet Chinook language. This language is no longer spoken (in fact, the last speaker died only a few years after Boas collected the story), and people who would have understood all the nuances of the story are long gone. Thus, while we have no hope of knowing fully what this myth dramatized, we can extrapolate from hints in the story, as well as customs and traditions of nearby related tribes, and reach a provisional understanding.

For one thing, we know that the Chinooks usually named their myths after the most important character in the narrative, not necessarily the one who appears most often. Thus, the focus in this myth is the Sun, and she is female. As an older female, she naturally provides nourishment and ritual propriety for her family. The baseline is ancient, continual, and traditional nurturance by a female head of family (and since she is the Sun, we may suppose this family includes us).

With that as a lead, let's take a look at the other females in the narrative: What roles do they play? The wife of the chief who wants to visit the Sun tries to dissuade him, implying that he's foolish to think he can go there. This is a subtle form of Native persuasion; since Native behavior is almost never prescriptive, mentors delicately suggest advice, but an individual's decision is his or her own responsibility. By rejecting or ignoring his wife's suggestion, the chief is taking personal responsibility for a rash decision. Like a traditional wife, she does not argue but helps him prepare. Later in the story, he encounters another younger, unmarried woman, and she, too, tries to give him guidance but to no avail.

All this is important for us to track because otherwise we might misread the story, which at first sounds like a Western "hero myth," in which a daring man goes into the world to bring back some kind of prize for his people. Instead, we must see this story as a man intruding his own egotistical agenda into a traditional way of life. The result? Not a blessing for his people but destruction.

The story, presented here in summarized segments, follows Dell Hymes's brilliant translation, which has been published several times with ever-finer tuning since its first appearance in the *Journal of American Folklore* in 1976. Hymes presents the narrative as a two-act play with distinct scenes; remembering Bierhorst's suggestion that these two acts may be restatements or reflections of each other, let's look at "The Sun's Myth," incorporating everything we now know (or think we know) about the cultural constructions of Northwest narrative. Granted, we are unable to deal with the actual language and its nuances, or the performance styles of traditional Kathlamet narrators, for all of that has been lost. But through Hymes's painstaking reconstruction of the original phonetic text in comparison with nearby dialects still in use, we have a pretty accurate articulation of the story line, and that's something.

The story opens with a couple of lines that seem to function like the first lines of "The Five Lummi Sisters"; they describe the normal setting, in and from which the action unfolds:

> They live there, those people of a town.
> Five the towns of his relatives, that chief.

It is not clear whether he is chief of all five villages or one village connected with four others by family ties. But in any case, there's our Northwest number *five*, which tells us that this chief is part of a considerable, complete family cluster. Keep in mind that in most tribes it is the family, not the individual, which constitutes the basic social unit; also remember that the chief of most Northwest coastal groups was an influential person who did not simply order other people around (as they are depicted in our movies: "Mmm! We go to war!") but presided over social events and rituals like hunting and fishing expeditions (which provided nurture for everybody) and arranged festive occasions when people gave goods away to others in their communities. Sometimes called "potlatches" (more commonly "giveaways" today), these events were chances for people to demonstrate their wealth and power by giving everything away. The Northwest tribes were surrounded by food: fish and mammals in the rivers and ocean; deer, elk, and moose in the nearby forests. They apparently spent a lot less time making their living than we do in our culture, and the bulk of their time went into producing gorgeous artistic items, ranging from totem poles and other carvings, to baskets and boxes, to cured hides and woven blankets. They loved material wealth, but in any tribal situation, one person accumulating extreme wealth can cause envy, so one of their favorite things to do with wealth was redistribute it to the entire community on ritual occasions such as maturation ceremonies, weddings, funerals, the dedication of a new house, the birth of a child, or virtually any important moment. The chief's job would have given him a central role in the enactment of these continual orgies of redistribution.

Our chief, in spite of these cultural expectations, wants to go on a personal journey.

He goes outside every morning and stares at the sun as it partially appears through the heavy clouds of the south Washington coast (where the Columbia flows into the Pacific). He asks his wife what she would think if he went to visit the Sun. She says, incredulously, "You think it is near?" and asks if he really wants to go there. Not accepting her hint that he's being unrealistic, he keeps going out every morning and finally tells his wife to make him ten pairs of moccasins (five times two pairs) and ten leggings. She complies without further comment (as if to say, "Okay, then; it's your decision").

He sets out in the morning, and over a long journey eventually wears out all of his moccasins and leggings, arriving at last at a large house (normally the indication of a family with an important place in the community). Inside is a young girl, alone, surrounded by culturally important items hanging on the walls in magnificent abundance. The storyteller catalogues these riches for the next fifty-eight lines, detailing the arrows, armor, axes, clubs, regalia ("men's property") on one wall, and the blankets, skins, and dentalia beads (presumably "women's property") on the other. The chief asks thirteen times who owns these items, and in every case he is told the same thing: They belong to the girl and her grandmother, the girl says, and they are being saved for "my maturity," that is, for the giveaway/potlatch that will be held when she celebrates her first menstruation—an event which will socially and ritually signal the fact that she is marriageable. The chief's response? "I will take her." He moves in with the girl and her grandmother (who, incidentally, is the Sun). He "takes" the young girl and lives there for a long time, watching the older woman come back every evening loaded with more blankets, arrows, and armor.

Let's stop for a moment to reflect on the first part of this drama: A chief who would normally be in the center of a culture, helping distribute goods on special occasions and encouraging proper behavior, has moved into someone else's house without invitation and appropriated goods which should have been distributed to others at a proper time by taking a prepubescent young girl who is not yet eligible to be married. What an irony: not just anybody but someone who should be the epitome of tribal propriety has now become, through his own selfishness and aggressive behavior, the icon of culturally destructive values. We should not be surprised if the second half of the drama expands on this idea by acting it out in bloody detail.

Part II begins with the chief sleeping, not getting up. The young girl and her grandmother recognize this as a sign of what we would call depression and conclude that he is homesick. The old lady, the Sun, asks him what he would like to take with him when he goes home: Some buffalo skins? Some mountain-goat blankets? She shows him virtually everything, but he refuses it all. He wants only one bright thing he has seen among her belongings, and he insists on taking it with him. The old woman refuses him several times, then finally gives in the same way his wife and the young girl have already done in response to his insistence—not, we must conclude, because they are weak but because it's a way of focusing our attention on the chief's willfulness, the fruits of which are about to be acted out with a vengeance. His moral defect is being dramatized against the backdrop of normal, nurturing, female deportment. Reluctantly, and with obvious misgivings, the old lady hangs the shining object on him (we are never told exactly what it is, but a later passage suggests it is a kind of blanket), gives him a stone ax, and after reminding him, "It is you who choose," sends him on his way home.

In contrast to the tedious outward journey, the homeward move is almost instantaneous. As he arrives near an uncle's town, the shining object begins to throb and speak: "We two shall strike your town." Losing his reason and using his stone ax, he crushes the entire town and everyone in it, covering himself with blood. As he recovers, he begins to blame the shining object ("Why was I made to love this?") and tries unsuccessfully to get rid of it. He tries shaking it off, but it seems attached to his flesh. As he approaches each of his uncles' villages, the same thing happens: He goes into a frenzy, crushes the whole village and its inhabitants, and then, still blaming the object and not his own selfishness, attempts to get rid of both the shining blanket and the stone ax, but "always those fingers of his would cramp." He cannot rid himself of the tools of destruction. Now he approaches his own town (where his wife and immediate family live), and he destroys it as well until "the dead fill the ground." Weeping, he looks back and sees the old woman, the Sun, standing nearby. In a lyrically quiet passage (after the frantic activity of destruction), she reminds him that he is responsible for what has happened.

In Hymes's carefully worded epilogue, the story ends like this:

He looked back   V1(A)
Now she is standing near him, that old woman   300
"You,"
    She told him,
        "You.
"In vain I try to love your relatives.   305
"Why do you weep?
"It is you who choose;
"now you carried that blanket of mine."
Now she took it,   (B)
    she lifted off what he had taken;   310
Now she left him,
    she went home.
He stayed there;   (C)
    he went a little distance.
There he built a house,   315
    a small house.

It is impossible to overlook the contrast between the long journey at the beginning of Part I and the quick return at the beginning of Part II. Similarly, it's hard to miss the contrast between the large, opulent house at the end of Part I and the small empty house at the end of Part II. If we assume the two parts are reciprocal in dramatizing an idea, what is that idea? One set of possibilities is this: A compulsive, energetic move away from your obligations just to satisfy a selfish whim is the fastest way to do something destructive to your culture. Taking over a large house full of objects you have no rightful claim to is the equivalent of impoverishing yourself. And if we compare the two most heavily descriptive and detailed segments of the story—the catalog of gorgeous stuff the chief first admires and then takes in Part I, and the village-by-village destruction of his own people in Part II—we can see the dramatization of the concept that the selfish, unritualized taking of culturally dedicated goods in violation of the culture's values (especially by someone who should know better, as implied by the women in this story) literally destroys the culture.

Assuming that the myth has a double structure allows us to see Part II as some kind of dramatization of Part I. But if these are indeed two halves, what happens to the young woman in Part II? Why does she seem to disappear? I suggest that she does not: she is the victim of cultural rape in both parts. In Part I, she is the demure prepubescent who should be protected by a chief and, instead, is simply invaded and taken over (colonized, if you will) by him; in Part II, her role is played by the villages and their inhabitants, who—similarly—should have been looked after by their chief and, instead, are invaded and destroyed by him.

In this powerful myth, women's constant and patient nurturing is the standard against which men's selfish adventures are measured (in high contrast to most of the hero stories in Western cultures). The Sun, whose myth it is, prevails; the chief, whose misadventure it is, fails and must start over, poor and alone (one of the most frightening scenarios in family-based tribes). Rather than achieving insight and a boon for his culture (as we would expect if we accepted Joseph Campbell's archetype for the hero), our chief's selfishness impoverishes him and kills his culture. This much, at least, we can see in the story—even without knowing anything about linguistic features (How many images in the story are cultural puns? How many are familiar metaphors?), or performance styles (Which passages were delivered rapidly or loudly? Where did the narrator pause and for how long? Was the narrator visibly or audibly moved by some part of the performance? Did the narrator tell the story well, or is this version just a tattered remnant of an older, even more magnificent portrait of human selfishness?), or even provenience (Was this a well-known story? Are there similar or parallel stories that comment on chiefs and their behavior, marriageability, gender, or individual impulses that might enlarge our sense of what this story means?). Indeed, this story contains some psychological insights that may seem quite modern or sophisticated to us: the recognition that unwillingness to get up may be a symptom of depression, or the tactic of denial or displacement in the chief's insistence that the coveted shining object itself, and not his craving of it, causes his troubles. Are there other insights in the story that are not so obvious?

As superficial as our understanding of the story is, it still emerges as a world classic, in my opinion, partly because of the eloquent and moving way it dramatizes a recognizable human dilemma and partly because the subject is universal and tenaciously contemporary: someone's reckless and single-minded addiction to a bright object he can't let go of is a topic that is just as gripping today as it has ever been. Dell Hymes said that when he was working on the first full translation of "The Sun's Myth," he could not help but think of his own culture's almost total addiction to the brilliance and power of atomic energy—especially as manifested in the destructive atom bomb (an issue taken up eloquently in Stanley Kubrick's film *Doctor Strangelove*).

But why did Charles Cultee choose to tell this story to Franz Boas in 1891? No doubt we will never know, but it is instructive to contemplate the question, for Native people don't just recite myths for the fun of it. Consider the context for Natives in the Northwest at the turn of the last century: they had been displaced, decimated, exploited, even gunned down. They themselves still tell stories and jokes about how stupid they felt in their first meetings with European goods and technology, which killed them even as they were fascinated by the novelty. Anecdotes like these (illustrated in greater detail in chapter 7), plus the strong admonition in stories like "The Sun's Myth" that people make their own moral choices and face the results, allow us to speculate that Charles Cultee saw his own people destroying themselves and their culture in a selfish rush to obtain the bright objects brought by the whites.

Consider the irony in this: one of the last three speakers of the myth's language narrates an old story of cultural disintegration (up until that moment a theoretical construct to be avoided, in large part by adhering to the values in the story) to a visiting white man who can't understand the language (Cultee later translated it phrase by phrase for Boas, using Chinook Jargon, which both of them knew). And consider the immediate scene: a powerful man arrives, presents himself to a powerless Native American who possesses immense narrative riches, and says, in effect, "Whose are these wonderful stories?"—then finally concludes, "I will take them." Did Cultee suddenly see himself unwittingly playing the role of the girl in the story, the innocent local on the verge of losing everything? The fact that Boas was a German Jew, whose people unknowingly stood only a few years away from their own annihilation by a culture they felt themselves an integral part of, makes the irony even deeper for us, if not for Cultee—though I suspect Cultee would not have been surprised.

"The Sun's Myth" is available because a dedicated anthropological folklorist and linguist, Dell Hymes, dedicated a good part of his life to resuscitating a dry, written text collected at Shoalwater, Washington, by a long-dead anthropologist and stored away in a dusty volume of Bureau of American Ethnology (BAE) reports. Using his knowledge of the extant Chinookan languages, he was able not only to translate the piece more thoroughly than Boas but also notice stylistic devices that highlighted certain actions and themes and even performance styles that brought scenes into sharp focus. But what about the rest of us who do not have a mastery of Native languages? Where can we go to discover even a part of the majestic Native literary heritage that was being shared with researchers a hundred years ago even as much of it was dying out? The BAE reports are full of wonderful texts, but they are not easy reading. They usually feature a transcription of someone telling a story (set down in a phonetic system that few can read today), followed by a phrase-by-phrase translation of the performed text (in syntax that makes it sound incredibly primitive), accompanied by a prose summary so dry it makes you wonder why anybody bothered.

Take a close look at one of these texts, though, and—even without linguistic training—you notice some connecting or transition words (then, again) repeated in regular positions at the beginning of parallel phrases. Take these phrases as signs of a delivery style (parallels, repetitions) and write down each of them on a new line, and you have a text that *begins* to look like "The Sun's Myth." You then see that sets of these phrases seem to fit together thematically or rhetorically, like paragraphs. But paragraphs are ways of marking closely associated ideas in writing, and we're not dealing with writing but oral delivery. We don't speak in paragraphs; we speak in aurally recognizable phrases. Thus, it's not as if we are trying to create poetry, per se, but what we perceive is that oral texts, like most poems, are addressed to the ear and not the eye. Forget about all those printers' conventions and think instead of the way someone might recite a long, complex narrative using a style that everyone in the home culture can recognize and understand. The result is a provisional rendering that is a lot more interesting than the ones provided by the early BAE texts. There are phrases you won't understand and others that can be interpreted in two or three different ways in English idiom. Remember that you are not pretending to translate a language you don't know but trying to suck a few drops of juice from a dry lemon: if you get any taste at all, it's more than you had before.

I followed this procedure with the members of a recent Native American traditional narrative seminar, working through Boas's transcription of a Tsimshian story called "The Grizzly Bear." We had been discussing the great number of stories in various Northwest tribes' traditions where young women inadvertently step in bear droppings (apparently a taboo) and are subsequently carried off (or seduced) by a handsome man who later turns out to be a bear. The woman lives with the bear as his wife in every respect, bearing his children and keeping his household, until, inevitably, hunters from her village (sometimes her own brothers) discover the bear and kill him. These are fascinating stories of intimate interactions and unavoidable frictions between humans and animals, and they are well worth reading and discussing. The Tsimshian story, in contrast, features a man who marries a female grizzly, so we decided it would be interesting to probe the story as far as our limitations allow us.

The following text is my best attempt to offer a conglomerate version of the suggestions made by the members of my class.

The Grizzly Bear
[told by Moses]

[Part 1:]

Four men:
    One the eldest,
    then the next eldest,
    then also the youngest;
    then one great chief, their father.
    Then their mother, the wife of the chief.
      Their town was large.
Well!
By the middle of winter,
everyone's food was gone.
Then, what could they eat?
One [of the brothers] was a hunter,
    And so was the youngest one.
Then they remembered what they used to do
    when there was no food.
Then they went, the two hunters,
    as well as the eldest, a great man.
Then they went in company.
The eldest one's wife did not go with him;
    only [one of] his brothers went with him.
And they went,
    a long way they went.
Then they found a house,
    and they stayed in it.
In the morning,
    the youngest one rose.
Two were his dogs,
    very powerful dogs.
Then he went.
He carried a spear;
    a blade was on it.
Then he put on snowshoes,
    and he went.
Then he reached the foot of a mountain,
    and he went up.
When he got halfway up,
    he heard his dog's voice above him,

but he couldn't get to it.
The mountain was icy.
Then he took a little stone ax,
    and crossways he chopped the ice of the mountain.
Then he reached the tail of a ridge
    where a tree was down.
That's where the dogs were making noise.
    And he reached them.
Look! In the ground was a great grizzly bear,
    two cubs, very large.
Then the man moved toward the hole;
Then she stretched way out and took the man.
Then the cubs took him,
    and they killed him.
Dead the man;
    then his brothers lost him.
When he had been lost about two days,
    then the next brother rose.
    He also had two dogs.
In the morning, he also went
    with his two dogs.
He, too, carried a spear with a blade on it.
Then he, too, went.
When he also found what his brother had found,
    the dogs also ran upwards.
Once more also he discovered what his brother had found.
He saw where the ice of the mountain was chipped crossways.
Then he, too, got toward [the hole].
Not long he did so:
    She took him in, too.
    Then the cubs killed him, too.
Then he, too, was dead,
    and his two dogs.
So again a younger brother was lost.
When only one [brother] was left over
    (a very big improper man),
    then he, too, rose.
Then he, too, went in the morning,
    also with two dogs;
    he also carried a spear.
    A blade was on it.

Then he put on snowshoes.
Then he, too, went on the mountain.
On the same path he went that his brothers had traveled.
Then he heard where the dogs barked.
Then he too reached [the spot].
Then just as he began to place himself,
    suddenly the great grizzly bear stretched out her paws.
The great man fell in headfirst.
Then this way he slapped it.
He got his hand right in the great vulva of the great grizzly bear.
Then said the great grizzly bear to her cubs,
    "My dears! Build up the fire;
    he begins to feel cold, your father."
Very embarrassed was the heart of the great grizzly bear
    because the man felt inside her vulva.
Therefore, it was very good for the man:
    She didn't kill him because he had felt inside [her].
Therefore, she liked him.
Then said the great grizzly bear,
    "I will marry you."
And the great man agreed.
The great woman grizzly bear was glad in her heart
    because the big Indian man married her.
Then always they lay down.

[Part 2:]

When he had done so many years,
    He was lost, the great man.
Then said the big man [that he was]
    lonesome for his father,
    and his mother,
    and his wife,
    and his little boy,
    and his little sister.
Then he said he would go out of the woods.
And the great grizzly bear agreed.
"I shall accompany you,"
    she said to the big man.
Then, when it was morning,
    then they went out of the woods.

And they traveled from there to the town.
Then the big man entered.
Then cried the great chief, his great father,
    and his mother,
    and his wife.
Then he entered and sat down.
Then he told [them] that his wife was standing outside.
Then his little sister went out to call his wife,
And she looked around for her outside.
Indeed, the little girl found where the great grizzly bear stood [and]
    fled inside shouting and crying and screaming
    very much afraid:
    "Great ugly thing!
    hohohoho!
    great monster!"
Then the man himself went out,
    the great grizzly bear's own husband.
    And he spoke [to her and] invited her inside.
Then she entered,
    and the great grizzly bear sat down
    where a mat was spread.
That large her paws.
The chief and his wife were very scared.
Then they ate salmon.
    Then the great grizzly bear ate some.
Then [they] put crab apple and grease in a dish,
    and it lay there.
Then the great grizzly bear ate it, too.
The town was very astonished at what he [the man] had done.
Later on, the great grizzly bear said to her husband,
    "Âdo, get your child,"
    she said to her husband.
    "I want to see it."
Then one man went to get the little child.
    And he made the child come;
    then the great grizzly bear wanted [to hold] it.
Then they gave it [to her],
    and the child did not cry.
Then the great grizzly bear said again one day,
    "It would be good if you would invite your wife."
Then the woman came,

formerly the wife of the man.
Then she entered
and sat down near the man, her own husband.
He [had] newly married the great grizzly bear.
One grizzly bear the wife of the man,
one also a woman of his own town.
The woman had one child,
and the great grizzly bear had none.
[But] there were her children in her house on the mountain;
They hadn't come with her out of the woods.
Well!
They lived this way for many months.
Then, when it came to be summer,
    then, before the berries were ripe,
    then said the great grizzly bear to the woman:
    "Perhaps [the berries] are ripe where I lived."
Then she asked her to go along,
    and they went.
Then they reached there,
    and a few berries were ripe.
Then they picked them:
    The woman put what she picked into her bag,
    [but] the great grizzly did not use a bag;
        her stomach was her bag.
    She ate what she picked.
Then they returned;
    they came from there to the house of their husband.
Then they entered.
Then said the great grizzly bear,
    "It would be good for you to invite the people,"
    she said to the man.
Then one man left who invited many men.
Then the woman took her bag to the middle
    of the house, where the great grizzly bear also was.
Then she said to her husband,
    "Put some dishes back from the fire,"
    and he put some back from the fire.
Then her anus became large,
    and out went the berries she had eaten.
    She said that she had picked them.
    What she ate, she put in [the dishes].
    It came out her anus.

Then the dish was full of the berries she prepared.
Then the Indians saw it;
   perhaps excrements were in it.
Well!
Then she ordered [someone to take] a dish full of the berries that came out
her anus,
   and she laid it before the people.
They were afraid to eat it
   because perhaps excrements were in it,
   because they saw where it had come out her anus.
They ate only the berries prepared by the Indian woman.
The rest they took home
   that the great grizzly bear had given them.
   Their wives ate it at their own houses.
Well!
Then the great grizzly bear was in good heart.
Well!
When the salmon swam in the water in front of the town,
   then the chief made a weir,
   and there was a trap;
   and there was still another kind of trap.
Then it was finished;
   they finished it,
   and it was evening.
Then the people lay down.
Just before daylight,
   then rose the great grizzly bear.
Then down she went to the weir,
   and she saw where the trap was full of salmon,
   and she emptied it completely.
Then she took them up inside the house,
   and she ordered the chief, the great father-in-law,
   To distribute them to the town.
So they distributed them.
Then again it was evening.
Again she did so,
   [but] the people didn't know it.
When she had done so for many days,
   she and her cowife had dried many [salmon]
   so that the house was full of what the great grizzly bear and her cowife
   had dried.
Then it was morning,

and down [to the weir] went one young man.
His heart stood still because he found no salmon.
He saw no salmon at the trap
    since the great grizzly bear had finished them
    and taken them to the house of her husband,
    therefore, he was sick in his heart [angry?].
Then he scolded.
The young man scolded the great grizzly bear.
He was sick in his heart because he did not get anything.
The young man said,
    "You wouldn't quit rising early, great drop-jaw";
    that's what he said to the great grizzly bear.
    He was scolding—that's why he said that.
Twice he scolded [her]:
    "Big Giving-Excrements-for-Food!" he said
    when he again scolded.
Then she took notice of it, the great grizzly bear.
Then she came,
    being sick in her heart.
Then she ran out [of the house],
    greatly angry,
    and she went to where the man was who scolded.
Then she stood in there [in the weir?],
    and she took the man,
    and she killed him all over.
The man was dead,
    his flesh was totally finished.
    All his bones were broken.
At once she left.
She remembered her people,
    where her two cubs were.
Then the great grizzly bear left,
    angry and sick in heart.
Then her husband followed her.
The great grizzly bear said:
    "Âdo! Turn back!
    I might kill you!"
But the man refused
    because he loved his great grizzly bear wife.
A second time the great grizzly bear spoke,
    sent back her husband.

And the husband refused;
   therefore, she did so:
   The great grizzly bear rushed back.
Then she killed him.
Then the man was dead, her own husband.
Then the great grizzly bear left.
The man was dead.

    I have an idea that the full meaning and emotional force of this occasionally humorous tragedy will elude us. Even so, many fascinating things are going on in the story, and we can ask some fairly pointed questions about them. For example, we notice several places where the narrator must have illustrated his story with hand gestures, such as when the man "slapped this way" when he accidentally struck the grizzly's vulva by thrashing around, or when the narrator describes the grizzly's hands as "that large her paws." What other gestures, volume levels, facial expressions, or eye contact did he use? We have little indication, for Boas was mostly looking for language examples, not performance styles, unfortunately.

    We can observe that the activities in Part I essentially depict male hunters going after meat, while those in Part II describe women harvesting berries and salmon. Part I is mostly about human behavior; Part II is mostly about the behavior of the bear. Part I takes the human characters away from the familiarity of a tribal town and toward unforeseeable, open nature in the woods; Part II takes a bear in the opposite direction: away from the woods and into town. The oldest, "improper" brother is welcomed into the family of the great grizzly bear (once the possibility of killing is converted by the female to sex) in Part I, while the great grizzly is welcomed into the family life of the town (once they get used to her odd way of carrying berries) in Part II. Yet, as we see toward the end, the berries episode is not fully accepted by the people, for the angry young man uses it to scold the bear. And even though the great grizzly works hard to harvest enough salmon to distribute to everyone, she is apparently doing it wrong—presumably by not letting anyone else help in a process that is normally shared among the townspeople. The man, who in Part I has saved his own life by accepting marriage with the grizzly bear (what options did he have, one wonders?), nonetheless eventually misses his family and wants to return to them. In spite of sexual intimacy, life among the bears isn't entirely satisfying; indeed, he is described as "lost." Similarly, though the grizzly in Part II gets along amazingly well with her husband's family and her cowife, calms the baby, supplies food (if you don't mind her processing method), and labors diligently at the fish trap, she somehow isn't fitting in. She is still a grizzly bear living away from her natural element in a human town. When the young sister first sees the grizzly and runs in fear, she is providing an important commentary found in many Northwest stories: The young can often see—and be honest about—something that the grownups are trying to overlook to be polite.

In the stories about women marrying bears, the union lasts a considerable time, and the woman has children by her grizzly husband. Nonetheless, sooner or later, realities seep into the story: hunters are out looking for bears—that's what hunters do. And eventually they find this bear and kill him (of course, they turn out to be her brothers; that's a kind of economy that focuses any good tale and provides irony). The implication seems to be this: Yes, the bears are our relatives, and yes, you could actually live with one and have children together, but nonetheless they're still bears, and we're still people. We don't act alike; we have different customs. Notice that it is the grizzly bear (not the chief) who tells her husband to summon people to eat berries, and it is she (and not the cooperating members of the tribal community) who gets up early and cleans out the fish trap. She's pushy, perhaps too insistent, unsocialized, and thus—even though she's trying to fit in—still an Other. And she sees it before her husband does. She recognizes the untenable relationship when the angry man at the weir yells at her for getting all the fish and then scolds her for having served them excrements. She realizes she is not at home there and would rather be with her cubs (just as her husband earlier wanted to return to his family). Why doesn't the story simply have her leave in disgust without killing the man? Is it because the vital difference between bears and people could be easily overlooked and romanticized without the tragedy? Is it to show that even bears recognize the gulf between us more readily than do humans blinded by emotion? I wish we knew, but we seem to be standing close to a human classic whose deepest nuances are unfathomable.

That said, it seems to me that the heaviest implication of the story is that while humans and bears are similar in many respects and considered related, they cannot naturally live together. Perhaps that is why the oldest brother (who—like the oldest sister in the Lummi story—should know better) is called improper. In accepting an unnatural sexual liaison to save his life, in effect trading his personal safety for the food he was supposed to bring back to his starving relatives, he acts improperly. It's as if Part II says to the listeners, "All right, let's play out this same convenient family drama back in the village, where the man normally belongs; let's see how it works in the fabric of tribal society, where the group—not the individual—decides what's normal." And we see that, in spite of the best efforts of the separate actors, the play is a cultural disaster, indeed, a tragedy of sorts in immediate terms. Yet in the long view, normality is restored to the world: The man forfeits his life—as he no doubt would have done had he refused the sexual partnership earlier; the grizzly goes back to her normal world; the town returns to its usual state. This is great stuff, even if we're only catching a small part of its total possibilities.

Our capacity to understand such stories increases immensely when we actually see and hear a performance by a gifted storyteller in the context of his or her own culture. We then can witness the gestural and vocal nuances of the performer and the responses of the audience, and if we're lucky, we can ask questions. I've spent countless long winter evenings listening to stories among Navajo families, everyone sitting around the perimeter of a hogan (or the living room of a house) as one or another adult slowly and quietly narrated a "Coyote story" while a fire snapped in the stove. Each story was followed by a respectful silence, and then someone—often a child—asked for some clarification, and a long conversation developed. Once, when I took a group of reservation high school teachers to such an evening, they came out into the cold night air at about 1:00 A.M. and said, "No wonder these kids are so tired when they get to school in the morning; they've been in a literary seminar all night!"

One evening in the winter of 1955 or '56, while I was living with the Little Wagon family in Montezuma Canyon, we had a visit from a small family which was traveling by wagon down the canyon from Hatch Trading Post. It had started snowing, and the family stopped overnight with us. Late in the evening, one of the children asked where snow came from, and old Little Wagon quietly responded with a story in which his own great grandfather found and returned some sacred fire to the *yei*, the Holy People, who had accidentally dropped it from their fireplace. As a reward to the young man, they dumped their ashes into Montezuma Canyon every year when they cleaned off their hearths and have done so ever since. When the little boy hesitantly asked his father why it also snowed in far-off Blanding, Little Wagon calmly said,"Well, you'll have to make up your *own* story for that." After the visitors left the next morning, the old man remarked that you can tell when children have been to school because they don't have any idea what stories are all about.

Well, what are they about? And how can we learn at least part of the answer by witnessing a live performance? Keeping in mind everything in this chapter thus far, let's take a look at my notation of an actual performance, a story told to his family by my friend Yellowman back in 1956. I had no tape recorder then, so I jotted down the story on scraps of paper as he told it. Fortunately, his delivery was very slow, and I had already heard the story several times. Although the words were not always the same, I had been able to put together a kind of outline, which I filled in with particulars as this performance took place. Here is an account of the live presentation and the responses of the audience.

Ma'i [Coyote] was going along there just as he has always been going along.
       [pause of several seconds; the audience is smiling]
Up ahead, near some trees, some junipers, in some junipers,
    he could see birds flying up.
       [slight pause]
They were flying up and looking all around;
    they could see everywhere.
       [pause; the audience is smiling in anticipation]
Ma'i said to them, "Come here, my relatives, give me your eyes
    so I can see as far as you can."
       [longer pause; some children are laughing quietly]
"No, you're not a bird. You can't fly."
       [general laughter, including narrator]
Ma'i said to them, "My relatives, please give me your eyes.
    Take mine out and give me yours."
       [pause; smiling]
"No [emphatically]! You're not a bird!"
       [pause; smiling]
Ma'i said, "My relatives, I want to see like you;
    please take my eyes out and put yours in!"
       [pause, deep breath]
"No! You're not a bird. You can't fly!"
       [pause; some laughter]
Ma'i said, "My relatives, please take my eyes out and give me yours!"
       [pause; smiling]
"Yaahdilah! [no translation; an expletive]"
       [general prolonged laughter]
They came to him. They took sticks and pried out his eyes.
       [loud laughter]
"Aah!" he was screaming. He cried. "That hurts!"
       [louder laughter, including narrator]
They pried out his eyes.
       [mild laughter]
They flew away.
       [smiling, nodding heads]
He was blind. He couldn't see anything.
       [pause; smiles]

He stumbled around in the junipers, feeling his way.
> [pause]

He was crying.
> [pause]

Ma'i felt some lumps on the side of the juniper,
>> that pitch that grows there.
>> [pause; someone says, "Hmm."]

He felt those lumps, and he pulled them off the tree:
>> Two lumps of pitch, the same size as his eyes, perhaps.
>> [short pause]

He put them into his sockets.
>> [pause; several people expel air through their noses]

Now Ma'i has yellow eyes; his eyes are pitch.
>> [long pause, several seconds]

That's what they say.

By now, I am sure you recognize that the main point of the story is not explaining how coyotes got yellow eyes; indeed, you're probably guessing (correctly) that, like the Lummi story, this one acts as a reminder: when we see a coyote, we note that he has yellow eyes and remember this story. So where's the action in the story? What is being dramatized? Coyote wants to be able to see from above ground, like the birds, and is unwilling to accept their admonition that his desire is not appropriate. Coyotes aren't birds. But Coyote insists four times (the key number in most Southwest Native stories), and at that point the birds abandon their advice and say "yaahdilah!"—the equivalent of "all right, dammit, you take the responsibility!" And his insistence on seeing what is not normal for him is turned into pain and blindness—a much more powerful form of instruction than the simple advice, "Children, don't overstep your bounds in nature, or it may be painful."

But what do we learn from the dynamics of the live performance? For one thing, we see that the Navajo narrator (in this case, Yellowman) pauses considerably between lines or phrases in a way that may make the telling a bit slow for people who are accustomed to reading or hearing stories delivered with greater verve and urgency. What accounts for this? Among many reasons, the Navajo narrator wants the images in each phrase to sink in, but more importantly, many Native speaking customs incorporate silence as a preparation for saying something important. If someone in a group is quiet for a noticeable time, it may mean that the person is about to say something especially noteworthy. In addition, many Native speakers and narrators repeat a key idea four times (the same practice often occurs in ritual songs, where the four-way repetition may remind us of the directions and thus sur-roundment). Interestingly enough, many Natives report that in conversa-tion they are always interrupted by non-Natives, who don't understand the rhythm in this kind of foregrounding. The fourfold repetition in this story appears in the scene where Ma'i begs the birds for their eyes and in each case is refused, until step four, when he reaches the limits of making his demand, and the birds feel obliged to teach him a lesson. You can tell from the responses of the audience that they know what's coming. They have not only heard the story before but are also familiar with the structural con-vention. But they are also laughing, so we need to consider what's so funny about prying out a coyote's eyes.

The Navajos often use laughter to comment on children's actions; it's a gentle way of correcting behavior since no one likes to be laughed at. Obviously, people laugh for other reasons as well, especially at jokes or sto-ries where someone does something outlandish. On one hand, it's register-ing amusement at something odd, and at the same time, it signals that we recognize the discrepancy between the normal and the odd. In the Navajo Ma'i stories, as I've argued elsewhere, laughter seems most pronounced just before or after Ma'i does something that is not only odd but also wrong: he betrays his best friends, he's gluttonous, he's oversexed, he insists on doing things inappropriate for coyotes. In recognizing that these actions are wrong (and they are wrong in *human* behavior; we're not talking about coyote morality), the audience laughs as if to say, "You wouldn't ever see me doing something like that!" And since audience members already know the story and can follow the fourfold structure, they can anticipate where these moments of moral concern surface in the narrative.

In addition, there are probably hundreds of Ma'i stories, some told more often than others, some told more regularly by some storytellers. Most of them are pretty widely known among Navajos and are told in a certain sequence over the course of the winter so that listeners hearing one story can easily remember others with similar motifs. They represent, in today's popular term, "intertextual" entities, although of course the people and the live performances activate the interchange (the idea that texts enjoy some kind of interaction derives from written, not oral, literature). A great num-ber of these stories depict Ma'i trying to do something appropriate for other living beings: he's trying to intrude on nature's norms. In one story, he begs the Lizard People to show him how to slide downhill on flat stones the way they do; they warn him he will be killed, and finally, after his fourth plea, they say "*yaahdilah!*" and show him how to do it, whereupon he promptly kills himself and has to be resuscitated by the Ant People. In another, he begs the Beaver People to let him gamble with them. They are throwing spears through rolling hoops, keeping score. Whoever gets the lowest score has to give up his hide. After his fourth entreaty, he is allowed to play, but of course he loses his hide and has to be buried in the ground for a year while it grows back (his coat is still scraggly today).

Two stories in particular are close in theme to the one already quoted, and the audience's laughter is based in part on its ability to bring the stories together. In one, Ma'i is trying to betray his hunting partner, Skunk (Gólízhii, literally "one with stinking urine") by getting him to take his eyes out so Ma'i can jump him and eat him. Ma'i suggests they play the old game of Throw Our Eyes Up in the Air, but Skunk doesn't know the game and has to be shown. Ma'i takes his eyes out and throws them into the air, saying, "Come back to my sockets!" but they get caught around the branch of a juniper tree (yes, in the same juniper grove as the first story), and Ma'i is blind. He gropes around the tree trunk, finds a couple of pitch balls, and puts them into his sockets. Still not able to see very well (appropriate, of course, since he almost never can "see" where his actions are taking him), he crawls too close to the campfire (where he originally had planned to roast Skunk) and melts the pitch, which runs down into the corners of his eyes (you may have noticed the brown matter in the corners of dogs' and coyotes' eyes).

In the related story, Ma'i is trotting along near a stand of junipers on the edge of a cliff. He sees the birds flying out of the trees and soaring over the canyon and then coming back. He begs them to teach him how to fly, but they point out that they have lightning under their wings, and he has none; moreover, he has no wings. He insists that it has to do with feathers and begs them to give him some. Finally, after the fourth plea, they say "*yaahdilah!*" and each bird pulls a feather out and sticks it to Ma'i's body with a small piece of, yes, juniper pitch. Ma'i launches himself off the cliff and tries to flap his arms but drops straight down to the desert floor to his death.

The story I've included, where Ma'i approaches the birds and begs to use their eyes, brings a whole cluster of Navajo beliefs and stories about Ma'i's selfishness and self-abuse to mind. For one thing, the juniper (*gad*) twists as it grows so it can watch the sun. Its seeds (called *gad bináá'*—literally "juniper's eyes") are used in necklaces and bracelets to remind the wearer of important relationships with nature, which Ma'i insists on breaking. When the birds remind him that he can't fly, they're referring to the story when he unsuccessfully tried flying. When he painfully loses his eyes because of his insistence, the audience can easily react by asking, "Won't he ever learn?" They shake their heads and look briefly at each other as if to say, "There he goes again!"

But even so, as Yellowman told me on several occasions, these stories are not about bad-boy coyotes but, rather, about those unmanageable actions of Ma'i which represent human inclinations, foibles, and acts of selfishness which are destructive to us. When I asked Yellowman why these stories differ about the appearance of coyotes' eyes (are they yellow because of the pitch, or are they melted—and thus no longer yellow or even eyes?), he grew quite impatient and gave his favorite explanation for my lack of understanding: the missionaries must have taught me to question Navajo beliefs. Those stories aren't about what coyotes look like, he assured me; they are ways of reminding us about our health. We bring most afflictions upon ourselves by our own actions or inattention to details. Ma'i's dramatizations (my wording, not his) act out a number of important moral issues about inappropriate behavior without actually naming them.

This has a double significance: 1) Navajo language is thought to create reality. Thus, we don't want to talk directly about things which we do not wish to have happen. A doctor telling a man he must take his medicine or he will die sounds to a Navajo as if the doctor is trying to kill his patient. Talking openly about witchcraft strengthens the very practice we do not want to have anything to do with. 2) The structure of the Navajo language contains much of this logic about volition and accountability. In a famous example cited by Gary Witherspoon, you can say, "The man kicked the horse" in Navajo, but you can't say, "The horse kicked the man" because the man is more articulate and intelligent than a horse, and therefore, a horse cannot kick a man. If a man is kicked by a horse, he has brought it on himself by being in the wrong place, handling the animal incorrectly, or just not paying proper attention to what he's doing. Thus, you have to say, "The man got himself kicked by the horse." The same logic applies to human health: If you are sick, it's not an accident that happened to you; in some way, you got yourself in the way of it or brought it on, or perhaps someone inflicted it on you intentionally. One way to encourage people—especially children, who don't consciously recognize all this yet—to protect themselves is to remind them not to mistreat their bodies, not to step outside the natural relationships in nature, not to betray friends and relatives, not to be selfish with resources. Rather than talk about these behaviors openly, which may have the effect of encouraging them, the traditional Navajo presents them through the dramatizations of that amorphous figure, Ma'i, ostensibly a coyote but really less *a* coyote than the epitome of coyoteness.

Of course, similar characters fill the stories of many tribes, especially from the Plains westward. Among the Sioux, it is Inktomi or Oktomi, who is depicted as a spider. In some tribes, he is a rabbit (as far as I know, he is always masculine, which probably reflects the tribal notion that aberrant behavior is most likely to be male). In the far Northwest, he is Raven. Though non-Natives have dubbed him Trickster, and some even believe the figure is a universal archetype, in fact you'll notice (if you encounter enough stories) that the American Indian Coyote character seldom tricks anyone the way that Anansi, the African trickster, does. Rather, he's mostly depicted as underfed, oversexed, unprincipled in selfishness, vengeful—in other words, the epitome of everything we should not be—and at the same time, he is a sacred creator who changes the nature of the world as he goes—the epitome of what we are not in a position to do. In this latter role, we find among the Northwest tribes accounts of Old Man Coyote creating the geographical world (to be sure, sometimes by depositing his turds, which can still be seen), teaching humans how to copulate (to be sure, by playing the active role himself), deciding which rivers will have salmon and which ones won't (to be sure, based on which chiefs send their most luscious daughters downstream to him), and even explaining minute human details like the white stuff in the corners of our eyes in the morning (he wipes his penis in his grandchildren's eyes so they won't notice he has been in bed with their mother, his daughter-in-law).

What virtually all these stories have in common is a strong, often unforgettable, central image, which reminds us again and again of the moral point of the drama. A pile of rocks on the Oregon coast marks the place where Coyote suffered from diarrhea caused by a small plant he ate in anger; the plant—used (sparingly) for constipation—can still be found there. The white stuff we clean out of our eyes every morning reminds us not to commit incest and also not to judge others before we can see clearly. A juniper grove may remind us to live within nature's system rather than challenge it. A far-off glimpse of a coyote with yellow eyes makes us remember not to abuse our body parts (or simply not make light of everything, as living coyotes seem to do).

A story told especially to teenagers by many tribes on the Northwest coast and along the Columbia River describes Coyote sitting on one shore of the river, lusting after a group of five women who are bathing on the other side. Not wanting to get cold and wet, he commands his penis to grow across the river and enter the women one by one. In one version of the story, the girls think they are being attacked by a water monster and immediately cut its head off with an obsidian knife. In another, he succeeds in copulating with the women, but as he tries to pull his penis back across the river, the sturgeon and other fish attack it and tear it to shreds. By the time he gets it back, it's all in tatters and can't be used. And of course, he almost immediately meets a pretty coyote woman who invites him home, an invitation he must decline because he can't function normally. Can you think of a more powerful image to drive home the idea that ignoring custom and misusing your sexual organs are self-destructive actions that prevent you from leading a normal life? Yet the narrative doesn't make this statement overtly; it embeds the concepts in a mental drama which depends on the audience for its realization.

A similar impression is created by tribal songs, even though they are usually far from narrative in their presentation. To put it most simply, what the narratives accomplish by dramatic patterning of cultural values the songs accomplish by musical and verbal nuance. Patterning is there, usually in the stanza format and four-way or five-way repetition of lines or phrases, but the weight is carried even more by recollections and associations in the listeners' minds, and the impact of most of these is difficult (unlike the narratives) to demonstrate in print. For example, a song made up entirely of *vocables,* syllables with no lexical meaning, may bring tears to the eyes of someone who remembers an aged relative singing it long ago, even though on the page it doesn't seem very provocative:

> *Hey-ey-ey-ey ha-ney ha-ney ya-a-a-a,*
> *hey-ey-ey-ey ha-ney ha-ney ya-a-a-a.*

If you attend a powwow, you'll hear many songs like this; each, however, has a different tune and is so unique in its sequence of verses that dancers can anticipate the end and stop dancing exactly with the last beat.

One Navajo song, often heard when a ritual stick is transported from one location to another during a sequence of ceremonies, has no words but is all meaning:

> *Hey yanga hey yo, hey yo hey yanga.*
> *hey yanga hey yo, hey yo hey yanga.*
> *Hey yo hey ya, hey yo hey yo hey,*
> *ya hey yo hey yo hey yanga.*

Repeated four times, the song is normally sung on horseback, so almost every syllable has two beats to it (like *hey-ey ya-anga-a hey-ey yo-o-o-hey yo-o hey-ey ya-anga-a).* Any Navajo who has heard it in its normal context immediately thinks of fifty to one hundred men on horseback, late at night, in the winter, singing this song in a high tenor voice together as they pass by on the way to where tomorrow's session of the ceremony will be held. Now, that's evocative. But the context is so musical that it is better illustrated by actually hearing the song live or on recordings, so I will focus on a few examples where words project culturally shared nuance.

At a powwow, you may hear this recent war-dance song:

> Mickey Mouse, Minnie Mouse, Pluto, too:
> They all live in Disneyland,
> *Hey ya, hey ya, hey ya yo;*
> Mickey Mouse, Minnie Mouse, Pluto, too:
> They all work at Disneyland,
> *Hey ya, hey ya, hey ya yo!*

Or intelligible lines surfacing in a song otherwise made up of vocables:

> Oh yes, I love you honey,
> *eeya han nigh yo*
> I don't care if you married sixteen times;
> I'll get you yet,
> *Hey ya, na eya han nigh yo.*

Sometimes at singing parties known as "forty-nines," you can hear very brief humorous verses:

> Shame on you,
> Shame on you, girl,
> your knees are floating along below your dress.

Apparently, this is a comment on minidresses. Or here's one from the 1930s, sung in English, "Wait for me, darlin'; after the dance is over, I'm coming to get you in my one-eyed Ford."

More serious are the songs which, in elliptical fashion, capture a process in nature. Judith Vander provides a number of striking examples in the Naraya (Ghost Dance) songs sung by several Shoshone women. One of them translates phrase by phrase into English as follows:

> Eagle's wing is skying,
> Eagle's wing is skying.
> Green water shiny under lying while moving,
> Green water shiny under lying while moving.

The singer, Emily Hill, comments, "That eagle's flying, his wings way up there in the sky, looking down to earth and seeing the water shining and the grass on the earth green." Vander rightfully uses the term "haikulike" for songs like this.

As provocative are the Deer Songs of the Yaqui, who live in the Sonoran Desert near Tucson, Arizona. The Yaqui sing of the *sea ania*, the

flower world which is thought to embody perfectly all the beauty of the
natural world, complete with all its plants, animals, birds, insects, and
water. On ritual occasions when the spirit of the deer is invoked (in part
by a dancer who wears a small deer's head on top of his own), the songs
describe the perfect deer moving through the utopian *sea ania* and being
hunted—phrased from the deer's point of view. In the morning, the deer
sings,

> You are an enchanted flower wilderness world,
>   you are an enchanted wilderness world,
>   you lie with see-through freshness.
> You are an enchanted flower wilderness world,
>   you are an enchanted wilderness world,
>   you lie with see-through freshness.

Later, while being hunted, the deer sings,

> Not wanting to die,
>   dodging through the wilderness.
> Not wanting to die,
>   dodging through the wilderness.

And later,

> Over there, I, in an opening
>   in the flower-covered grove,
>   as I am walking,
>   alongside
>   the flower-covered grove,
>   as I am walking,
>   with my head hanging down
>   toward the ground,
>   as I am walking,
>   with foam
>   around my mouth,
>   as I am walking,
>   Exhausted from running, you are walking;
>   exhausted from running, you are moving.

And finally, after he has been killed, the deer finds himself upside down,
being carried back on a pole by the hunters:

Over there, I, in an opening
   in the flower-covered grove,
     as I am walking,
Just I, flower person's wooden bow
   has taken me.
Flower person's flower bamboo arrow
   has overpowered me in an enchanted way.
What happened to me that my hands
   are over my antler crown?

Such a song allows listeners to think of nature and vicariously experience it from the perspectives of the animals and plants which animate the world. For the singers, of course, giving voice to the words and music becomes an even more personal experience requiring concentration, breath, muscle, voice, commitment. For the Deer Dancer and others involved in the ceremonies, the experience becomes even deeper through the intensified use of the body and its gestures. None of this has to do with explaining anything about deer or nature or commenting philosophically about ecology. This is a process which uses words and tones to touch off shared values among closely associated people: it is a culturally structured way of thinking and experiencing together the patterns which make us real. As Yellowman insisted, "We need a strong way of thinking about things; stories make things possible. Without stories and songs, nothing would be possible, nothing would exist."

Notes

Paul Zolbrod, *Diné bahane': The Navajo Creation Story* (Albuquerque: University of New Mexico Press, 1984). His "Ałtsé Hástiin" appears in Brian Swann, ed., *Coming to Light: Contemporary Translations of the Native American Literatures of North America* (New York: Random House, 1994), 614–23. Sam D. Gill, *Sacred Words: A Study of Navajo Religion and Prayer* (Westport, Conn.: Greenwood Press, 1981) discusses the active, hortatory ways in which Navajo ritual speech is thought to bring about real change in the human condition. Gladys A. Reichard, *Navaho Religion: A Study of Symbolism* (Princeton: Princeton University Press, 1974) provided the first thorough discussion of Navajo narrative ritual acts. Leland C. Wyman, *Blessingway* (Tucson: University of Arizona Press, 1970) offers an analytical and comparative study of three different versions of the basic "main stem" of the Navajo ritual system.

The assertion that the capacity for story is uniquely expressive of human behavior and thinking was put forward by Professor Renee Fuller at a meeting of the

American Psychological Association in the 1970s and reported to the general reader in *Brain and Mind: Frontiers of Research, Theory, and Practice* 5, no. 2 (December 1979): 1–2. John Niles's brilliant *Homo Narrans: The Poetics and Anthropology of Oral Literature* (Philadelphia: University of Pennsylvania Press, 1999) deals mainly with the northern European heritage of oral narratives, but many of its assertions relate to what we discuss here. A collection of essays edited by Joseph F. Trimmer, *Narration as Knowledge* (Portsmouth, N.H.: Boynton/Cook, 1997), explores the application of this concept to the field of teaching in the contemporary world.

Dell Hymes's "The Sun's Myth" also appears in Brian Swann, ed., *Coming to Light: Contemporary Translations of the Native American Literatures of North America*, 273–85. His article, "Variation and Narrative Competence," appears in Lauri Honko, ed., *Thick Corpus, Organic Variation and Textuality in Narrative Tradition*, Studia Fennica, Folkloristica 7 (Helsinki: Finnish Literature Society, 2000), 77–92.

John Bierhorst's concepts of double myth structure are proposed in his anthology, *The Red Swan: Myths and Tales of the American Indians* (New York: Farrar, Straus and Giroux, 1976), especially pp. 9–10.

"The Grizzly Bear" was told by Moses (no other name is provided) to Franz Boas near the mouth of the Nass River in British Columbia in 1894. The text (along with many others like it) is printed in *Tsimshian Texts*, Smithsonian Institution, Bureau of American Ethnology Bulletin 27 (Washington, D.C.: 1902), 200–210. The names of the students in the class who did the translation are as follows: Reed Cornia, Kim Fitzgerald, Steve Hatcher, Dan Haws, Fayth Marrelli, Eric Nankervis, Robin A. Parent, Krystel Poulsen, Paulette Roberts, Trevor Smith, Michael Spooner, Wynne Summers, Tomoyo Tamayama, Donna Vance, Harriet White, and Nora Zambreno.

Melville Jacobs discusses the various personality traits of grizzly-bear women in *The Content and Style of an Oral Literature: Clackamas Chinook Myths and Tales* (Chicago: University of Chicago Press, 1959), but it is risky to assume that the superficially similar characteristics found in narratives of a tribe so far south of the Tsimshian will illustrate specific issues central to our tale.

Gary Witherspoon's amazing study of the Navajo language is *Art and Language in the Navajo Universe* (Ann Arbor: University of Michigan Press, 1977). In it, among other things, we learn that the Navajo verb system has 356,200 distinct conjugations for the verb "to go" (p. 21) and that "in the Navajo view of the world, language is not a mirror of reality; reality is a mirror of language" (p. 34).

For information on Coyote and Coyote stories, see William Bright, *A Coyote Reader* (Berkeley: University of California Press, 1993). The term "trickster" is not really descriptive of the complex character (who seldom tricks anyone).

For the "Mickey Mouse" song, I am indebted to Craig Miller of the Folk Arts Program at the Utah Arts Council, who recorded it at a powwow in southern Utah.

More Ghost Dance songs, as well as powwow and social songs, can be found in Judith Vander's rich and sensitive study, *Songprints: The Musical Experience of Five Shoshone Women* (Urbana: University of Illinois Press, 1988). The concept of musical *experience*, not just recitation, is germane to our discussion. The eagle Naraya song and the singer's comment on it appear on page 19.

The Yaqui songs are published in Larry Evers and Felipe S. Molina, eds., *Yaqui Deer Songs/Maso Bwikam: A Native American Poetry* (Tucson: University of Arizona Press, 1987). The songs quoted partially here can be found in their complete form on pp. 104, 164, 165, and 167. The Yaqui evocation of a lush, dewy "flower world" as the epitome of their Sonoran desert environment is one of the most striking examples of the triumph of poetry and song over everyday reality.

5

Patterns and Themes in Native Humor

Why should we attack them? They're finally headed in the right direction!

> —A Yakima spokesman, responding to an invitation to stage a mock attack on the 1976 Bicentennial Wagon Train as it moved east through the state of Washington

It was Custer who originated the Bureau of Indian Affairs; as he left for the Little Big Horn he said, "Now don't do anything 'til I get back!"

> —A Native joke in wide circulation during the 1970s

We're just lucky that Columbus wasn't searching for Turkey!

> —Larry Calica, Warms Springs leader, commenting on the aptness of the name "Indian"

STILL ALIVE IN THE ORAL TRADITIONS of elderly Native people in the Pacific Northwest are stories about negotiations between the United States government and the many tribes around Puget Sound. Large, outdoor meetings were held so that tribal members could hear what offers (or threats) were being made, and a principal speaker at these events was Isaac Stevens, the army major appointed governor of the newly created Washington Territory. Apparently, Stevens was self-conscious about his short stature and made up for it with long, impressive orations where he called the Indians "our children" and referred to their leader, Suiattle, as "my son." They say that when it came Suiattle's turn to respond on one occasion, he drew himself up to his full height (he was about six feet, six inches tall) next to the diminutive Stevens, put his hand on the shorter man's head, looked down at him and began, "My father . . ." to the open amusement of the Native audience.

Subtle (and not so subtle) critiques of the whites and their juggernaut system range from biting remarks (e.g., the bumper sticker: "We gave an inch; you took three thousand miles") or one-liners like "Custer died in

146

an Arrow shirt," and "Custer was disappointed: He heard that blondes were supposed to have more fun," to deliciously funny stories about intercultural "events," both real and imagined.

We are not surprised at the vitriolic political remarks—given the history of conflict between the invaders and original inhabitants—but our convenient stereotype of the stoic Indian often blinds us to the ongoing expressions of humor which in many ways are even more pointed in their critique. In this arena of subtlety, humor coalesces and gives dramatic shape to culturally shared Native attitudes and experiences. For example, Native people around Pendleton, Oregon, still reminisce about the year when the Indians played a grand trick during the Pendleton Roundup's famous (and tacky) *Happy Canyon* outdoor pageant by reversing their assigned roles. Scheduled to come out whooping and attacking the pioneer stagecoach as it lumbered across the arena, the Indian riders actually captured the coach and rode out of the rodeo grounds with it and its white-actor occupants—and didn't bring them back until the next day. During a Kiowa Gourd Dance (performed by veterans), you can hear the strange sound of a bugle playing. According to the story, during the Plains wars, Kiowa warriors would capture an army bugler, bring him home, and make him blow "Charge!" while they danced; if he did well, they let him go back to his unit (one wonders how he could even pucker up, never mind sound a note or blow "Charge" in the middle of a lot of dancing Indian enemies!).

In spite of many recorded instances like these, in spite of hundreds of photographs that show laughing Indians, in spite of numerous studies of Indian clown societies, in spite of all the well-known Coyote stories, many non-Indians persist in believing that Native Americans have no sense of humor. On the polite level, a colleague of mine, hearing me mention this chapter, gingerly suggested I should merge it with other material since obviously there would not be enough Indian humor to make a whole chapter. On a less polite level, I recall a southern Utah gas-station owner in the 1950s telling me in puzzlement, "I just don't see how you can live with those Navvies—they aren't like other people. Why, I've lived here all my life, and I've never seen one laugh or cry!" I couldn't summon the words to tell him that there was a good reason: Navajos usually only express personal emotions in the company of good friends (fig. 60); in front of strangers, laughing may possibly be interpreted as an insult. He had lived in his hometown for some forty years and had—apparently—never become friends with any of his Navajo neighbors.

In this chapter, I want to explore the proposition that folk humor is one of the best and most revealing ways to learn about the shared values

Fig. 60. Maryann and Mike Johnson laugh over a Navajo joke;
Dinnehotso, Arizona, 1956. Photo by the author.

of any culture. Corollary: Our continuing belief that Indians have no
humor is a serious sign that we have not come very far in understanding
the cultural values of the people on whose land we Europeans have
established our transplanted societies. And while some may naïvely hold
onto the stereotype of the stoic Indian simply because they've had no
opportunity to test it, others have maintained the intentional, or at least
convenient, stance that Indians are just too difficult to know. The
unwillingness to understand is not limited to gas-station attendants in
the rural Southwest, either. In 1969, anthropologist John Greenway
characterized the leaders of the American Folklore Society and its
Journal like this:

> Several were the greatest folklorists of their day. Franz Boas, for
> example, is the father of American anthropology. He is also the father
> of abominable editing of a scholarly journal, the father of interminable
> Indian myths. . . . During his fifteen years and the fifteen years of his
> protegee, student, and fellow indiscriminate lover of Indians, Ruth
> Benedict, the *Journal* was the refuge for the dispossessed redskin. Some
> think it was the Depression that cut the list of subscribers in 1935 to
> 191; I think it was those incessant Coyote Trickster stories. . . . Things
> have improved since World War II, which was a terrible conflict bring-
> ing much suffering upon the world, but worth it in that it put an end to
> Coyote Trickster tales in the *Journal of American Folklore*.

Perhaps you can understand why, when I began editing the *Journal of American Folklore* in 1972, the first piece I published was an article on humor in Paiute Coyote stories written by a Paiute woman, Judy Trejo. Greenway responded immediately with an angry letter, suggesting first of all that the article was counterfeit, then following up this way:

> . . . I am pleased to see you are retaining some of my rules [for *Journal* style], grieved to see you are reinstating others I banished. Among the latter are those Coyote Trickster tales. I say nothing further about them, except that they will be in themselves your punishment. . . . Instead of a sense of humor—or anything else—Indians have feathers. And whoever heard of an Indian who was anything other than 1/32 Cherokee? You may give her [Judy Trejo] a copy of this letter—I give you a carbon for that purpose. . . . To say nothing more to the point, I ask you whether it is not bad enough to have Indians in real life without having them in the *Journal*. Tell her if she is ever out this way I will take great pleasure in pulling all her feathers out.

What is it that otherwise-intelligent and witty people like John Greenway are missing? (And why do they get angry when it appears that they are wrong?) Let's look at some different kinds of Native humor and speculate about the way they embody serious cultural issues in coded form. We already discussed some examples in chapter 4, where we noted that even when Coyote stories are uproariously funny, the laughter (often with implied ridicule) points our attention to culturally moral issues. Old Man Coyote uses (misuses?) his magic power to make a hollow tree close around him so he can be comfortable during a hailstorm; when he can't get out, he has to cut himself in small pieces, push the pieces through a small hole, and then reassemble himself outside (and during this process, Bluejay flies away with his anus). The story is performed as if it's funny, but the moral implications about the self-destructive result of using magic for personal comfort are far from humorous.

In one Navajo story, Ma'i (Coyote) proposes a race against Skunk to see who will get the most prairie-dog meat (planning, of course, to get back to the campfire in plenty of time to eat it all himself). He gives Skunk a head start, but the smaller animal just runs up a nearby hill and hides under a rock until Coyote goes rocketing past (with a torch tied to his tail to show arrogantly how fast he's running). Coyote runs all the way to a distant mountain and back, arriving exhausted at their hunting camp to find only the four skinniest (and by now sandy) prairie dogs. It's difficult to say which is funnier: his duping of himself because of gluttony, his hubris, or the final scene, where Skunk, from a ledge above, drops occasional bones down to him but refuses to share the meat. Obviously, the cultural moral about sharing food is not funny but quite serious.

In another Navajo story within a longer myth, Ma'i is being pursued by larger animals because he has disguised himself and has been sleeping with their sister (in some versions, it is the woman herself who changes into a bear and tries to catch him). Close to being captured, he nonetheless stops to taunt a pair of spiders down in a canyon. He yells, "You're ridiculous! You don't even know how to screw properly!" The moment in the story is hilarious, but it brings a number of serious issues to the forefront: sexually active Navajo couples who live in crowded, single-room hogans *often* go out for some privacy, and people are expected not to call attention to them—much less shout critiques or instruction about their style. Moreover, spiders are the ones who taught us about weaving and string games, and we should show them respect. And Ma'i, who has just been having sex with someone else's sister and is about to be dismembered for it, is in no position—either morally or tactically—to stop and make disparaging remarks about another's sexuality. Notice that the text does not say any of these things overtly, but it suggests them all so that they have a combined effect on the knowledgeable audience.

The following story is an even more striking example of what a performed text can say without actually stating it. In the 1970s, this story was told to me several times, usually by teenagers, who called it "the funniest Navajo joke":

> Long ago, they say
> (a man off to one side):
> "Which of you dreamed something last night?" he said.
> Another said, "I don't know."
> Another said, "I don't know."
> "I dreamed last night," another one said.
> "Last night I dreamed I was sitting on [hatching] four little birds,
> and three weren't mine;
> only one was mine," he said.

What can this possibly mean? In any case, it's clear that the bare text isn't going to tell us, so we need to discover what such a sequence of statements may signify to Navajos: What does it make them think about or remember? Why does it start with "long ago"? Is this equivalent to our "once upon a time," thus a stylistic hint that the story is fictional and not a report of a "real" event? Why is the questioner described as off to one side? Are we to see him as somehow marginal? Do Navajos ask each other about their dreams? Do they talk about dreams openly with others? What about the phrase, "I don't know"? In Navajo the term is *hóla*, which basically means "I don't know," but it's often used in conversation to avoid answering an uncomfortable question, as if to say, "I don't know what you're getting at." Are the two men uncomfortable at being asked? And why is it the fourth person in the sequence who answers; why didn't he speak up at once? We may guess that the cluster-of-four logic is working here: Just as in Western culture Cinderella is the third (and not the first) to try on the glass slipper, here the key line is spoken in the fourth position, after we have been presented with the problem. The final position is held by the speaker who "solves" the puzzle (or gives the punch line). But what does his answer mean? Is there anything funny (or culturally loaded) in the image of a man sitting on birds' eggs? Why are there four eggs/birds? And what can he possibly mean by saying that one of them is his? Is he talking about children and not birds? And why, in a female-centered culture, are the actors all men? These few questions give us a place to start, at least, but they don't tell us everything.

Taking some cues from Navajo culture, we can supply at least some of the life values and attitudes to which the joke refers. For one thing, Navajos usually don't talk about their dreams to others (though grown-ups sometimes joke about what a restless child must be dreaming); so those who answer *hóla* are giving the culturally correct response to the first man's question. The fourth man describes a dream which is full of natural discrepancies: a human is playing the role of a bird, a man is playing a woman, something heavy is sitting on fragile objects. Discrepancies in nature are usually signs to Navajos that things are not in order, symptoms that indicate potential sickness or fragile mental health. In this case, since the man dreams that the young birds are his responsibility, though only one of them is "mine," there is the hint he suspects three of the four children he is raising have other fathers. When I asked some Navajos, they said, "Well, yes, that's in there, but of course that's not what's funny about it." Part of the humor, it seems to me, is that since Navajo women are considered the owners of their children, Navajo men sound ridiculous if they show concern about paternity.

So we have an apparent breaking of the custom of not sharing dreams, a cluster of discrepancies in nature suggesting mental or spiritual imbalance, and an odd concern about infidelity. Navajo friends tell me there are other nuances, among them the fact that when the man says he has been hatching *tsídii yáázh* (literally "young birds," but by implication eggs, since they are being sat on), because of the Navajo logic about who can do what to whom, most Navajos picture not a man but a bird sitting on the eggs.

Their conclusion? The joke appears to depict a dangerous situation, but in fact there is no threat because the audience (unlike the speaker in the joke) realizes the man did not really dream *he* was sitting on eggs but that he was a *bird* sitting on eggs—thus, there is no discrepancy (it's a bit like a pun that appears to say something questionable or a so-called pretended obscene riddle).

Even after this clarification, however, the non-Navajo is unlikely to find the joke suddenly very funny and start laughing, and this is probably because the discrepancies in jokes need to reflect concerns in the listener's own language, culture, and experience. Just knowing intellectually about another culture's issues does not confront the outside listener with an emotionally recognizable dilemma and its resolution. Building on this, I suggest that the humor in Coyote stories does not lie in a depiction of ridiculous behavior but a response to what in that behavior makes deep cultural values palpable. For this reason, even though we may think we see the humor in a Coyote story (or in that long-lived cartoon character, Wiley Coyote), we can be confident that we are missing the depth that makes the laughter culturally meaningful to Native people.

When my friend Yellowman told Ma'i stories to his family in the winter, their laughter was made up of several layers of acquaintance with the tradition: On the surface, of course, the story is entertaining (Ma'i's mannerisms, his foibles, his rationalizations are all funny in and of themselves the same way that, when we see Bugs Bunny appear in a cartoon, we humorously anticipate everything that's coming); as we've seen, however, the real bursts of laughter come during particular scenes where Ma'i is not just being quaintly idiotic or goofy but challenging an important Navajo value or breaking a taboo. When a singer (medicine man) refers to a particular Coyote story during a break in a healing ritual, the audience's laughter includes these two levels but adds a third: the realization that the ceremony is addressing an imbalance that may have been caused by the kind of behavior depicted in the story. If someone tells, or refers to, a Coyote story before a political or educational meeting, the laughter recognizes and mitigates the bothersome possibility that some human weakness (like competition or selfishness, for example) may come up during the ensuing gathering. Clearly, while such articulations may be funny, the issues behind them seldom are.

Today jokes and humorous remarks are among the most common "tools" Native people use to register their perceptions of cultural frictions between themselves and other tribes, between Natives and non-Natives, and between tribes and the U. S. government. Even a brief anecdote can carry an immense burden of meaning, such as the joke going around Navajo country during the heavy winters of the mid-1950s: "Did you hear about the [Navajo] woman who heard a plane circling her place and ran out to see what it was? She got out there and was killed by a case of condensed milk." The Air Force and National Guard were indeed dropping supplies to snowbound Navajos, but no one thought to ask if they wanted or needed milk. Most of them do not metabolize milk very well, so the joke dramatizes the irony of getting bombarded and killed by a kind of help you can't use, epitomized in a commodity food someone else assumes is good for you. In this vein of being surrounded by people who don't pay attention to your culture, Lakota friends tell me that there is an old story about women who went over the Custer battlefield after the fighting was done to see what useful items they could retrieve. Some of them recognized Custer, and two of them ran their sewing awls into his ears, saying, "Now can you hear us better?" Whether or not either of these two events actually happened, retelling such anecdotes testifies to the way Indian humor expresses the almost inexpressible dimensions of living among the whites.

Less macabre, but equally telling, was an event I witnessed in Montezuma Creek in the spring of 1955. Government scientists (from the Soil Conservation Service, as I recall) called a meeting to propose an idea to local Navajos. They had set up a couple of long tables, each loaded with stacks of paper anchored against the incessant wind by chunks of sandstone. They suggested a complex combination of alternate sheep grazing, limited local irrigation, and reseeding as an attempt to retard soil (to be honest, *sand*) erosion in Montezuma Canyon. For some reason I couldn't figure out, the local people were not charmed by the plan, though I could tell that part of their resistence had to do with anyone telling them what to do with their sheep—advice that brings back terrible memories of the devastation of the government's sheep-reduction program during the 1930s. But there was something else hanging in the air, and I was not enough of an insider to catch what it was. After a long and uncomfortable presentation and tedious, negative discussion from the petulant crowd (made even worse by the reluctant translation of the sullen Navajo interpreter), my adopted father, Little Wagon, got up and grimaced at the white visitors for more than a minute. The crowd got still, apparently anticipating that this short, bandy-legged man would put their thoughts into funny words (he was famous for doing so). Finally he said, very slowly,

> A long time ago, people came here from Washington [a kind of pun because the Navajo term, *wááshindoon*, means both the city and the federal government] with a pile of paper to show us [the Navajo word for paper, *naaltsoos*, means "a flat, flexible (therefore potentially impermanent) object is carried about"]. They said they wanted to stop

soil erosion in Montezuma Canyon, and they asked if we would help.
We said we would, and they went away. A long time after that, some
people came here from *wááshindoon* and said they had a plan for soil
erosion, and they asked for our help in this area. We thought maybe
the first ones didn't hear us, so again we said we'd help if they'd tell us
what they wanted us to do. A long time after that, some other people
came, carrying even more paper, and they told us they had a plan for
soil erosion in Montezuma Canyon. And then we decided to wait and
see what you people were really up to. Then nothing happened until
now. Today you people carried lots of paper to us here, and now we
understand that you want to control our sheep; but *wááshindoon* killed
most of our sheep a long time ago, and the ones we have left are
being scared by the oil hunters and the uranium prospectors. So we've
decided you're really not interested in soil erosion; all you've done for
a long time is carry paper here.

He took a long pause and then continued, "Now I have a plan for
stopping soil erosion here in Montezuma Canyon, and I want to tell you
about it. You take every piece of paper on that table and wipe yourselves
with it [he used the phrase *naaltsoos bee 'ádít'oodí*, "flat and flexible
(thing) with which one wipes himself"], then throw them all into the
canyon. There's so much of it that it will keep the sand from sliding
away." The audience laughed heartily, and the soil experts picked up their
packets and retreated. For years I recounted the story to friends as an
example of Little Wagon's wit, but I later found out that essentially the
same comment had been made by others at numerous meetings across the
reservation from the 1940s on. Little Wagon was applying a well-known
joke to the immediate situation.

A common comment during the 1960s and 1970s was "whites get
headaches; we get anthropologists" (fig. 61). People tell of an elder who puts
his arm around his grandson's shoulders, sweeps his other arm across the
horizon, and says, "My son, someday *none* of this land will belong to you."
A tourist asks, "Where does this road go?" and an Indian answers, "Road
stay; you go!" Columbus tells his first mate, "Throw those Indians a line!"
An older Native explains a puff of black smoke on the horizon as proof of a
government requirement to make a carbon copy of every message sent.

But despite the widespread use of such vignettes, some of the most
finely honed commentaries on the differences between whites and
Natives are expressed in narratives. According to one widely told story,
an old Indian is sitting comfortably in the shade of a tree next to a government office building when the whites come out on lunch break. A

Fig. 61. Perry Johnson with a Geiger counter at the ruins in Chinle Wash. He told the author, "You can tell people you found someone living in here." Photo by the author.

white man sits on the grass next to the old Indian, nods hello, and reaches for his sandwich. The old man suddenly sneezes, then blows his nose on the ground. The white, nauseated by this behavior, throws his sandwich back into the bag and starts to lecture the old man about proper behavior. "This is what's wrong out here," he rails; "we've been here for more than a hundred years and still haven't even been able to teach you people something basic, like how to blow your noses! You're primitive!" The old man doesn't say anything; he just looks off at the horizon. After a while, the white gets ready to eat again, but the sun shines in his eyes and makes him sneeze. He takes out his handkerchief, blows his nose, and puts the handkerchief back in his pocket. The old man looks over in disgust and says, "My God, you white people save *everything*, don't you?"

This parody of the white mania for owning and saving things—as viewed from the Native perspective—gets at least part of its humor from the gesture of cultural disgust allowed the old man at the end, so the assumed cultural superiority of white behavior is turned on its head. Indians return things to nature; whites keep everything, even snot. The whites think they know how to behave and assume the right to instruct others, but the Indians get the last word.

A parallel story is told by the Nez Perces on the Colville Reservation in central Washington (where Chief Joseph and his band were banished after the Nez Perce War). They say that in early times, a group of white explorers came through Nez Perce country and made camp there for a while. Some Natives argued that they were dangerous and should be killed, but others—led by a young woman who had been treated well by whites on an earlier occasion—argued for hospitality. The consensus finally favored being friendly to the whites. Having watched the explorers in the meantime, the Indians had noticed that many of them were blowing their noses into pieces of cloth, and someone got the idea that it would be a friendly gesture to help them out. A deer bladder was rinsed out, passed around so people could blow their noses into it, and eventually presented, fully loaded, to the strangers. Is this an episode that somehow missed getting into Lewis and Clark's journals? Did it ever really happen? Lewis and Clark scholars have told me privately that they doubt its authenticity, partly because many whites in those days also blew their noses on the ground—and besides, we don't have a written confirmation of the event. But all that means—in terms of historical accuracy—is that we simply don't know if it happened or how it happened.

Folklorists know that the story carries its own cultural comparisons whether the event occurred or not: if the story didn't mean anything to the Nez Perces, they wouldn't keep telling it. So what does it mean? It does not seem to focus on cultural superiority but on the naïveté of the Natives—again from their own point of view. It is very much like the stories told by Natives along the Oregon and Washington coast which emphasize how little their grandparents knew about the new culture by ridiculing the awkward Native efforts at trying to understand it. The Chehalis and others tell about their first encounter with a white hunter carrying a rifle: They see him shoot a bird out of a tree, and they immediately demand that he shoot at them so they can prove their powers are greater than a bird's. Before the scared white can escape, he shoots and kills several Natives at their own insistence (a bit reminiscent of "The Sun's Myth"). In Coos anecdotes, people encounter coffee for the first time and keep boiling the beans, pouring off the evil-smelling liquid, but never manage to get those beans soft enough to eat. Self-parody of being easy victims for whites is also apparent in such stories as the one about a young urban Indian who spends weekends with his grandfather on the reservation learning old methods of tracking and hunting. One day he arrives and finds his grandfather spread out on the highway with one ear to the ground. "Grandfather! What is it?" he yells. The grandfather replies, "Red Cadillac, 1980. Blonde woman with a sundress. Male driver. Two kids." "Grandfather, that's amazing! How can you tell all that just by putting your ear on the road?" "I can't, you idiot! I just got run over by a car full of white people!"

It is said that as astronauts were trying out some of their hardware in the southwestern desert, they noticed some Navajos watching them from a distance. Their public-relations man asked the Navajos if they wanted to meet the astronauts, and when the two groups were introduced, one old Indian asked if he could send a message in case the astronauts met some Navajos on the moon. The message, slowly and laboriously translated by a young (and nervous) Navajo, was, "Be nice to these people, but whatever you do, don't sign any papers and don't accept any beads," acknowledging the ease with which early whites were able to flimflam the Indians.

Self-critiques also include Natives making fun of their problems at mastering the invader's strange language and idiom. According to Neet Brown, a Navajo emergency medical technician, a man phoned the Navajo police and yelled, "My hogan's burning! My hogan's burning!" When the operator asked, "How do we get there?" he yelled, "You got that big red truck, i'n't it?" A Hopi mother overhears her young son doing his mathematics homework: "Two plus two sonofabitch is four; four plus four sonofabitch is eight," so she goes to ask the white teacher why her son has been taught to swear. The teacher answers, "I said, 'Two plus two, the sum of which is four. . . .'" A coastal Indian goes out to get crabs with some white friends, and they notice that the crabs all stay in his bucket, while they try to climb out of the others. He explains, "Well, I only pick up the Indian crabs; that way, when one tries to climb out, the others hold him back," a subtle and complex reference to the way traditional Natives sometimes treat younger people who adopt white concepts of competition and upward mobility.

Of course, another kind of humor involves parodying white behavior seen as odd or compulsive. Some years ago, for example, Hopi clowns used to wear alarm clocks strapped to their wrists and, during an otherwise religious ceremonial dance, ran around the crowd yelling, "It's time to be tired!" (then they laid down and pretended to sleep), or "It's time to be hungry!" (they pantomimed shoveling food into their mouths). Larry Calica at Warm Springs Reservation in central Oregon tells the story of a white anthropologist who was trying unsuccessfully to collect Coyote stories from local residents when he suddenly discovered a coyote caught in a trap. He was about to shoot it for the bounty, but the coyote spoke to him, promising to give him money and help him get all the stories he wanted if he would only spring the trap. The anthropologist accepted a roll of bills, freed the coyote, and was then treated to several hours of authentic Coyote tales narrated by the coyote himself. But when he got home that night, the big wad of bills the coyote had given him had turned to a handful of mangy fur, and the next day, when he opened his tape recorder to play the precious stories for his colleagues, he found his machine was stuffed with coyote turds.

Sometimes the humor acknowledges simultaneously the Native's own modest position in contrast to the white tendency to brag. In one story, a Texan stops his Cadillac along the highway in Montana and asks an Indian, "How much of this land do you own?" The Indian replies, "I own the land from here down the highway to that next road down there, then up the valley about a mile, then across to those hills, and back to here." "That's nothing," says the Texan; "Why, I can get in my pickup at the house and drive two days before I come to my property line!" "Yeah, I know what you mean," says the Indian; "I had a pickup like that once."

In another story, a white hunting enthusiast in Farmington, New Mexico, saves up and buys an expensive English pointer. He asks his next-door neighbor, a Navajo, if he'd like to go out bird hunting and if he has a bird dog. The Navajo replies that he has a Navajo pointer and goes out to hunt for him in the dusty backyard. He kicks the dog awake, throws him into the back of the white's pickup, and they drive off in a cloud of dust. When they reach a good bird area, the white goes out first, the expensive pointer walking ahead and freezing into pointing position every now and then, followed by a bird flying up and the hunter shooting it. The white comes back with six pheasants and tells the Indian to try his luck: "But I don't think that dog of yours has any real talent for this." The Navajo walks out with his dog following him; the dog just looks calmly around in all directions, sitting behind the hunter. Every now and then, the Navajo looks back at his dog; then a bird flies up, and he shoots it; then another, and another. He comes back with twelve birds. The white hunter says, "It must have something to do with you being an Indian; you just have a sense of where the birds are. Your dog didn't do anything but just sit there and look around!" The Navajo responds, "I told you he's a Navajo pointer: You just have to watch his lips *real* close!"—a reference to the custom among many Southwest tribes to point with their chin or pursed lips rather than a finger.

Even the contemporary debate about gender gets into Native inter-tribal humor. From my Lakota son-in-law, Peter DeCory, comes the following story: Three Lakota men are stranded on one side of the Missouri River and don't know how to get across. The brother from Eagle Butte makes tobacco ties and prays to Wakan Tanka (Great Holy) to make him smart enough to think of a way to cross the river. Wakan Tanka turns him into a Ponca Indian, and he swims across. The brother from Rosebud prays to Wakan Tanka to make him even smarter, so he can think of a better way to cross the river. He gets turned into a California Indian, and he makes some fry bread and floats across on it. The brother from Pine

Ridge prays to Wakan Tanka to make him the smartest of all, so he gets turned into a woman, and she walks across on the bridge.

Conflicts with other ethnic groups also register in Native joke lore. A Navajo sitting in a bar in Gallup gets into an argument with an Asian and suddenly finds himself on the floor, recovering consciousness. He asks the Asian, "What in the world did you hit me with?" and the Asian replies, with a curt bow, "Judo. Blackbelt. Tokyo. 1980." The next day the Navajo comes in and sees the Asian sitting there again; he rushes up to him and slams him into unconsciousness on the floor. The Asian gets up saying, "What in the world did you hit me with?" and the Navajo replies with a bow, "Tire iron. Green Chevvy pickup. Gallup. 1960."

Intertribal differences, cultural variations, and frictions are common themes in Native humor. Western Native people joke about the Sioux being dog eaters by asking, "What's a Sioux seven-course meal?" (answer: a six-pack of beer and a puppy), or "What's a Sioux's favorite sandwich?" (answer: BLT—black Lab on toast). Two Sioux went into town for the first time and couldn't find anywhere to eat. Finally, they saw a sign that said "Hot Dogs" and went up to the stand and ordered two, politely looking away as the proprietor prepared them. After they got down the street and one guy opened his napkin up, he said to the other, "Hey! What part did they give you?" As if in retaliation, the Sioux counter with "What do you get if you cross a Navajo and a sheep?" (answer: a retarded sheep), or "What can you get at Navajo Community College?" (answer: a BAA degree). At Warm Springs, you may hear the question, "What does a Hopi give to his wife on their wedding day that's long and hard?" (answer: his name). Navajos, who consider the Hopis to be short and ineffectual, ask, "What's four feet tall and a mile long?" (answer: a Hopi parade), while Hopis, many of whom consider the Navajos to be aggressive bullies, ask, "Why do Navajos prefer to buy used police cars?" (answer: So they can see what it's like to ride in the *front* seat).

A Navajo, ruffled by anthropological notions that his people had come to North America by the Bering Strait "land bridge," told a committee I was serving on, "We didn't come over by any bridge. It was the Hopis. In fact, their own stories talk about it: They were on their long migration, and they were caught by freezing storms in the far North. They noticed some animals swimming in the water nearby, and they went over and asked them, 'Excuse me! Is the Bering Strait land bridge around here anywhere?' and the seals said, ' 'Aoo'!'" The word *'aoo'* is Navajo for "yes," and if enunciated properly with volume, sounds a bit like a seal's grunt. In this story, the seals are already speaking Navajo by the time the Hopis arrive in North America.

Whites who want to be Indians (or who claim they are) come in for humorous treatment as well, as the Wanna-be Dance anecdote in chapter 3 illustrates. Someone who claims (as millions of whites do, apparently) to be part Cherokee may be told, "Oh yeah? If you had a nosebleed, you'd lose all your blood quantum." According to one story, a white tourist came back from the Navajo reservation overjoyed that the Indians liked him so much they gave him an Indian name, *bilagáana* ("white person"). Lakota columnist Tim Giago recalls that when he was in a mission boarding school, a young Jesuit teacher was being visited by his mother, who asked if the Indian kids liked him. He said, "Of course they do; they even have a nickname for me in their own language, and, although I shouldn't allow it, since they are forbidden to speak their native tongue, I just let it go because it shows they appreciate me. . . . The boys call me *ooahloh* [*ooahloh* means 'Watch out, he's coming!']."

Parodies of white fads and fascinations are common on the Internet today; you can find out, among other things, what kinds of things Indians can say to a white person when being introduced, including, "How much white are you?" and "I'm part white myself, you know," and "My great grandmother was a full-blooded white princess," and "What do you think about those riverboat casinos your people are building? Do they really help your people, or are they just a quick fix?"

Through the Internet, you also hear about NDN Barbies (reflecting the colloquial western Native pronunciation of the word "Indian"). According to recent messages, you can get a Commod Barbie doll (referring to welfare commodity food), who comes with a can opener and cheese slicer, plus pliers and thread so you can make a jingle dress out of the lids (the latter bonus is available only on the Cree Reservation). The Rez Ball Barbie comes with sports bra, knee brace, wristbands, and sports goggles, plus her own oxygen bottle. The Forty-nine Barbie sits in her pickup until her beer is gone, then "closes in on the next snag." The Wanna-be Barbie comes with jet-black (Clairol) hair, a brown corduroy dress, made-in-Japan moccasins, a turkey-feather fan, "and an attitude that is intolerable." The New Age Barbie has her own crystals, beads, and "sacred" smudge shell. Wolf Woman Barbie (a Cherokee version of the Wanna-be Barbie) includes a pet mutt alleged to be "part wolf." And the My-Great-Grandmother-Was-a-Cherokee Barbie is an exact replica of regular Barbie, "no different from all the Barbies in the store." The extra commentary, plus sarcastic reference to common white misperceptions, makes it clear that these Barbies are not just clever Indian parallels to the dolls but rather, observations on white, especially New Age, misunderstanding and commodification of Indian attributes.

Recently circulated on the Internet was an Indian version of the popular survival television series where a limited number of people are left on an island to see if they can survive. The Native author proposes to drop ten white people onto a reservation, where they will have to endure "one week of hardship, gossiping, back stabbing, jealousy, teepee creeping, forty-nining" and be able to survive on high-cholesterol commodity foods. The ten contestants will be given five sacred rocks, a rez rocket (reservation car) with no doors and no back window, an unwinterized HUD house, and three-days' worth of food stamps, plus moccasins, headbands, and feathers "to wear around the rez to demonstrate cultural sensitivity to reservation inhabitants." The last one to survive will be awarded a casino coupon booklet worth ten dollars, an authentic Indian handmade dream catcher, homemade tattoos from an ink pen, and a Princess Pale Moon special-edition Pendleton blanket.

All this humor suggests superficially that the Indians have been jolly good sports about everything that has happened in America—and I do think the Indians have maintained a better sense of humor about whites than whites have about Indians on the whole. But the images and styles, the themes, and the nuances of Native expression show us pretty clearly that—like the humor of most cultures—what's being communicated is not pleasure but anxiety. Think about the most common themes in Euro-American humor, especially jokes: religion, sex, politics, race (to name the most common). There is nothing particularly funny in these topics. Indeed, they represent exactly those issues which are far from settled in our society, issues that cause interpersonal and intercultural friction, issues that provoke fear and anxiety. The same is true of Native humor, which tends to dramatize a continuing and perhaps even intensifying sense of disequilibrium and anxiety about personal and tribal existence, about maintaining stability in a world that requires people to act like witches or crazy persons to succeed, about Indianness itself in a political and economic setting where tribes and other ethnic groups are victimized by their own government or provoked into corrosive competition with each other.

In the processes of what we have politely called "assimilation" (which, incidentally, has not taken place), we have continued with remarkable naïveté to ask the Indians' help in securing their own cultural demise—along with their language, heritage, value systems, and religion. We seem to control all the rewards: jobs, school, money, reputation, financial stability, upward mobility. The temptations for Indian people are great, and the tensions are more complex than anyone can easily articulate in intellectual or sociological terms. In James Welch's *Winter in the Blood*, the protagonist spends most of the novel discovering that he's more Indian than

Fig. 62. Dancers break into laughter at the Bethel Dance Festival, 1989. Photo by James H. Barker.

he thought, even though he has not been leading a traditional Native life. Indeed, for most of the book, he leads an apparently empty, meaningless life. The one clear Indian gesture he makes, which lets us know that he is acknowledging his identity, comes right at the end of the novel when he tosses his grandmother's medicine pouch into her grave. But the scene where this serious, symbolic moment occurs is framed in hilarious terms since his mother and her second husband, aping white ways, are wearing too much lipstick and garish double-knit clothing. The hole they dig for the grave isn't big enough, so the expensive, lacquered coffin sticks, requiring them to jump up and down on it. When the scene was dramatized by a Native theater group at the University of Montana, Indians in the audience howled with laughter, while whites in attendance were offended by their behavior and wrote letters to the student newspaper advising Indians to learn proper theater manners and "respect for their own culture." Obviously, the whites didn't understand the important way Native humor functions in dramatizing dead-serious issues.

Native humor—ranging from funny aphorisms and wry comments, to old Coyote stories, to contemporary jokes—provides a culturally structured system through which shared anxieties, fears, and concerns can be played out, foregrounded, dramatized, and—most importantly—reexperienced and mastered. Like all poetry, the forms of humor utilize a style and imagery that speak to us of issues far deeper than a simple story line. Like all jokes, their content is not really funny, but they become funny if performed for a knowledgeable audience because the imagery dramatizes and stimulates personal responses to shared values and fears (fig. 62). Humorous expressions in any culture are sensitive dramatic documents, barometric readings, pulse soundings which give us a sense of cultural worldview by projecting abstract emotional systems onto a human stage. By paying serious attention to Native humor, we can finally learn something really deep and genuine—and most of all, human—about our Indian neighbors, and—if we're attentive—about ourselves as well. But it's a subtle process: we've got to watch each other's lips real close.

Notes

The sources of the Chief Suiattle story are anthropologist Jay Miller, Agnes Ferdin, and Terry Tafoya. An early version of the "Kiowa Gourd Dance with Captured Army Bugle" can be heard on the record that accompanies John Bierhorst's *A Cry from the Earth: Music of the North American Indian* (New York: Four Winds Press, 1979).

John Greenway's comments on the *Journal of American Folklore* appear in *Folklore of the Great West* (Palo Alto, Calif.: American West Publishing Company, 1969), 8–9; his letter to me, on University of Colorado stationery, is dated 24 June 1974 and signed "John Greenway, Professor of Anthropology."

The story of Coyote's dismemberment is given in full, with collaborative discussion, in George Wasson and Barre Toelken, "Coyote and the Strawberries: Cultural Drama and Intercultural Collaboration," in Larry Evers and Barre Toelken, eds., *Native American Oral Traditions: Collaboration and Interpretation* (Logan: Utah State University Press, 2001), 176–99.

The Navajo story of Ma'i, Skunk, and the prairie dogs can be found in Barre Toelken and Tacheeni Scott, "Poetic Translation and the 'Pretty Languages' of Yellowman," in Karl Kroeber, ed., *Traditional Literatures of the American Indian: Texts and Interpretations*, 2d ed. (Lincoln: University of Nebraska Press, 1997), 88–134.

The "funniest Navajo joke" was collected from Matthew Yellowman, then a teenager, on 12 December 1974. For more on the several levels of meaning in Navajo Coyote tales, see my essay, "Life and Death in the Navajo Coyote Tales," in Arnold Krupat and Brian Swann, eds., *Recovering the Word: Essays on Native American Literature* (Berkeley: University of California Press, 1987), 388–401. For a whole treatment of Coyote across several Native tribes in the West, see William Bright, *A Coyote Reader* (Berkeley: University of California Press, 1993)

The term "i'n't it," as used in Navajo vernacular English, is a contraction of "isn't it" in the sense of "isn't that so?" or "isn't that correct?" One is likely to hear "you're going to town today, i'n't it?" or "they're crazy, i'n't it?" The pronunciation is almost exactly like "in it?" I am obliged to Chiyo and Pete DeCory, George Wasson, James Florendo, and Denny DeGross for keeping me supplied with examples of NDN humor on the Internet. Tim Giago's article on Native humor appeared in his syndicated column in *The Idaho Statesman*, 14 July 2001, p. 7.

James Welch's *Winter in the Blood* (New York: Harper & Row, 1974) is the first in a line of extremely penetrating fictional works about Native Americans caught in a meaningless, threatening, confusing white world.

6

Cultural Patterns of Discovery

*Just about everything the old-timers knew, it was given to them by
the animals and the plants.*
> —Charlie Ashcraft, Seneca, responding to my question about
> how the Indians figured out how to make maple syrup

*Roger, if a treasure is lost, it isn't gone. It's still there, where it has
always been. . . . The knowledge isn't lost. We are. The truth never
sleeps . . . but for a moment we don't know about it—just as it was
when we had the willow but didn't know about the willow.*
> —Fool Bull, Lakota, refusing Roger Welsch's request to
> record the old man's medical knowledge before it died out
> and became lost

Who taught you to ask questions like that: the missionaries?
> —Yellowman, Navajo, responding to my asking how the
> Navajos found out that *chiiłchin* (the bitter red berry of
> the desert sumac) could prevent colds

SOME YEARS AGO, when I taught at the University of Oregon, I was asked
to join a group of colleagues who were visiting high schools to speak with
seniors about coming to the university. Among other things, we suggested
courses they might take in high school to prepare themselves for the university experience. Aaron Novick, director of the university's Institute of
Molecular Biology and one of the country's foremost scientists, astounded
everyone by telling the students that if they anticipated going into the
sciences, they should take every literature and art class they could get.
"For one thing," he said, "we already have enough overtrained and under-
educated scientists." Beyond that, he pointed out, we now have calcula-
tors, computers, electron microscopes, and other tools to aid scientific
observation and analysis.

Most important, though, we need people who can think. Literature
requires you to deal with imagery, subtle characterizations, various

levels of meaning, ambiguous plots, even puns—all of which make
you think and imagine beyond what you personally believe you know
as fact. Art requires you to be creative, be aware of relationships, of
patterns beyond yourself—maybe even create new ones. We will not
be asking you to recite the periodic table of the elements; we will be
asking you to think.

In the earlier chapters of this book, we have considered Native
American literature, expressive arts, culturally structured dance, and the
subtleties of humor. I've suggested that even though Native tribes are not
all alike, their traditional expressions provide us with a thumbprint—if
you will—of shared assumptions about relationships in the world, their
view of normality. In this chapter, following Aaron Novick's lead, I want
to go further and point out some ways in which these artistic and narrative
patterns also illustrate distinctive Native ways of thinking and discovering.

Let's begin our speculation about Native discovery by looking carefully at the logic behind Fool Bull's comment to Roger Welsch at the head
of the chapter. In that conversation, Fool Bull told Welsch, "If everyone
were to forget for a moment that aspirin cures a headache, does that mean
that aspirin no longer cures headache? No, it simply means that for a
moment we don't *know* that aspirin cures headache. . . . The knowledge
is still there to be found again. The truth never sleeps." In addition to the
reciprocal logic we've noticed previously, I think the Native assumption
behind this kind of statement is that the world around us abounds with
information waiting to be found, experienced, and, by inference, passed
on to others. If people happen to forget or misunderstand, well, the information is still there, waiting for someone else to discover it. This attitude
describes an environment that is not opaque, stoic, or reluctant, one that
does not require us to pry out its secrets by force and at great expense;
rather, the environment is seen as an ongoing walk-in laboratory, a living
library, a nurturing family.

Now, admittedly, this is a very easy image to romanticize: We can
imbue it with personality, and suddenly we have the Earth Mother hover-
ing over us, complete with beatific smile. While some Native cultures
indeed envision a Mother Earth—or at least an Earth whose basic role is
female (in spite of some scholars' assertions to the contrary), I think the
main point is that humans have the responsibility to glean nature for its
information and then apply it. Such an assumption is so obvious to most
traditional Native Americans that if you appear not to know it, you are
suspected of having been influenced by missionaries or schoolteachers—
whose main function seems to be undermining traditional Native precepts

(hence, Yellowman's acerbic response). The world of information and nurturing surrounds us, and it's ready to share.

I'm not suggesting, of course, that Natives are automatic gurus of natural principles that are invisible to the rest of us. Nor, at the other extreme, do I think Native discoveries were fortuitously stumbled upon by someone accidentally chewing on willow twigs. Rather, I argue that there is a particular frame of mind, encouraged by attitudes like Fool Bull's and perpetuated in stories that continue to provide dramatic structures and patterns conducive to creative thought. Indeed, all cultures have a similar frame of mind, a shared worldview, or they would not have survived and flourished. If the natives of the Americas were actually as primitive as they have been made out to be (admittedly, the term "primitive" is seldom used by students of culture these days, but it's still on the loose in everyday chatter), how could they have developed rich cultures with such extensive arts, oral literatures, rituals, and metaphorical expressions as we have been discussing?

In this chapter, we'll look deeper at some of these culturally situated patterns to see how they function on the complex level of evaluative thought, following Norwood Russell Hanson's assertion that critical insight is not totally dependent on individual brilliance: "We are set to appreciate the visual aspects of things in certain ways. Elements in our experience do not cluster at random. . . . Seeing is not only the having of a visual experience; it is also the way in which the visual experience is had." The way we are "set," Hanson points out in his *Patterns of Discovery*, has to do with our assumptions, our own experiences, and our turn of mind, and although the author doesn't pursue the issue, I think we can argue that these assumptions include patterns provided by our culturally shared worldview. That worldview not only makes particular discoveries "thinkable" to begin with but often makes it difficult to appreciate, or even see, the discoveries of others whose way of thinking is distinctly different.

Thus, because the Indian tribes had no technology for weighing, measuring, and timing, our scientists have been skeptical of their discoveries until very recently. They had no real science, in our sense of that term: laboratories, the scientific method of objective analysis, double-blind testing, a writing system, a means of tracking replicable results over time. They must have inadvertently stumbled on ideas that they somehow managed to duplicate occasionally, however, even though they lacked schools, writing, and technology.

This attitude persists despite the fact that many foods now nourishing the world's population were developed by Native Americans and Native medicines are the source of many of our culture's pharmaceutical "discoveries." Indians knew of vitamin C and its relation to scurvy well before the white arrival; in fact, we know about it mainly because Native people saved Jacques Cartier and his men from scurvy when they were icebound in the St. Lawrence River in 1533 by giving them a tea made from evergreen needles (probably northern white cedar, *Thuja occidentalis*, also known as *arbor vitae*—the tree of life). Later, back home in France, Cartier tried unsuccessfully to promote this tea (as a cure for syphilis), and we know that because he recorded it in his journals, and the idea was picked up more than two hundred years later by James Lind, a British naval surgeon seeking a cure for scurvy. His recommendation that ships carry citrus fruits and issue juice to long-haul sailors not only revolutionized British survivability at sea but also led to their long-standing nickname, Limeys. Ironically, it also facilitated major conquests, invasions, the Empire, and migration; led to the successful long voyages of Captains Cook, Bligh, and Vancouver; and resulted in major displacement and eradication of Native populations. In hindsight, perhaps a higher level of secrecy about Native medicines would have served the world better, but the Natives, in the typical style we'll see in this chapter, shared their information freely.

More recently, Frederick Banting, the discoverer of insulin, gave credit to Indians for their original pharmaceutical experimentation. The birth-control pill, antibiotics, digitalis, and the rubber syringe for enemas and injections all have their antecedents in Native medicine. Some two hundred Native drugs are still listed in the *Pharmacopoeia*, not to mention hundreds of others categorized as home or folk remedies.

Even though Euro-American scientists have been interested in Native plant use since the earliest contacts (they were hoping to find everything from the cure for syphilis to the remedy for old age), Western cultures in general have minimized Indian discovery because it does not conform to the familiar systematic generalizations of Western worldview. Home remedies and "snake-oil" medicines have been popular through the years, but seldom have everyday Americans availed themselves of the vast medicinal repertoire that surrounds them in the customs of their Indian neighbors. We seem to feel that discoveries have to be ferreted out of an unfriendly—or at least reticent and inarticulate—environment, and then—to become acceptable—they must be weighed, measured, and analyzed in distant, objective laboratories where professional scientists guard against wishful thinking and coincidence.

The Native American ways of seeing result in experiential data becoming generalized in entirely different ways. No doubt originating sometimes in coincidence, their discoveries have grown empirically from experimentation within a consistent and widely shared body of experience and cultural worldview. This way of looking at the world encourages people not to view experience as coincidence but be alert to relationships and processes which are embodied in—and interpreted by— tales, myths, songs, dances, and beliefs, whose patterns, congruent with one another, stress integration, reciprocation, and cooperation among all members of a dynamic system. Humanity is not separate from nature in this model; indeed, very little is removed from anything else. Rather, everything is assumed to belong together in balance. Knowledge about this integrated process is archived and continually dramatized in story, sacred customs, religious rituals, art forms, and dance, not simply recorded in objective, explanatory, data-centered commentary.

If the world is a constellation of interdependent relatives, Native Americans assume that sickness, for example, must result from a failure or imbalance of processes, and thus, logically, somewhere among all the plant and animal relatives in nature must be some way of restoring balance and harmony (the Navajos call it *hózhǫ́*). Armed with this assumption, Native people "experimented" with various plants, animals, and rituals until they discovered how to regain the necessary balance. Aided (or at least supported) by neighbors who probably felt the imbalance, too, and guided by stories and extensive botanical traditions, they enjoyed a culturally structured hunting license.

Once the balance point was found, it is unlikely that it would have been easily forgotten. There is ample evidence that in hundreds of instances, it was quickly invested with story and ritual and incorporated into the performance repertoire of the tribes. If a medicine did prove continually efficacious, why shouldn't the people have seen the results as firsthand (isn't this "empirical"?) evidence that their assumptions were valid and the world did operate as the stories indicated?

To be sure, in all Native societies gifted individuals have specialized in learning, discovering, and disseminating medicinal processes. Thus, even though everyone was attentive to the cues in nature more than most of us tend to be today, there were those who knew a lot more than the ordinary person, and these people were—and still are—sought out when extraordinary medical problems require a specialist. For convenience, these practitioners can be described as belonging to two large (and partly overlapping) categories: shamans and doctors. A shaman is usually understood to be the kind of practitioner, male or female, who has personal magical or spiritual power which can be focused on the dilemma at hand. The problem may relate to human health (including psychological), but since most shamans are found among hunting cultures and are thought to have a strong influence on life-and-death processes, they often function as spiritual liaisons between the human world and that of the game animals. Many shamans claim to have gained their power by apprenticing themselves to a senior shaman who, among other things, killed them and brought them back to life. Others self-induce a traumatic moment (in a rigorous vision quest, for example) when an animal or other spiritual helper announces that it will aid them in healing if proper ceremonies are conducted. Shamans often use botanical and animal medicines, of course, but their intersection with their patients—both human and animal—seems to be primarily magical, spiritual, psychological.

Native doctors, on the other hand, spend years learning an extensive range of medicines, rituals, and diagnostic procedures in the belief that these factors, and not the personal force of the practitioner, bring about healing. For example, it is typical for a Navajo doctor to spend ten or more years learning the details of a particular healing system (each one called a way) which can be applied to a limited assortment of ailments. Red Antway, for example, concentrates primarily on stomach problems but can occasionally be used for upper-respiratory-tract ailments. In every tribe, the term for what I'm calling a "doctor" is different: in Hopi, it's *tuuhikya*, "healer" (and the Hopi have specialists like the *oqatuhikya*, a bonesetter, and the *tipkyatuhika*, who deals with uterine ailments); in Lakota Sioux, it's *pejuta wicasa*, "medicine man" (as compared to *wasicun wakan*, literally "sacred white person," the white doctor); in Navajo, it's *hataałii*, a "singer"—one who knows the songs of the restorative ceremony or way. Almost all of these practitioners have been called medicine men by the whites.

The Native doctor is a person of accumulated learning and ritual competence, coupled with extraordinary memory (some Navajo curing ceremonies last fifteen days and nights, each day requiring a different complicated sand painting, specific medicinal applications, hundreds of ritual songs, and responsive interactions between singer and patient, all timed by star constellations that allow each night's ceremony to end before dawn). The cure cannot occur if the details of all these interactive steps are not performed correctly. The Native shaman is a person of striking psychological and spiritual force; the cure cannot happen if his or her power fails. In reality, both of these domains overlap because—as recently discovered by Western medicine—the psychological state of the patient is a key factor in any cure. In both kinds of medicine, one of the main goals is the restoration of balance and harmony between the patient and the total environment. In both kinds of practitioners, the exercise of too much personal power (especially to benefit the healer) is looked on with suspicion and even fear. Yet there is still a distinction: In one kind of heal-ing, the operative elements are chiefly known medicines and rigidly memorized rituals; in the other, they are psychological power and magic. In neither case do the names medicine man or shaman help us understand the rich complexity of knowledge and psychological know-how that con-nects Natives with the world around them.

As we have seen, the Native world is not distant and inarticulate; rather, it is inhabited by relatives whose activities are packed with mean-ing. Ongoing observation of animal and plant characteristics is not regarded as idle curiosity but paying attention to meaningful, articulate patterns where humans play an important role (just as in art, song, dance, and story). Moreover, animals and plants continue to articulate the truths of their existence whether we're watching or not. Or, to put it another way, they constitute a consistent baseline of natural relationships which we may consult anytime we need to know anything. It's for that reason that old Fool Bull ridiculed Roger Welsch's desire to document (and thus fossilize) his tribe's medicinal repertoire before it was "lost" with his death. In the Native view, there is no *it* which exists or dies out; there is a continuum of natural truths which are always there. Thus, as old man Fool Bull noted, even if everyone happened to forget a cure, the evidence is still living, waiting for someone else to notice and recall it to others.

But human inventiveness and cultural insight are also important: For example, many of the northern California tribes (and, indeed, tribes across the country) burned the forest's underbrush each year. For years, whites, including forestry specialists, considered the practice damaging to the ecosystem. Even Aldo Leopold, the early conservation pioneer, railed against the destructiveness of what he called "Piute Forestry," claiming that it "is the very negation of the fundamental principle of forestry, namely, to make forests productive not only of a vegetive cover to clothe and protect our mountains, but also of the greatest possible amount of lumber, forage, and other forest products." We now realize that by burn-ing off forest undergrowth, Native people were able to reduce the fuel to support greater forest fires, encourage the growth of grass and small plants and thus the immigration of deer and small animals into areas close to tribal lands, increase the ash in the soil, and produce local moisture through combustion.

By providing better browse for animals in forest clearings, this system allowed protein to be acquired at a minimal expenditure of human calo-ries: inviting animals toward human environment instead of chasing them across the hills meant burning fewer calories in pursuing others, thereby promoting caloric conservation. How it was reflected in expressive folk traditions like song and story, we may never fully know, for these northern California tribes are among the groups that were hunted and destroyed wholesale by the white invaders before we were able to learn much about them (one Ishi is not enough of a basis for broad spiritual and cultural generalizations). But some of these people remain, and their beliefs today suggest that they actually saw the fires as a way of creating deer and causing the trees to produce more seeds.

In a modern sequel, the Bureau of Land Management and the Forest Service now burn off undergrowth in some areas to reduce the possibility of fires reaching high enough to set forest canopies ablaze. Government experiments have shown as well that lodgepole and ponderosa pines produce noticeably more cones and seeds after being challenged by controlled undergrowth burns. It is now common knowledge in forestry that some trees are "fire dependent" for full natural propagation.

Another example of a scientific process embedded in culture is the botanical development of corn. Maize (*zea mays* or *z. mays*) evolved with human help from an early hard-seeded grass into a pod corn where each seed was enclosed in its own chaff, allowing it to be dispersed by wind or passing animals. Early gatherers would have gotten their hands most easily on those few seeds that had not been dropped by the grass—in botanical terms, the less-successful seeds—and planting these would have encouraged a particular strain that did not cast its seeds so readily. The pod-corn gene was eventually lost, and the result was a cob of seeds wholly dependent on humans for survival, for corn cannot disperse its own seeds; for that reason, it has been called the "hopeless monster" by botanists. But maize hybridizes so easily that it is said to have more variations than any other crop species, and its development as a major food source must have been noticed by those responsible—especially because they had to plant it! Virtually every story and myth about corn attributes energy and fertility to it and describes the plant as a reciprocating relative who nurtures us in return for us nourishing it. Even the word "maize" seems to derive from the Arawak word *mahiz*, "life giver," which is not surprising when we think of the sudden burst of energy available to humans from this new plant.

In many tribes, the interdependence of corn and humans was characterized by the now-familiar terms of sacred balance, reciprocation. Recognizing this strong relationship, humans seem to have made their own gods by investing this botanical creation with sacred power. Yet godliness here, as with the Sioux and other tribes, is expressed fully only through a reciprocal process— not the one-way power of a superior being. Not only were there maize gods and goddesses but there was a delicate concern for the safety and sacredness of the corn itself: said the Zunis, "Love and cherish your corn as you love and cherish your women." Knowing how central the creative power of women is in Pueblo society, one can glimpse the significance of this sacred equation.

In fact, in one passage in the Zuni emergence story, "The First Beginning," the newly arrived people, led by the Ahayuuta twins, ask "the Mexicans" what they are good for. One replies,

> "When you come to the middle, it will be well to have my seeds. Because we do not [yet] live on the good seeds of the corn, but on wild grasses only. Mine are the seeds of the corn. . . ." He showed them an ear of yellow corn. "Now give me one of your people." Thus he said. They gave him a baby. When they gave him the baby it seems he did something to her. She became sick. After a short time she died. When she had died he said, "Now bury her." They dug a hole and buried her. After four days he said to the two [the Ahayuuta], "Come now. Go and see her. . . ." When they got there the little one was playing in the dirt.

It would be difficult to find a more succinct, dramatic rendering of the geographical origin of corn, its replacement of wild seeds as food, and its apparent death and rebirth through burial, described as the death and rebirth of a girl—the epitome of potential fertility and nurturing. Maize was developed in northern Mexico more than seven thousand years ago; in its development and later ritual functions, we see a botanical and ecological fact (obligatory reciprocity and concern in the survival of people and corn) phrased in cultural terms; yet, at the same time, they are terms based on systematized knowledge derived from empirical observations.

Evidence of Native deduction and discovery is never difficult to find. Many tribes, as revealed by the Fool Bull anecdote, chewed willow twigs to relieve the pain of headache or toothache; they had discovered a principle they could employ with highly consistent results. Today, we know that the salicin ($C_{13}H_{18}O_7$)in the bark of the willow is changed to salicylic acid ($C_7H_6O_3$) by the enzymes in human saliva. It's the salicylic acid, not the willow itself, that addresses the pain. Of course, Native people did not use these terms, but they discovered the process nonetheless, and they had to discover it by biting on the willow twig, noting the effects, and passing the word to others. Fool Bull's comment gives us part of the answer to such questions as, "Why did they even bother to experiment?" or "Where did they get the idea?" for we know they saw themselves surrounded by a living world of information, of "truth," to use Fool Bull's words. Beyond the belief, widely held among Natives, that nature is ready to share such truths is the proviso that human seekers must be motivated by a genuine desire for healing, not hopes of personal aggrandizement. Tom Yellowtail, former leader of the Crow Sun Dance, believed that medicinal plants would reveal themselves to those who prayed appropriately but not those who wanted to gather them for commercial exploitation.

An articulate ecosystem obviously requires an attentive audience, but do we dare—at least for purposes of discussion—take the Natives at their word and consider the possibility that, in addition to their own sensitive deductive logic, they were also instructed by the animals? In Euro-American cultural terms, the idea seems untenable: Did they really get lectures from bears and ravens as described in children's literature? Unlikely. So then, what do they mean when they say they were taught by the animals?

I remember hearing in school that the Pilgrims learned how to make maple syrup and sugar from the Indians. They may have brought a small amount of honey with them, but they would have run out eventually, and honey bees had not yet made the voyage from Europe. So of course they must have learned eagerly from their Native neighbors (who, by the way, also kept them alive by teaching them almost *everything* about plants and planting in continuing instances of inexplicable generosity). But something always gnawed at my understanding of this cultural exchange, for, growing up in New England, I had also learned that making a gallon of maple syrup requires boiling down about forty gallons of sap. Easy enough (maybe) for the Pilgrims and their iron kettles, but how had the Indians done it, and how had they learned to do it? Making maple syrup, especially if you have to do it by putting hot rocks in little birch-bark baskets over and over again for ever so many days until you've boiled forty units of sap down to one unit of syrup—and still further if you want sugar—isn't the sort of thing you would logically think of: "I think I'll go gather and boil a bunch of maple sap for several weeks just to see if anything will happen to it. After all, it's spring, and nothing else is going on."

The point is that maple sap itself is usually tasteless (oddly enough, some people find it terribly bitter), so what would give anybody the idea to start boiling it, and keep boiling it, for a very long time? I think it was a combination of animal instruction and human comprehension, and the key to the puzzle came to me in a conversation with my friend Bernd Heinrich, who teaches biology at the University of Vermont. Heinrich makes it a point to pay attention to what's happening in nature and ask questions about what he sees. He was sitting on the back porch of his cabin in Maine one spring when he noticed a red squirrel running across the lot; the squirrel dashed up the trunks of several maple trees, stopping only long enough to bite a small incision under a branch or two, then ran to the next tree. Was he after moisture, Heinrich wondered? He didn't stay long enough in any one place to lick the sap, and besides, there was plenty of moisture on the ground. So was he after sweetness? Typical of Heinrich, he went and licked some of the places where the squirrel had bitten. No taste. No answer to the puzzle.

A few days later, he saw a red squirrel—probably the same one, but who knows?—running up the same trees and licking at the small incisions. When he was gone, Heinrich immediately went out and did some licking himself. This time, it was sweet. Apparently, some of the water in the sap had had time to evaporate, leaving a slightly sweet taste—probably one that was more interesting to the squirrel than to a human, except for one factor: natives were aware of evaporation because they knew how to boil water and make soup in birch-bark baskets. How much of a leap would it take to reason that if water evaporating from maple sap over a few days made the sap sweeter, then by evaporating a lot of it at one time (as happened when you made soup, for example), you might get a denser, sweet-flavored fluid? Heinrich thinks Natives may well have learned about the principles of making maple syrup from the animals, just as they have always said. And I think he's right. But it was a joint venture: it took a brilliant deductive leap on someone's part to connect the animals' behavior to human experience with the results of evaporation.

In his best-selling (and controversial) book, *Of Wolves and Men*, Barry Lopez devotes a whole chapter to the proposition that, while we cannot talk to wolves directly, we may learn about their patterns of life by interviewing and observing people who have known wolves for thousands of years and in many ways continue to pattern their actions as hunters and family members on the behavior of wolves. Attitudes toward death, nature, family responsibility, travel, and relationships with other animals are all culturally interpreted "wolf values" among the Nunamiut and Naskapi (to name only a few of the Arctic people who consciously know and interact with wolves); they result from millennia of close observation and imitation of what Elaine Jahner calls "wilderness mentors." Many Plains tribes have legends and tales of wolves who discover lost humans (children or women, usually—that is to say, utterly defenseless) and guide them back to their villages, and regardless of how one evaluates them, the stories dramatize a set of relationships which can be inferred from empirical observation (including the widespread knowledge among Indians, now slowly spreading to skeptical white people, that wolves don't attack people, while they *do* lead nurturing family lives). But do they "talk" to us?

Barry Lopez comments, "The idea that animals can convey meaning, and thereby offer an attentive human being illumination, is a commonly held belief the world over," and adds, "The eloquence of animals is in their behavior, not their speech. . . . To 'hear' wild animals is not to leave the realm of the human; it's to expand that realm to include voices other than our own."

Obviously, for Native peoples, who already regarded the animals as relatives, this realm already included what Lopez terms the "voice of the indigenes." Calvin Martin, in *Keepers of the Game* (1978), argues that we will never fully understand Native involvement in the fur-trade era unless we pay serious attention to the Natives' belief that they spoke with animals. The Lummis of northwestern Washington, having watched the behavior of migrating salmon for generations, learned how to attract them to spawn in, and therefore return to, areas closer to their village. Today the Lummi tribe supports itself largely with aquaculture and an extensive shellfish-propagation program—paralleled since the 1970s by academic programs in biology offered by their community college. The Yupiks of Alaska are so convinced of the delicate communication between humans and fish that they avoid even speaking about a decline in fish population for fear of offending the fish. Similarly, they find catch-and-release sport fishing repulsive because it is insulting to the fish who have willingly offered themselves. Such examples (and one could quote hundreds more) suggest that Native peoples see the ecosystem not simply as biologically integrated but as a communicative constellation where all participants are articulate.

How eloquently animal behavior dramatizes indigenous truths can be seen in a Navajo belief relating rain to burrowing animals. Government agents were forced to learn about it during the 1950s when they proposed getting rid of prairie dogs on some parts of the reservation to protect the roots of the sparse desert grass and thereby maintain at least marginal grazing for sheep. Navajos objected strongly, insisting, "If you kill off the prairie dogs, there will be no one to cry for rain." Of course, they were assured by the amused government men that there was no conceivable connection between rain and prairie dogs, a fact that could be proven easily by a simple scientific experiment: a specific area would be set aside, and all burrowing animals would be exterminated. The experiment was carried out, over the continuing objections of the Navajos, and its outcome was surprising only to the white scientists. A few years later, the area (not far from Chilchinbito, Arizona) had become a virtual wasteland with very little grass. Apparently, without the ground-turning activity of the prairie dogs, the sand in the area became solidly packed, causing massive runoff whenever it rained, and the already-sparse vegetation has since been carried off by the annual flooding waters. No doubt it would be incautious to suggest that the Navajos had a clear, conscious, objective theory about water absorption and retention in packed sand. On the other hand, it would certainly be difficult to ignore the fact that the Navajo myth system, which includes a long Coyote story about prairie dogs' connection with rain, anticipated more accurately than our science the results of an imbalance between principal communicants in the rain process.

Just as animals and plants "instruct" people, so do still larger phenomena of nature—especially the weather, the sun and moon, the night sky. Native stories and customs make it clear that people are not only surrounded by living relatives close by but enjoy reciprocal relations with the visible universe. A Kiowa story told by N. Scott Momaday relates that seven sisters being chased by their angry brother were taken up into the sky by a helpful tree trunk. They became the stars of the Big Dipper, and the brother became a bear. Ever since, Momaday says, the Kiowas have known they have relatives in the night sky. What's the point of having relatives in the sky? Well, for one thing, relatives help you and guide you. Certainly for these early navigators on the Great Plains, a standard reference to the North Star must have been important. And, although Momaday doesn't mention it, the Kiowas must also know they have relatives on the earth around them in the form of the bear, an animal Momaday himself has a unique relationship with.

Native stories abound about hero twins visiting the sun, or a warrior getting revenge against the sky people, or people being carried into the night sky to become stars, sun, and moon, all of them dramatizing certain assumptions about ongoing relationships between people and the forces which surround them. Most of them can be taken as metaphorical (unless one wants to believe it is possible to visit the sun by floating up there on an eagle feather, or for humans to become stars), but even so they testify to the unlimited imaginations of the storytellers, who invented space travel before it was technically possible. A Navajo story relates that an incestuous family was put inside a gigantic arrow and shot to the moon. In a Coos story that clearly comes from the prejet era, Old Man Coyote's violent farting propels him up off the trail so high that he bumps his head on a tree limb (a comical enactment of the principle behind Newton's second law). So we are not surprised to encounter imaginative stories about immense journeys, strange animals and spirits, stunning transformations, and miraculous returns from the land of the dead. But, that said, we also now and then come across a detail that goes beyond imagination and drama and presents the possibility that some narratives are actual accounts of intentional or accidental journeys of discovery.

For example, the Kiowas, according to N. Scott Momaday, have a story about a group of young men who decide to see where the sun spends the winter. They saddle their horses (which means that the journey must have happened within the past five hundred years) and ride south into country they've never seen before. While camped in a forest, however, they notice that "men were all about in the trees, moving silently from limb to limb. . . . they were small and had tails!" This is too much for the Kiowas, and they head for home. How far south did they have to travel to encounter monkeys? Well, to about twenty-one degrees south, somewhere around Vera Cruz. And if the Kiowas didn't actually make this trip, why (and how) could they have invented the idea of monkeys? A common motif in stories of this kind is that the travelers see—and must cope with—some feature of life quite unfamiliar to them, and this feature is then incorporated into the traditional stories, as well as speculations about the nature of the world. Already in 1823, an Iroquois (Tuscarora writer David Cusick) had suggested that monkeys were predecessors to human beings.

In a Tillamook story, the people of a coastal village see what they think is a large whale floating in the bay with birds sitting on it. When they go out in their canoe to investigate, it turns out to be a huge boat full of people from the other side of the ocean. The villagers retreat toward shore, followed by the bigger boat, and some of them are captured and taken across the ocean. The Tillamooks follow in an attempt to rescue their brothers:

> They fitted out their largest canoe and started out the next morning. At nightfall they stopped far out at sea. The mountains of their home had disappeared from their view. . . . Thus they traveled for many days, steering towards the sunset. Finally they saw the land at the other side of the ocean. They found a kind of wood which they did not know. It looked like reed, but was as tall as a tree.

They have arrived in a land where bamboo grows. The story goes on, describing subsequent trips across the ocean and eventual marriages between the two peoples. Is this—among other things—a record of travel to the Orient, or did the Tillamook people simply dream up the idea of a hollow plant as tall as a tree? If it were the only example of such an imaginative act, we might remain skeptical. But it isn't.

In the Tlingit tale of "Kaax'achgoók," a leader and his friends are out hunting and fishing in their boat and are caught in a storm that lasts several days. They find themselves cast up on an island covered with bamboo, far from home—so far, in fact, that it takes their leader a year to figure out where they are by referring to the star constellations they know. There is no water on the island, but the broken stumps of the bamboo are full of rainwater, so they survive. Kaax'achgoók studies the stars every night until he falls asleep and finally determines a course for their return. "We'll start out while the handle of the big dipper is still visible," he says. Are they so far south down the coast of Asia? How far do you have to go to find bamboo big enough to hold water? In any case, using bamboo poles and seal stomachs for sea anchors to keep them from drifting off course at night, they eventually reach Tlingit country and are reunited with their families. After noting that bamboo does not grow in Alaska, Nora and Richard Dauenhauer suggest that "the implication is that the men crossed the Pacific to Hawaii or possibly the Kuril Islands. The voyage of Kaax'achgoók belongs in the annals of small craft navigation such as Captain William Bligh's saving his crew after the mutiny on the Bounty, the voyages of the Vikings, the wanderings of Odysseus, and the traditional chants of Polynesian navigation."

Such lengthy voyages require a complex combination of know-how, navigation techniques, boat-building skills, and guts. Just think of the boats: Northwest coastal tribes built gigantic dugouts which could withstand the pounding of the sea far from shore and which they used to successfully pursue and kill the world's largest mammal before European boats could even cross the Atlantic. Eskimo kayaks and umiaks, made of driftwood, bones, and seal or walrus hides, could carry anywhere from one to twelve persons out to sea to hunt seal, whale, and walrus (an aeronautical engineer told me that the umiak's structure sustains the pressure of the water with more struts than are in a modern jetliner's wing; efficient, maneuverable, flexible, and resilient, the boat is an engineering marvel). The Aleut *baidarka* was similarly capable of carrying large groups of people on long sea journeys. The efficiency of the kayak design is verified by its widespread use today in sports—pretty much unchanged except the materials from which it is made. Eastern Native boats—like the birch-bark canoe—provide other stunning examples of human inventiveness: lightweight, waterworthy, and maneuverable, the birch-bark canoe was also incredibly thin and vulnerable. How did people travel long distances, carrying considerable loads, without sticking their feet through the bottom? Such works of art and engineering—in addition to the agility required to ride in such a boat without ruining it—can be created consistently only by people who have a clear, ongoing conception of what they're doing.

And think of the navigation. Though we don't know much about its principles, we know from innumerable stories that star lore played a large role in it, and this means that people had noticed the consistency of

heavenly movements and learned how to orient themselves to the patterns in the sky. Ethnoastronomy—as this field of study is known
today—shows that virtually all tribes had an extensive knowledge of the
night sky and patterned much of their lives by the regular movements
they saw there. In addition to navigation (a body of knowledge used not
only by seafarers but all wanderers and migrators), tribes like the Hopi
begin and end most Kachina Dances by the appearance of certain constellations in the entryway of a kiva; Navajo all-night healing rituals
("sings") end "just before dawn," a moment computed by the singer, who
checks the stars periodically all night during the ceremony; the Pawnee
patterned their councils after the "star that does not move" (Polaris),
surrounded by nearby stars. Most tribes keep track of the solstices and
equinoxes and orient their various seasonal activities and rituals to them.
The Navajo hogan is conceived as a model of the sky, and the Maya used
constellations as guides to architectural planning. The Mesoamericans
paid so much attention to the rhythms in the sky that they were able to
construct complex calendars—some of them more accurate than
European models.

Native exploration and discovery did not cease with the invasion of
the Europeans, either. Adapting themselves to the newly arrived horse,
several small woodland tribes (like the various Sioux groups, the Kiowas,
and others) rode out into the Great Plains and evolved entirely new cultures which changed the nature of inland North America forever. A number of eastern coastal people accompanied early European explorers back
to the courts of France, England, and Spain, some, to be sure, as captives,
but others as willing travelers. In 1498, for example, Sebastian Cabot
brought several Indians to England, at least two of whom were reported
two years later dressed like Englishmen and doing well. During the 1530s,
Jacques Cartier either invited on board or kidnaped the two men who had
taught him the cure for scurvy and took them to France to exhibit at
court. When he brought them back on his second voyage, these two
(Domagaya and Taignoagny) guided him up the St. Lawrence. Jean
Ribaut's 1562 expedition was ordered by the queen of France to bring
back some Natives. In 1687, some Iroquois leaders, who had been invited
to Montreal to confer with the governor of Canada, were captured and
sent to France to serve in the galleys.

Probably the best-known mass abduction took place in 1614, when at
least thirty Natives were taken by Captains Frobisher, Weymouth, and
Harlow, who tried to sell them in Spain as slaves. But some local friars
heard of the pending transaction and put an end to it, turning the captives loose and harboring some of them until they could find ways to

return home. One of these, Tisquantum, had already been to England with Captain Weymouth in 1605 and had lived there with Sir Ferdinando Georges, learning English language and customs before sailing back to North America in 1614 to help sea captains with mapping and interpreting. Now, captured and rudely hauled off again to Europe, he stayed with the liberating friars in Spain from 1614 until 1618, when he was able to sail to Newfoundland. There he was recognized by one of Georges's captains and taken back to England, but soon headed back to North America with another expedition, landing near his home near present-day Plymouth in 1619 to discover that his whole tribe had been wiped out by an epidemic. Taking refuge with the Wampanoags, he had barely settled in before the Pilgrims arrived and gladly took advantage of his ability to speak English (a friend of his, Samoset, who also spoke English, had—in a way—introduced them).

Tisquantum, or Squanto, as the Pilgrims and most of us ever since have called him, is a favorite character in our account of the Pilgrims' survival in the New World, and he is known to virtually every schoolchild in the United States. But I don't recall Squanto ever being described as an intellectually gifted, multilingual, brave world traveler and diplomat, just as I don't remember hearing that Pocohantas, the legendary savior of Captain John Smith, married a man named John Rolfe and moved to England, where she lived out her life as an Englishwoman until she died of smallpox. And whatever happened to all those other travelers—both voluntary and kidnaped—who went to Europe in those early days? How many got home and played some intermediary role during the European invasion that soon followed? How many became ancestors of today's Europeans? Our knowledge of these discoverers is slim indeed.

Clearly, one of the most stunning examples of Native exploration is the comparatively recent story of Ranald MacDonald, a man virtually unrecognized in his native United States but renowned in Japan (and among historians) as the first American to enter Japan after it had been closed to outsiders for 264 years by the leaders of the Tokugawa era (1603–1867). MacDonald was a Chinook Indian from the Pacific Northwest coast who had grown up hearing stories about castaway Japanese fishermen being adopted and enslaved by his ancestors and noticed there were Japanese loan words in his Native language (one example: *hy-yak*, from Japanese *haiyaku*, which means "to hurry"). Fascinated by the possibilities of relatives in Japan and apparently convinced that his own Asian features and small collection of loan words would overcome the Japanese threat to execute all foreigners who set foot there, MacDonald contrived to make the journey.

In the fall of 1847, after having worked on sailing ships bound for London and the Far East, MacDonald signed aboard the U.S. whaler *Plymouth* under the command of Captain Lawrence B. Edwards and sailed out of Kalakakna Bay, Hawaii, having made a deal with the captain that if they came close enough to Japan, he would forego his pay (usually a share of the whaling profits) in return for a small boat and a few provisions. They did reach the vicinity of Japan, and the captain, wary of Japanese defensiveness, quickly lowered MacDonald over the side in his boat and made a hasty retreat. MacDonald landed—actually, shipwrecked himself—on Rishiri Island in Hokkaido on July 2, 1848, and was immediately arrested by coastal guards. Instead of dispatching him on the spot, however (apparently impressed by his Asian looks and his insistence on repeating those Japanese words), they contacted authorities, who, in turn, sent him to the capital at Edo (Tokyo). There he was held under house arrest while two and sometimes three leading scholars interrogated him and tried to figure out just who he was. In the process, he taught them a good deal of English.

In 1853, when Commodore Matthew C. Perry steamed into Edo harbor with a letter from President Franklin Pierce to the emperor demanding that Japan be opened, curiously enough three Japanese scholars were able to serve as interpreters—all of them trained by Ranald MacDonald, a Chinook Indian from Astoria, Oregon. But MacDonald was far away by that time; he had managed to obtain permission to leave Japan and was prospecting for gold in Australia. Born in 1824, he died at Fort Colville, Washington, on August 24, 1894; his grave can still be seen along the highway on the Colville Indian Reservation, but his intellectual and exploratory triumphs remain unknown to most of his countrymen.

For Natives, having relatives across the ocean would have seemed no odder than having them in the night sky. Native people knew the earth was round (Black Elk pointed out that everything in nature was round), and they believed all its inhabitants were related in one way or another. Perhaps they sensed that if they went and looked, they'd find someone. Perhaps that explains why others from across the ocean came looking for them. There are legends among the Tlingits of relatives who sailed off in boats with people who came from the South Seas, for example. At a recent meeting of Native elders in Alaska, I met Lela Oman, an eighty-five-year-old Yupik elder from Nome, who told me an incredible travel story. According to her family's tradition, her great-great-grandfather—named Kaiana—fought on the losing side of an uprising against King Kamehameha in Hawaii. Afraid of being banished or executed (he was a close relative of the king), he and some friends "just got in their boat and sailed north," landing somewhere on the coast of British Columbia about

1840. One wonders why the escapees headed north, away from warm weather. In any case, they later decided to go even farther north (apparently through the Aleutian chain) and eventually landed near Nome. They took Yupik wives, settled in the Kobuk Valley area, adopted the local hunting and subsistence lifestyle, and raised their families—whose descendants still inhabit the area. In recent years, Lela told me, she and some family members visited Hawaii so they could check out the family names and various Hawaiian phrases that had been passed down in oral tradition. They were welcomed as long-lost, royal relatives. "So. Now then," she said to me, lips pursed in a coquettish smile," you knew I was a Yupik elder, but I bet you didn't know I was a Hawaiian princess!"

The Coquelles on the southwestern coast of Oregon tell of relatives who visited Japan during military service after World War II and found Milluk-speaking people there, corroborating an old story about a whole Coquelle village that disappeared long ago. When they couldn't pay a debt to a neighboring village, incurred when the neighbors helped them catch and kill a miscreant, they began to fear their own demise. According to the old story, the whole village built a big canoe, and—in the words of Coquelle elder George B. Wasson—"they just climbed in it and traveled across the ocean to Japan." Presumably, someone must have come back eventually, or no one would know if they survived or where they went, but the story—still told by people who find sea voyages unsurprising—does not say.

Clearly, in any case, ocean voyages—with all their demands of navigation and grit—were not the exclusive invention of Europeans. Moreover, since virtually all Northwest coast cultures have stories of prodigious sea journeys, it would not be a stretch of the imagination to add boat travel to the possible ways Natives moved into North America. This approach would alleviate the restrictive dates when the Bering Strait land bridge was open for travel (a thorny dilemma because glottochronology—the rates at which languages change—and the evidence for far earlier settlements along the coast of North and South America have never matched the Beringian "tourist seasons"). And it would also help explain why Native Americans keep insisting that they were already "here" and thus did not need to migrate from somewhere else. Look down at a globe from the North Pole toward the coast of western America: it is the clearest line in world geography, running along the coast, along the Aleutian Islands, along northern Asia, and on to the lands of bamboo. People traveling along this coast by boat would only need to keep the land on their right on the way to Asia, and on their left on the way back. People living along the coast—where, by the way, they would have been surrounded by food supplies—would have been pushed one way or another by the outward movements of the ice packs and might have gone one way or another by boat as well. Apparently, the polar region has been inhabited for an exceptionally long time, with every retreating glacier exposing even more evidence. Ancient tenure along this coast, and ancient movements in both directions (chasing food, being chased by ice), could certainly have formed the traditional concept that "we have always been here." Of course, such puzzles will not be resolved by speculative books, but—as we've already seen—we always gain perspective by taking the Native voice seriously.

I think it is clear that Natives and non-Natives alike have benefitted immensely from this cultural accumulation of Native discovery, speculation, and invention; and the process is not over yet. Just to mention a few Navajo examples, take Fred Begay (once the subject of a documentary called *The Long Walk of Fred Young*), a physicist at Los Alamos doing research on the bombardment of heavy water with laser beams. By utilizing the vocabulary from the Navajo story of the Twin Brothers (one of whom receives from the Sun a spear of jagged lightning to combat monsters, the other a beam of pure, straight light to cure diseases), Begay finds that he can describe the motion of light beams more articulately than he can with English verbs, which are—to the Navajos—far less capable of detailing fine movements. Naturally, discussing his work with his colleagues must be difficult, but the point remains: by using the perspectives inherent in a Native language, one can see and discuss issues that are not totally understandable in English. Take the modern field of ethnomathematics, where researchers have found surprising resources in most Native languages; in particular, anthropologist Rik Pinxten suggests that the Navajo language presents the ideal base to study space navigation and topology (the mathematical study of geometric forms in motion).

And take the case of Tacheeni Scott, now a professor of biology at California State University at Northridge. When he was a graduate student at the University of Oregon, he phoned me late one evening to say he was frustrated by the way his laboratory work was going. "I just want to spit on my slides," he said, which I took to mean he was ready to dump his project. But no: he thought he had detected two totally different kinds of movement by one microscopic specimen and suspected spitting on the slide would prove it. I asked how that would help, and he replied—as if answering an obvious question from a child:

"You know, it's like when we butcher a young goat or sheep; all those little pieces of meat on the front legs are hard to get loose without cutting them, but if you spit on your hand and pat the legs, that thin membrane comes loose, and you can pull all those little pieces right off the leg. I have a hunch that if I spit on my slides, the cell wall will be at least partly digested, and these two different animals will float out separately where I can photograph them."

"Go ahead, then," I said, "why not?"

"Well, how can I explain that in scientific terms? My committee will kill me. 'I applied some spit to the specimen, and I discovered x, y, or z?'"

"Why don't you go ahead and try it," I said, "and if it works, then test your saliva to see what enzymes may be there. Then you write, 'I applied x amount of x enzyme, and the result was whatever.'"

It worked, and he was able to determine that the specimen—a kind of algae, as I recall, that had never been properly categorized—actually featured two different entities sharing one cell wall. But these small animals moved so differently that he had to use two totally different verbs in Navajo to describe them, and there was no way to translate the variation into English. His committee was baffled because they couldn't understand the nature of his discovery. One result was that I, a professor of English, was added to his biology doctoral committee so we could negotiate the nature of the discovery, and we eventually worked out a way of describing it so others could understand.

Today Tacheeni Scott and Fred Begay, in addition to their own ongoing research, regularly visit schools on the Navajo Reservation to persuade students to hold onto their language and think about going into the fields of science. Begay and Scott, addressing an assembly of Navajo students a few years ago at Red Mesa High School in Arizona, said, "Your language and your culture are resources. Don't let anyone tell you they are burdens. They are the basis for the way you look at the world and discover things. Listen to your elders and the stories: they are your treasures. You will be able to see things that others haven't noticed. You already know things that others haven't thought about. Don't lose this!" I am sure that molecular biologist Aaron Novick would agree.

Notes

Roger Welsch's discussion with Fool Bull can be found in *It's Not the End of the Earth, but You Can See It from Here: Tales of the Great Plains* (New York: Villard Books, 1990), 50–51. Welsch has played a significant role in my understanding of this topic.

Sam D. Gill's passionate argument that the Mother Earth concept is of recent (and largely non-Native) vintage is set forth in his *Mother Earth: An American*

Story (Chicago: University of Chicago Press, 1987). I have heard too many traditional Native references to the female earth and the male sky to find Gill's position convincing, however.

Norwood Russell Hanson's *Patterns of Discovery: An Inquiry into the Conceptual Foundations of Science* (Cambridge: Cambridge University Press, 1958) demonstrates the extent to which even our most scientific observations are channeled and defined by the way we are set. The quoted passage is on page 15, but the whole chapter, titled "Observation," is well worth reading as we try to understand that cultural worldviews are not simply differences of opinion or interpretation but represent a different mode of thinking and seeing.

See Virgil J. Vogel's *American Indian Medicine* (Norman: University of Oklahoma Press, 1970) for an extensive description of the many medicines and procedures developed by Native Americans. Robert and Michele Root-Bernstein's *Honey, Mud, Maggots, and Other Medical Marvels: The Science behind Folk Remedies and Old Wives' Tales* (Boston: Houghton Mifflin, 1997), despite its condescending title, provides a number of modern explanations of the way folk and tribal medicines work; many of their examples are from Native American medical practice. On the subject of Jacques Cartier and vitamin C, I am much indebted to Calvin Martin for sharing with me his year-long research at the Johns Hopkins Institute for the History of Medicine. His many books, especially *In the Spirit of the Earth: Rethinking History and Time* (Baltimore: Johns Hopkins University Press, 1992) and *The Way of the Human Being* (New Haven: Yale University Press, 1999) are exceptionally rich conceptualizations of Native thought and practice.

An interesting sidebar on Richard Evans Schultes, "the father of ethnobotany," appears in *Natural History*, February 2002, 22, along with a longer piece, "Flowers of Evil," by Rob Nicholson (pp. 20–24), detailing present research into psychoactive plants in South America. Nicholson describes the fleshy flowers of *Brugmansia sanguinea* and comments, "One feels compelled to fondle the flowers and inhale the complex perfume that wafts from the long trumpets. No wonder some native trailblazer was drawn to sample the taste of the plant; what an interesting meal that must have made" (20). The modern field of ethnobotany is well described and illustrated in Michael J. Balick and Paul Aslan Cox, *Plants, People, and Culture: The Science of Ethnobotany* (New York: Scientific American Library, 1997).

One of the standard comparative studies on shamanism is Mircea Eliade's learned *Shamanism: Archaic Techniques of Ecstacy*, translated by Willard R. Trask (New York: Pantheon Books, 1964), but modern books on the subject, especially by New Age seekers, are produced by the hundreds, spawning, among other things, a thriving tourist business for those who wish to visit practicing shamans. Anthropologist Bonnie Glass-Coffin has written brilliantly about the phenomenon in "Anthropology, Shamanism, and the 'New Age,'" in *The Chronicle of Higher Education*, 15 June 1994, p. A-48. Native commentary on white "wanna-be shamans" is predictably (and justifiably) negative. Among others, see Ward Churchill's *Indians Are Us? Culture and Genocide in Native North America* (Monroe, Maine: Common Courage Press, 1994) and Wendy Rose's "The Great Pretenders: Further Reflections on Whiteshamanism" in M. Annette Jaimes's *The State of Native America: Genocide, Colonization, and Resistance* (Boston: South End Press, 1992), 403–21. Anthropological opinion is equally negative: see Alice B. Kehoe's "Primal Gaia: Primitivists and Plastic Medicine Men" in James A. Clifton, *The Invented Indian: Cultural Fictions and Government Policies* (New Brunswick, N.J.: Transaction Publishers, 1990), 193–209.

The ritual and rationale for the Navajo Red Antway ceremony is described (with photos—many of them covering items which must not be photographed) in Leland C. Wyman, *The Red Antway of the Navaho* (Santa Fe: Museum of Navajo Ceremonial Art, 1965). The Blessingway, considered the main stem of Navajo ceremonial practice, is given in three different versions with substantial elucidation by Wyman in *Blessingway* (Tucson: University of Arizona Press, 1970). The tribal doctor's extensive learning of ritual detail, the memorization of thousands of chants and their complicated sequences, the retention of lengthy mythic and historical narratives that inform the ceremonies, and the deep acquaintance with particular plants and minerals used for healing are all quite different from the traumatic events that usher the shaman into an active healer's life: One hears accounts of everything from a dream animal appearing during a vision quest to the young trainee being starved for a month in a snow hut or suspended under Arctic water and ice for forty days or even being killed and sent to live with the walruses for a year before returning to life in the human community. Among others, see Knud Rasmussen, *Across Arctic America* (New York: G. P. Putnam's, 1927), 82–84; and stories like "Sigvana" and "The Boy Who Went to Live with the Seals," both in Brian Swann, ed., *Coming to Light: Contemporary Translations of the Native American Literatures of North America* (New York: Vintage, 1996), 8–10, 57–74.

Aldo Leopold's opinions are succinctly expressed in his essay, "'Piute Forestry' vs. Forest Fire Prevention" (1920), in Susan L. Flader and J. Baird Callicott, eds., *The River of the Mother of God and other Essays by Aldo Leopold* (Madison: University of Wisconsin Press, 1991), 68–70. I am indebted to my colleague, Professor James J. Kennedy of Utah State University's College of Natural Resources, for calling this essay to my attention, as well as bringing me up to date on current forestry practice with regard to fires.

Ishi, the last of the Yahi tribe, lived out his last days working as a janitor at the Lowie Museum at the University of California, Berkeley, and died in 1916. His life is chronicled by Theodora Kroeber in *Ishi, Last of His Tribe* (Berkeley: Parnassus Press, 1964).

The past and present existence of corn is described in layman's terms by Betty Fussell, *The Story of Corn* (New York: Knopf, 1992); see especially pp. 15, 20. A more succinct botanical account is given in Jacquetta Hawkes and Sir Leonard Wooley, *Prehistory and the Beginnings of Civilization* (New York: Harper & Row, 1963), 274–77. Botanists do not agree about the details of this development, but in any case, it seems clear that the relatively sudden appearance of maize in the food supply must have had a tremendous impact on Native nutrition.

The account of the Zuni emergence story, "Talk Concerning the First Beginning," is taken from Ruth Bunzel, "Zuni Origin Myths," in *Forty-seventh Annual Report of the Bureau of American Ethnology* (Washington, D.C.: GPO, 1929), 584–602; reprinted in Karl Kroeber, ed., *Traditional Literatures of the American Indian: Texts and Interpretations*, 2d ed. (Lincoln: University of Nebraska Press, 1997), 81–87; the quoted passage is on page 84.

Tom Yellowtail's account of traveling to a remote canyon with Sun Dance leader John Trehero and stopping to pray so the medicines would reveal themselves appears in Michael Oren Fitzgerald, *Yellowtail: Crow Medicine Man and Sun Dance Chief* (Norman: University of Oklahoma Press, 1991), 46–47 (all of chapter 6, "Hunting Stories," 37–49, is full of examples where animals and plants respond to human gestures).

Bernd Heinrich provides a compelling report on the squirrel "tapping" maple-sugar trees in "Nutcracker Sweets," *Natural History*, February 1991, 4–8. For Barry Lopez's comments on wolves and arctic cultures, see *Of Wolves and Men* (New York: Scribners, 1978). Elaine Jahner's examples of animals helping humans are given in "Wilderness Mentors," in Brian Swann, ed., *Coming to Light: Contemporary Translations of the Native American Literatures of North America*, 423–31.

Barry Lopez's comments on the eloquence of animals appear in his essay, "The Language of Animals," in Polly Stewart, Steve Siporin, C. W. Sullivan III, and Suzi Jones, eds., *Worldviews and the American West: The Life of the Place Itself* (Logan: Utah State University Press, 2000), 10, 11, 12, 14, 15. Calvin Martin's *Keepers of the Game: Indian-Animal Relationships and the Fur Trade* (Berkeley: University of California Press, 1978) is a fine exposition of the many interactive, reciprocal models in Native thought relating them to their food supply and ecosystem. Anthropologists Phyllis Morrow and Chase Hensel have generously shared their insights into the cultural world of the Yupiks with me; I am indebted to them for examples throughout this book, especially on the articulated relationship between humans and animals.

The experimental killing of prairie dogs near Chilchinbito was recounted to me by Ray Hunt, longtime trader to the Navajos, who, because he was operating the Chilchinbito Trading Post at that time, did the translating between the government soil specialists and the Navajos.

N. Scott Momaday's story of the seven sisters who became stars can be found in the introduction to his *The Way to Rainy Mountain* (Albuquerque: University of

New Mexico Press, 1969). His story of the young men's exploration into Mexico is retold in part 18 of the same book (page numbers vary in different editions). Early Tuscarora writer David Cusick's musings on the relationship between monkeys and humans is mentioned in Gordon Brotherston, *The Book of the Fourth World* (Cambridge: Cambridge University Press, 1992), 293.

The Tillamook account is taken from Franz Boas, "Traditions of the Tillamook Indians," *Journal of American Folklore* 11 (Jan.–March 1898): 23–28, 137–50; a rephrased version is provided by Jarold Ramsey, ed., in *Coyote Was Going There: Indian Literature of the Oregon Country* (Seattle: University of Washington Press, 1977), 167–70. The fascinating Tlingit tale of traveling to Asia is called "Kaax'achgoók" and was told by Andrew P. Johnson. See Nora Marks Dauenhauer and Richard Dauenhauer, eds., *Haa Shuká, Our Ancestors: Tlingit Oral Narratives* (Seattle: University of Washington Press, 1987), 82–107.

For more on Native navigation and attitudes about the heavens, see Anthony F. Aveni, ed., *Native American Astronomy* (Austin: University of Texas Press, 1977) and Ray A. Williamson and Claire Farrer, eds., *Earth and Sky: Visions of the Cosmos in Native American Folklore* (Albuquerque: University of New Mexico Press, 1992).

A basic book on enslavement of Indians is Almon Wheeler Lauber, *Indian Slavery in Colonial Times within the Present Limits of the United States* (1913; reprint, New York: AMS Press, 1969); it gives detailed accounts of the many voyages, mostly unwilling, of Native people to Europe, among them the well-traveled Squanto. A succinct and well-researched account of Tisquantum (Sqaunto) can be found on the Internet at http://members.aol.com/calebj/squanto.html.

Accounts of Japanese crossing the Pacific are discussed by Katherine Plummer in *The Shogun's Reluctant Ambassadors: Sea Drifters in the North Pacific*. The remarkable adventures of Ranald MacDonald are recounted in *Ranald MacDonald: The Narrative of his Life, 1824–1894*, edited by William S. Lewis and Naojiro Murakami (Portland: Oregon Historical Society, 1990), and in Jo Ann Roe's *Ranald MacDonald: Pacific Rim Adventurer* (Pullman: Washington State University Press, 1997).

For the past fifty or sixty years, the archeological cliché for the peopling of North America was that a channel of land was open for foot traffic across the Bering Strait about twelve thousand years ago, and therefore, the migrations into the New World could not have occurred before that time. However, recent discoveries in South America (e.g., Monte Verde in Chile) of active settlements far to the south even before the standard date for the Bering Strait land bridge suggest that other means of migration—boats, for example—must be considered. (See *National Geographic* 192, no. 4 [October 1997]: 92–99.)

For more on the Native conception of science, mathematics, and space, see Michael P. Closs, ed., *Native American Mathematics* (Austin: University of Texas

Press, 1986); James F. Hamill, *Ethno-Logic: The Anthropology of Human Reasoning* (Urbana: University of Illinois Press, 1990); Rik Pinxten, Ingrid van Dooren, and Frank Harvey, eds., *The Anthropology of Space* (Philadelphia: University of Pennsylvania Press, 1983); and Marcia Ascher, *Ethnomathematics: A Multicultural View of Mathematical Ideas* (Pacific Grove, Calif.: Brooks/Cole Publ. Co., 1991). Jim Barta, a colleague of mine in Utah State's College of Education, has been developing approaches for teaching mathematics to Native children by using the precepts already present in tribal cultures; see his "Native American Beadwork and Mathematics" in *Winds of Change* (Spring 1999): 36–41.

Black Elk told John G. Neihardt that "everything the Power of the World does is done in a circle. The sky is round, and I have heard that the earth is round like a ball, and so are all the stars. . . . Birds make their nests in circles. . . . The sun comes forth and goes down again in a circle. The moon does the same, and both are round" (John G. Neihardt, ed., *Black Elk Speaks: Being the Life Story of a Holy Man of the Oglala Sioux* [1932; reprint, Lincoln: University of Nebraska Press, 1961], 198–99). Such an assumption, prevalent among the Native peoples of North America, helps explain the relative ease with which they understand topology and space navigation more readily than lineal algebra, as current research suggests.

My acquaintance with Tacheeni Scott began when we were both at the University of Oregon, he as a graduate student in biology, I as a professor of English. His interest in the perspectives of Navajo oral tradition led to his sitting in on several of my classes and finally to our collaboration on an essay, "Poetic Retranslation and the 'Pretty Languages' of Yellowman," in Karl Kroeber, ed., *Traditional Literatures of the American Indian: Texts and Interpretations*, 2d ed. (Lincoln: University of Nebraska Press, 1997), 88–134. As national faculty advisor to Red Mesa High School on the Navajo Reservation, I had the pleasure of inviting both Tacheeni Scott and Fred Begay to address the students, almost all of whom were Navajos and none of whom had heard the idea that their own language might be full of scientific perspectives.

Epilogue

"Gleaning" and the Active Audience

ALL THAT REMAINS is for us to take a look back over the vast array of implicit and explicit cultural meanings we have been discussing and contemplate how Native people derive significance from performed texts, artifacts, and movements which don't announce their meanings openly. How do they know what they mean—and more problematic—how can we be sure we know? After all, Native Americans do not go around giving explanatory lectures to each other, mostly, I presume, because the interpretations are seldom perceived consciously. I have been arguing that knowing more about a culture's assumptions and traditions helps us—Native and non-Native—immensely in gaining a sense of what is performed, and what those performances mean in their cultural contexts. To be sure, the argument is complicated by the tremendous range of cultural differences among tribes in North America, yet it is mitigated to some extent by certain similarities that allow us room for speculation and comparison. We have tried to avoid "reading into" our texts, yet we have to admit that much of what we have shared in this book is interpretive and tentative, rather than certain.

What we need is a good model for understanding just what happens when a talented storyteller, singer, or basketmaker performs a story, song, or basket for people who recognize the cultural codes in the genre. John Miles Foley uses the phrase *immanent art* to characterize the kind of artistic expression which comes into being as a traditional artist performs a traditional expression in the presence of a traditional audience in a traditional context: the art does not reside in the text or performance but emerges in the interaction between the artist and a knowledgeable audience as the event takes shape. It's a wonderful concept, and it resonates with the reciprocal systems we have encountered. But how does it work?

In a 1982 prepublication photocopy distributed to friends and colleagues, Ron and Suzanne Scollon discussed a number of special linguistic features and insights they had encountered while doing field research in Northern Athabascan communities. One of these caught my attention because of its compelling metaphorical quality: in Chipewyan Athabascan, a verb stem identified later by Suzanne Scollon as *-sas/-zas* is used to describe a dog gnawing a bone until it is clean, a woman picking berries, and someone listening to—and understanding—what another person is saying. We can surmise that using this verb for these apparently disparate actions dramatizes a set of cultural nuances and assumptions about earnestness and thoroughness that may be approximated by the English term "gleaning" and that listening to others—not just obtaining food— falls into that important range of concerns.

Because bushes produce varying amounts of berries, the job of finding and properly harvesting them is the responsibility of the hardworking berry picker; in the subarctic, berries are not always abundant, and the picker needs to know where they are, as well as how and when to get them without losing or crushing any. Along with the berries, of course, there is the accumulation of leaves, twigs, and spoiled berries; in other words, the process of gleaning also produces materials which are not nutritious and need to be sorted out and discarded as superfluous.

The job of getting every last morsel from a bone is the responsibility of the dog who wants to eat, polish his teeth, and exercise his jaws. The more resilient parts of the bone may eventually be discarded, but the surviving dog is the one who can consistently glean the most nutrition out of what he gets. With an oral performance (let us say a traditional story, a hunting anecdote, or medicinal instructions), the job of "getting it" and obtaining its cultural nutrition is the responsibility of the listener, who has learned by experience to recognize and glean the important references, metaphors, nuances, and cultural assumptions, while carefully discarding the anecdotal leaves, stems, and other nonnutritive elements.

Listening, like gathering berries and gnawing a bone, is not easy: it requires effort and knowledge on the part of the gleaner. Another implication is that the process is evaluative as well as interactive: it is much more complicated than the old cliché about the tree falling in the forest where no one can hear it, for /*-sas*/ describes more than the physical registration of sound by an ear or the arrival of data at its intellectual destination (as suggested by various information and conduit models of communication). The *active reception* of an oral performance requires a conscious and energetic engagement which includes selection, scrutiny, sorting, interpretation, and digestion. Moreover, the concept of /*-sas*/ not only relates to survival but also encompasses a range of relationships within the cultural and natural world: plant/human, bone/animal, human/human. The categories are different, but the principle of gleaning remains the same across them; thus, the verb is not denotative as much as it is metaphorical. It provides for the vivid, physical rendering of a culturally understood abstraction.

First, let us take a more detailed look at the implications of /-sas/ in English as applied to actively receiving and processing what others say. In the grain fields of northern Europe, after the reapers cut the wheat and barley, and the farm laborers took the bundles of grain away to be threshed, others came into the fields to glean the seeds of grain that had fallen to the ground. Just as the Athabascan woman painstakingly searches for, identifies, and carefully plucks the smallest isolated berry, the gleaners went through a field in a careful, thorough, painstaking attempt to find and keep every last kernel of grain. In early Europe, of course, gleaning implied social status and customary privilege: some had rights to glean in certain fields after a harvest; others did not. The process was central not only to their physical survival but also their identity. Thus, the cultural meaning of gleaning (with all its associated nuances of position, custom, relationship) was multivalent, just as the cultural meaning of Arctic subsistence berry picking today is every bit as significant on a political and ethnic level as for the actual number of berries collected.

The analogy with gleaning is limited, of course (as are all attempts to exploit other cultures' wonderful phrases). Gleaning basically refers to discovering and utilizing leftovers, while /-sas/ relates to the central act of "harvesting," in all senses of that term. Anyone who has watched subarctic Native people picking berries or choosing blades of grass for baskets has been impressed by the keen deliberation, the care, the delicacy, the almost fierce attention to small detail that characterize the process. And even a dog that is not hungry will "worry" a bone until it is almost gone—just on principle, it seems. The central quality of this action is total and energetic (but careful) commitment to getting all there is.

As it applies to an audience, gleaning suggests that the listeners (who, in a traditional society, very likely know the story or song—and could perform it themselves) are proactively absorbing every nuance of a performance, using what they know of their culture's customs, values, and traditions—along with their own familiarity with the song or story—to bring the full referent of the text dramatically into their minds. The term *referent* suggests that the text itself is not the focal point of a folk performance; rather, the performed text stimulates or creates a rich constellation of culturally significant associations in the minds of the listeners, and that's where the meaning is located. The listeners must identify, sort, bring up related cultural, contextual, and experiential possibilities and apply them to the performance. This attitude was discovered by Phyllis Morrow when she tried to get Yupik narrator Elsie Mather to comment on the meaning in her stories. Mather replied that Yupiks don't explain their stories; instead, they listen to them throughout their lives and continually try to understand the stories as they accumulate the personal and cultural experiences to interpret them.

As I look back on some forty years of working with Navajo narratives, I realize that my understanding of what was going on would have benefitted immensely from a better grasp of what the Navajos were gleaning—not only from their telling of their stories but from my continuing interest in talking about their motifs and nuances. For I discovered about thirty years into the process that not only did my friend and adopted brother-in-law Yellowman skillfully shape brilliant dramas that embodied positive moral and ritual values for an audience who already knew those ideas and stories, but a constant threat of invoking evil and destructive forces existed when the stories were being discussed. When I finally asked Yellowman directly why he hadn't warned me we were treading on dangerous ground, he replied with some distaste, "We don't talk about those things." And perhaps that's an important point to make about this kind of gleaning in general: it is so basic, so common, so self-evident that people don't talk about it; they simply do it.

Yet the transmission of culturally important information also depends on the aggregate gleaning efforts of a community, a fact nowhere more eloquently illustrated than in an Arctic experience shared with me by filmmaker Leonard Kamerling. While he was filming in the Nelson Island village of Tununak in the early 1970s, he went with a small group of Yupik hunters on snow machines to set blackfish traps under the ice. They had been traveling across what appeared to be featureless frozen tundra for more than an hour when suddenly the weather changed. A dense white mist surrounded them, blotting out even the distinction between the sky and the ground. The hunters, apparently lost, stopped their snow machines and gathered for a lengthy discussion about the nature of being lost, how to discover which way to go, the meaning of subtle landmarks in this area, the particular shapes of willow clumps, and where the river should be. They joked, and they compared stories and anecdotes. Kamerling remembers that the conversation mostly centered on details which he could not see. A younger hunter admitted that he couldn't recognize anything in the vicinity, and an older man responded jokingly, "I know this area like the back of my hand."

"But clearly," Kamerling writes, "they were lost. Finally, they picked a route and started out, snow machines and sleds in close formation one behind the other, and found a slough that they all agreed was 'So and So's slough,' and which looked exactly the same to me as where we had just come from. They were right—we traveled on and they found the place they were looking for, where the blackfish nets went in under the ice." Fortunately, Kamerling filmed all this, and the event makes up one section of the resultant film, *Tununerimiut: The People of Tununak* (in Yupik, with English subtitles, 1972). Just as clearly as they were lost, the hunters shared everything each one knew about the area and its idiosyncrasies, and by gleaning they came up with a composite set of understandings that no individual commanded separately.

In a similar instance, Dennis DeGross tells about a group of Yupik hunters who, suddenly caught in a furious snowstorm, built an impromptu snow hut, sat inside telling anecdotes and jokes about the area (sometimes sticking an arm outside to bring in snowflakes for close inspection), and—having decided which way the wind was blowing and where the ice must be—abruptly stood up, got a grip on each other's jackets and belts, and hiked resolutely through the storm for an hour to find themselves in the middle of a village. Whether vernacular gleaning results in survival or cultural enrichment, its exercise is clearly conscious, interactive, and multivalent; it depends upon the seriousness with which people regard their stories.

Well and good for the Native insider who has been able to hold onto cultural traditions in spite of the forces exerting contrary pressure. Where does that leave us, the viewers of the snail shell from the outside? What kind of help does it give us when we try to explain a fast, but puzzling, break within our own culture? Rather than select a complex and lengthy example from our own or another culture, let's take a common occurrence in all cultures: a stroke, something I experienced on July 5, 2002. From the Western point of view, this is easy; we only need to consult a dictionary. According to *Random House Webster's College Dictionary*, a stroke is "a blockage or hemorrhage of a blood vessel leading to the brain, causing an inadequate oxygen supply and often long-term impairment of the sensation, movement, or functioning of part of the body."

That tells us what a stroke is; it doesn't tell us what causes it, what forms it may take, and how long it may take to recover. It only says what a dimly opinionated victim can already surmise. What's to be done against it? Should one focus on large muscles, small muscles, the voice, or all three (why three categories, one wonders)? Doctors lift their eyebrows and say, "Well, it takes various people different amounts of time to get out of such a fix or heal. You may or may not recuperate from the stroke." But you try, and a little bit at a time, you do come back from the stroke to some extent. With the exception of dietary or life style choices, Western society does not believe that there are any reasons other than physiological for a stroke, including where it actually takes place. Japanese physicians have reported at conferences that the Japanese suffer strokes within the vessels of the brain, not in those leading to the brain. In my case, the stroke occurred in my right temple, puzzling my doctors (is it because I've been eating Japanese food for forty years?).

The Navajos would take another healing approach, peopled with those who are interested in your illness and physical well-being. The questions would be more psychological and focus on the patient's relationships with other people. You may have done something wrong to someone or something, or been the victim of witchcraft (forget about whether you believe in such things or not), or you may have simply done something which wasn't wrong but that interfered with someone else's plan for events unknown to you. Add another couple of hundred possibilities (the number doesn't matter). What you see developing is the difference between the scientific answer based upon scientific facts and the human answer based upon human facts. One isn't right and the other wrong. They are both right in their own way, and just as many people probably get cured from strokes among Navajos as whites.

Western traditional medical prescriptions for recovery from stroke include a low-salt diet, rest, no alcohol, physical, occupational, and speech therapies, and various medications for depression, high blood pressure, and elevated cholesterol. Navajo remedies involve sweat baths and healing ceremonies with other people, and medicines taken by others as well. The principal difference is whether one's stroke is treated as a personal affliction or a group-oriented one. Which cure to follow? They both yield results. The difference is that if I go to my doctor, I'll get another appointment within a month or six months, and if I go to a Navajo medicine man, I will get a long, thoughtful description and schedule another ritual. It's a matter of whether I want to face the thing alone or with someone else.

I'm simplifying considerably, but I am buoyed by the knowledge that my Navajo sister stayed home this summer from the Northwest and is waiting for me to call. From my Western doctor, I get a list of dates he will be in his office, a list of medications to take, and a list of therapies to pursue. If you add this scenario to the hundreds of others available from ethnic groups in America, you will see that the choice is mine: I can go with one answer or with five or ten or twenty. When will we give up our one answer for the world of the many which surrounds us? I, in any case, will be reaching for at least two telephones, one to call my Western doctor and one to commune with my Navajo sister.

Notes

On immanent art, see John Miles Foley, *Immanent Art: From Structure to Meaning in Traditional Oral Epic* (Bloomington: Indiana University Press, 1991). The collaboration of Elsie P. Mather and Phyllis Morrow is discussed in "There Are No More Words to the Story," in Larry Evers and Barre Toelken, eds., *Native American Oral Traditions: Collaboration and Interpretation* (Logan: Utah State University Press, 2001), 200–42.

Ron and Suzanne Scollon's paper later appeared as "Language Dilemmas in Alaska," *Society* 24 (1984): 77–81. See also S. B. K. Scollon, "Reality Set, Socialization, and Linguistic Convergence" (Ph.D. dissertation, University of Hawaii, Honolulu, 1982).

Filmmaker Leonard Kamerling's and Dennis DeGross's stories are based on personal communications with me; respectively, letter, 20 November 2001, and letter, 18 December 2000.

For the author's work with Navajo narratives, see Barre Toelken, "Life and Death in the Navajo Coyote Tales," in Arnold Krupat and Brian Swann, eds., *Recovering the Word: Essays on Native American Literature* (Berkeley: University of California Press, 1987), 388–401, and "From Entertainment to Realization in Navajo Fieldwork" in Bruce Jackson and Edward D. Ives, eds., *The World Observed: Reflections on the Fieldwork Process* (Urbana: University of Illinois Press, 1996), 1–17.

Index

Page numbers in **Bold** refer to photographs.

The following friends, colleagues, and fans of Barre Toelken made financial contributions (as of the press deadline) to support printing of color illustrations in *The Anguish of Snails*:

Lila Abersold
Brian & Jennifer Attebery
Louie W. Attebery
Sonja Bahn
Iren Bencze
Margaret K. Brady
Prof. Dr. Helmbrecht Breinig
Mary Ellen Brown
Jan H. & Judith Brunvand
Terrie Buhler
Hal Cannon & Teresa Jordan
Helen & Lawrence O. Cannon
Star Coulbrooke
Daniel M. Davis
Anne Cullimore Decker
Melody Graulich & Brock Dethier
Charles Doyle
Norine & Harold Dresser
Carol Edison
John Elsweiler
Lawrence J. Evers
Frances J. Fischer
Lydia Fish
Kathryn R. Fitzgerald
Harry A. Ford & Lisa Bardwell
Julie R. Foust
Janet C. Gilmore & James P. Leary
Carol Goodson
Andrea M. Graham
James S. Griffith
Gabrielle Hamilton
Joseph C. Harris
Bess Lomax Hawes
Elizabeth Hearne
Joanna Hearne

Elissa R. Henken
Claudia Hernandez
Joseph C. Hickerson
Charlene Hirschi
Christine Hult
Jean Tokuda Irwin
Edward D. Ives
LaVerna B. Johnson
Thomas Wayne Johnson
Elaine Jones
F. A. de Caro & Rosan A. Jordan
Marilyn A. Jorgensen
Sharon MCF Kahin
Nancy Kavanaugh—National
   Storytelling Network
Cozette Griffin-Kremer & Robert Kremer
Joseph Kulin
Janet Langlois
Ann Leffler
Li Li
Patricia Limerick
Carl Lindahl
Elizabeth M. Locke
Barry Lopez
Glen A. & Rhoda M. Love
Barbara & Timothy C. Lloyd
Jens Lund
Margaret Read MacDonald
Ekkehart Malotki
Frank & Marjorie McEntire
Donald J. McMahon
Norman L. Jones & Lynn L. Meeks
Richard E. & Lottie L. Meyer
Margaret A. Mills
Alice Morrison

Patrick B. & Roseanne Rini Mullen
Sarah B. & Richard W. Munro
Michael L. Nicholls
Ruth Olson
Elliott Oring
Daniel & Beverly Patterson
Cathy Lynn Preston
Michael J. Preston
Robert M. Pyle
Charlotte Reynolds
Leonard N. Rosenband
Aden Ross
The Rutt Bridges Family Foundation
Twilo Scofield
Anne Shifrer
Steve & Ona Siporin
Society for the Study of Myth &
    Tradition, Inc.
Diana Major Spencer
David H. Stanley
Anne & John Stark
Polly Stewart

Ruth Stotter
Stephen & Stacy Sturgeon
Douglas H. & Laraine Swenson
Frances M. Tally
Taylor Mountain Group LLC
Elaine Thatcher
Peter I. Tokofsky
Patricia Turner
Utah Museums Association
James W. & Sharon L. Van Loan
Linda Degh Vazsonyi
Roger Welsch
George Wickes & Louise Westling
Randy & Terry Williams
Susan Tucker Williams
David S. Wilson & Sarah Newton-
    Wilson
William A. & Hannele Wilson
Nora J. Zambreno
Charles G. Zug III
Rosemary Levy Zumwalt & Isaac J.
    Zumwalt